SOCIOLOGY OF WORLD RELIGIONS

Important Books of Similar Interest Published Recently

Encyclopaedia of Sociology of Politics, in 3 Volumes
Edited by Motwani and Saksena

Encyclopaedia of Sociology of Religion, in 3 Volumes
Edited by Nayar and Nayar

Encyclopaedia of Tribal Religion, in 12 Volumes
Edited by S. M. Channa

International Encyclopaedia of Anthropology, in 12 Volumes
Edited by S. M. Channa

Encyclopaedia of Ethics and Logic, in 10 Volumes
Edited by Piet and Prasad

Landmarks in Indian Anthropology, in 74 Volumes
Edited by Several World Famous Authors

Untrodden Fields of Anthropology, in 2 Volumes
By A French Army Surgeon

SOCIOLOGY OF WORLD RELIGIONS

Edited By
V. G. Nayar
&
M. G. Nayar

COSMO PUBLICATIONS
2001 INDIA

SOCIOLOGY OF WORLD RELIGIONS

First COSMO Print 2001

ISBN 81-7755-152-3

Published by
MRS. RANI KAPOOR
for COSMO PUBLICATIONS Div. of
GENESIS PUBLISHING PVT. LTD.
24-B, Ansari Road, Darya Ganj,
New Delhi-110 002, INDIA

Composed at
Cosmo Publications

Printed at
Mehra Offset Press

CONTENTS

Chapter-1

Durkheims Attitude to Traditional Religions

Chapter-1

1. Introduction

Durkheim's analysis of religion was in the main based on ethnographic data relating to beliefs and practices of primitive peoples. But as he repeatedly showed and so often implied, he intended that his findings could be generalized and seen to be universal, and therefore it was legitimate to extend them to modern society. Indeed, the test comes in applying his theories to modern religion. He did not, however, directly examine the religious scene in Europe in his day—a scene marked by social differentiations and a plurality of denominations, nor is there any evidence to indicate that he ever intended to embark on such a task. It might well be argued that his conclusions, contrary to his own position, cannot be generalized and that his findings do not in fact apply to contemporary western society with its religious pluralism (but see Hammond 1974:116ff.).

Although Durkheim wrote no systematic treatise on contemporary religion, he did frequently consider it (for example, Protestantism and its relation to suicide), and he made a large number of references to Christianity and Catholicism. Nor was he loath to talk about contemporary religion in more general terms (see especially 1919b). To Judaism, strangely enough, his allusions were rare and brief (see ch. 1.2). But what must not be forgotten is that, in connection with the present day, Durkheim saw emerging in Europe a new religion based on humanism, which would transcend old, dying forms, namely, that of traditional western religion. Many were his references to this.

The intention of the chapters which follow is to outline Durkheim's attitudes towards the traditional religions of Europe, with the exception of Judaism; to examine his writings on what might loosely be called secularization; and finally to look at his analysis of what he believed was the religion of the future.

2. Christianity praised

Despite Durkheim's rejection of the creedal assertions of Christianity, he nevertheless displayed a high regard for it as a religion. In this respect, as we have already noted, he is markedly different from some atheistic rationalists, who saw little good in religion of any kind, let alone Christianity .

Durkheirn's (on the whole) generous appraisal is seen throughout his entire life, but never more so than in the early period. In the *Division of Labour,* he defends Christianity against those extremists who would attack it on grounds of its intolerance of other religions and alien thought. In contrasting Christianity with the religion of the Romans, he held that, in the matter of freedom and tolerance, the then emerging religion far exceeded those religions which had gone before it, or which might be seen to be its rivals (1893b/1902b:137/t.1933b:163). Durkheim was attempting to show that societies characterized by organic solidarity, such as those in our modern western world, paid less attention to penal law than societies marked by mechanical solidarity, such as primitive societies. In Christianity, ritual crimes which can be classified as penal crimes are given a smaller place than in other religions. And 'sacrilege, of which blasphemy is only one variety, [and] heresy under various forms, are hereafter considered the only religious forms' (ibid.). Indeed, Church leaders only resorted to penal sanctions when the fabric of Christian society was threatened by some infamous action or when it was openly attacked. They did not demand repressive action for offences of a minor kind, but only those which threatened its fundamental principles. Hence, with the passing of time, the list of crimes committed in the name of religion becomes less numerous. In a footnote Durkheim observed that the death penalty for heretics was introduced for the first time as late as 1226 and he held that this was part of the normal development of Christianity' (ibid). He concludes that as 'everybody knows ... the Christian religion is the most idealistic [*idéalistie*] that has ever existed' (ibid.). Its central beliefs were broad generalizations and not rigid or narrow doctrines and practices.

In a later observation, Durkheim noted that what Christianity was able to do politically was to separate 'the temporal and spiritual, the theological and political' (1918b/1966a: 192/t.1960b: 133). With other religions there had been no such split—religious crime was a political crime and vice versa; and to be a member of a state meant to be a practitioner of its religion. That Christianity was responsible for the creation of two spheres gave rise to the possibility of flexibility of thought in political and moral matters, and so there emerged freedom of thought itself, which is thus directly descended from Christianity. More specifically, this freedom gained its impetus in the Middle Ages as scholasticism appeared. Here was the first deliberate attempt to create open argument in which the rights of discussants were freely admitted. In passing, one would add that the councils of the Church were doing this long before.

Durkheim developed the notion that Christianity was an idealistic' religion in his lectures on French higher education (1938a). *L'Évolution pédagogique en France* is a book of considerable importance in attempting to understand Durkheim's thought, not least on religion. Using a wide historical canvas, he covers the development of educational ideals and theory in the western world. The lectures demonstrate his ability as a historian who at the same time derives sociological insights from his material. Not surprisingly, he shows how certain aspects of western culture have developed in accordance with Christian ideals. His references to Christianity are extensive and detailed, and we can only hope to mention some of his more pertinent observations in conjunction with his other writings. Once again, as in his doctoral thesis, he contrasts Christianity with classical religions and notes its idealistic qualities, by which he means both a concern with personal moral values and also an emphasis on belief. For Christians, God is believed to reign over the soul of man and not over his body (1938a/1969f:323/t.1977a:282). God is not to be worshipped with material things (for example, in offerings of food), but rather he is to be the subject of the soul or mind and to be loved. Hence the Christian turns his thought inwards, to within himself as the source of life, and hence there arises the most common practice of prayer which is basically something interior. The soul—the principle of the inner life—is a direct manifestation of the divine. Christianity broke with the notion that the centre of religious activity is the material world, and so prominence was given to the spiritual, personal, the intellectual. Durkheim wrote elsewhere:

> Gradually human duties are multiplied, become more precise, and pass to the first rank of importance, while others on the contrary, tend to become attenuated. One might say that Christianity itself has contributed most to the acceleration of this result. (1925a:7/t. 1961 a/r. 1975:194)

This theme was also stated in *Professional Ethics and Civic Morals* (1950a/1969g:94/t. 1957a:58).

The emphasis on the interior life, basic as Durkheim saw it to be to Christian theology, had many consequences. First, it meant that the human personality, which can be identified with the soul, became of the utmost importance and hence received ultimate status. In *Suicide* he wrote that it 'has become sacred, even most sacred in their [the Christians'] eyes, something which no one is to offend' (1897a:378/t.1951a:333). It had one practical result which was of concern to Durkheim at the time. Because what was essential in man, his psyche, was sacred, it was therefore sinful to damage it wilfully as by an act of suicide. And the Christian Church, from its early days through to Catholicism and Protestantism, has always held that suicide constituted a sinful act. It is thus nothing less than sacrilege. Durkheim's own judgment against suicide as being an immoral act is based on very similar arguments. He believed that the religion of his day – a religion of humanity – was based on such doctrines, so that suicide 'must be classed among immoral acts; for in its main principle', suicide denies the ideals of such a religion (ibid.:383/337). In brief, suicide is the violation of the personality. The person is and must be considered to be sacred, neither the individual nor the group is free to dispose of it at will. Hence an act of suicide causes society to be injured 'because the sentiment is offended on which its most respected moral maxims today rest' (ibid.).

Another consequence of the Christian doctrine of the

supremacy of the individual soul was that it gave rise to modern humanism, to the cult of the individual. Durkheim noted that no matter how remarkable was the place given to the individual in Roman times, it was insignificant compared with what was developed in Christianity (1950a/1969g:94/t. 1957a:58). In Durkheim's moving article on individualism, written under the shadow and alarm of the Dreyfus affair, he said that 'the originality of Christianity has consisted precisely in a remarkable development of the individualist spirit' (1898c:11/t.1969d/r.1975:68). As a result of Christian doctrine, the individual was given integrity, personal rights, and allowed to express himself, within limits, as he wanted to. Durkheim held that such restricted individualism constituted in part the teaching of Christianity (ibid.). He could not identify himself with Christian morality in its entirety, nor, on the other hand, with that form of individualism which bordered on egoism.

Also, Christians were commanded to love one another and indeed mankind. Because of the sacredness of all individuals, and because their God was a god of the spirit and of love, they were encouraged to be concerned for their neighbours and, as a consequence, Durkheim held that there was a decline in the number of duties addressed specifically to the deity. On one of the rare occasions that Durkheim referred to the atonement, he wrote:

> An essentially human religion since its God dies for the salvation of humanity, Christianity teaches that the principal duty of man toward God is to love his neighbour. (1925a:7/t.1961a:6-7/r.1975:194)

Durkheim saw that the history of western society could not be understood apart from a Christian doctrine which lay at its root. Christianity was the main force in forging that culture which was to become dominant in Europe and which is the foundation of modern society. It was the Church alone that was able to influence, educate and civilize the barbarians and invading Germanic peoples in the ninth century. No other comparable force was able to exert itself and to give Europe moral unity. It was without a rival, especially in the absence of any national civilization which might have opposed it.

Christianity at this period was essentially international, transcending locality and region. And the monk had a definite part to play, since he was mobile, and carried the pervading culture from one country to another. He was a truly universal figure in so far as he was in one sense of no particular country, being in the service of a universal religion (1938a/1969f:49/ t.1977a: 39). On such a foundation arose the Carolingian renaissance and the concept of Christendom itself.

For Durkheim, what Christianity had to offer was in sharp contrast to that of rival religions around the Mediterranean, for at its heart was a contempt for the joys and pleasures of the world, a rejection of material luxury and the refinement of pleasure. In their place it substituted the joys of renunciation (ibid.:27/20). It did not praise asceticism for its own sake or embark on extreme renunciation. It extolled the virtues of humility and unpretentiousness in material and intellectual spheres, and thus it upheld the ideal of a simple way of life. This had an obvious attraction for the poor. As Durkheim said: 'Christianity was supremely the religion of those who were not great' economically or culturally (ibid.:28/21 also 1897a:282/ t.195la:254). The Church thus found itself attracting peoples who were poor, who were of non-Roman origins, and it was able to weld them together by a common faith and culture.

Quite logically the Church took the initiative in the matter of education. One reason for this was the success of the Church in its mission of converting the barbarians, notably the Germanic peoples. But at the same time, it was rooted in Roman civilization and culture, and the Latin language was at the very centre of its life. This language had therefore to be taught to the converts. Another reason, as has been noted, was that a Christian doctrine laid emphasis on faith, and therefore on thought. Hence the contents of its doctrine had to be rationally imparted to others and understood by them, and this called for educational institutions. The Church, as no other body could, entered the field of education and thoroughly developed it. Realizing this, Durkheim gave a considerable place to the role of the Church in his lectures on higher education (1938a; see especially chs 2-4, 26-7, and the following section of this chapter on the work of the Jesuits).

Within Christian education itself, Durkheim noted that it was not just concerned with facts but with basic values and indeed the whole of life. He wrote:

> Christianity was aware that the forming of a man was not a question of decorating his mind with certain ideas, nor of getting him to contract certain specific habits; it is a question of creating within him a general disposition of the mind and the will which will make him see things in general in a particular light. (1938a/1969f:37/t.1977a:29)

And the agents of education – indeed its leaders – were for the most part members of religious communities and orders. As so many others have had occasion to observe, Durkheim emphasized the fact that the religious life in Christianity was never one that was totally contemplative in outlook. It was essentially communal and had been greatly influenced by the rule of St Benedict, who placed emphasis on work as well as on prayer and worship (ibid.:31, 46/24, 35). In the medieval period the monasteries were not only centres of 'research' in letters and philosophy, but were also institutions in which aspiring intellectuals were taught (1950a/1969g:95/t.1957a:59).

We have described in a somewhat cursory fashion Durkheim's attitude towards Christianity in general, and by that we mean the development of the religion up to the time of the Reformation. The subsequent history of Catholicism and the Protestant churches interested Durkheim in various ways, and it is to this later period of Christian history that we now turn and consider the ways the leaders of these religious groupings had occasion to refer to his sociology.

3. Roman Catholicism: Durkheim's admiration and disgust

Durkheim's attitude towards modern Roman Catholicism, from say the time of the Counter-Reformation, was very mixed. His fleeting attraction in his teens towards this form of Christianity has already been mentioned. Although he withdrew from the possibility of conversion, there were aspects of Catholicism he greatly respected and continued to do so to the end of his life.

In an early essay his first to appear in the *Année sociologique* on the subject of incest and its origins, he noted with apparent approval that the Roman Catholic Church saw sexual relations as having an immediate end in the creation of a family and he went on to observe that the same church prohibited sexual intercourse on holy days. Strongly implanted in Durkheim's mind was the conviction that uncontrolled sexual drives stand opposed to family morality. This was most apparent in a discussion of the Société' Franchaise de Philosophie on sexual education, in which he openly stated his opposition to extra-marital sexual relations on the grounds, amongst others, that it had a disruptive effect on family solidarity (1911a:46/t. 1979a:146). Durkheim, academically and personally such a strong supporter of the family, believed that the home in the past and the present had a religious character, which of necessity was based on collective discipline (1898a(ii):67/t.1963a:111; and see Lukes 1972:263 n.45, etc.).

But discipline is required not only within the family, but in every area of social life. This concern with discipline is based, in turn, on Durkheim's doctrine of man. From his early writings and extending to those which appeared just before he died, there is a repeated demand for the need of discipline which is based on the firm assumption that man's instincts need to be controlled (see relevant sections in 1897a, 1925a; etc.). Man is not a creature to be liberated from social or economic oppression, from the shackles of fear and guilt, from the crippling effects of institutions, or from the degradations of capitalism. To the contrary, man's freedom comes from ensuring that his instincts are controlled by moral limits which are set by society. What makes a man a human being, and not a quasi-animal, is his acceptance of, and incorporation into what his fellow creatures have made – the culture or the civilization in which he is born. Socialization, which begins at the time of birth, is the process by which man comes to a position of acceptance and compliance; and therefore of humanness. When, however, the process is inadequate, when man openly rejects the norms and limitations set by society, when the sky is the limit, a state of anomy emerges, for man now runs wild without the boundaries within which he can operate. A position of limitless freedom and ambition gives rise to social chaos. The guarantee of social order and prevention of the anomy, which society so deeply fears, are thus dissolved when the moral limits and disciplines of society are rejected for one reason or another.

Such a doctrine of man has affinities with that of certain classical writers, for example, Plato and Aristotle. However, Durkheim chose not to mention these parallels, but to go straight to Christian sources, speaking in general terms and, surprisingly, making no reference to St Paul's writings. It is beyond doubt that Durkheim's own doctrine of man is derived from orthodox Christianity as Felix Pécaut noted (1918:4). (Pécaut (1828-98) had once been a Protestant minister, was chosen in 1880 by Ferry to organize an important teacher training college for women, and as a liberal Protestant tried to base moral education on religious feeling.)

Another aspect of the Christian doctrine of man that Durkheim adopted with modification was the notion of man's duality (see 1913b and 1914a). Man, he upheld, was possessed of two components or elements within himself, body/soul, sacred/profane, egoistic appetites/moral action, and so on. Needless to say, such a position, metaphysical in its assertions, has been widely criticized both in his day (see 1913b) and again more recently (Sumpf 1965:66ff.). The point here is not to expound Durkheim's doctrine or to criticize him, but to demonstrate his borrowing of certain Christian ideas.

Whereas the orthodox Christian doctrine of man is common to both Catholics and the majority of Protestants, we have mentioned it within the context of modern Catholicism because Durkheim was of the opinion, evident in his *Suicide,* that the spirit of discipline and moral constraint which are a necessary element of his doctrine of man, were in modern times better upheld by Catholics than by Protestants. At various periods Protestants had been subject to influences which granted considerable authority and autonomy to the individual (see the next section of this chapter), whereas the Catholic Church, in rejecting such doctrine and later setting its face against liberalism, was able to exert over its followers a clear-cut morality and to administer it through the confessional. Never let it be forgotten that Durkheim's attachment to liberalism in morals and politics was one that maintained the necessity of self-discipline and the imposition of social discipline. Any notion that liberalism should veer towards egoism or libertinism was strongly repudiated.

The thought and practice of the Jesuits occupied a considerable place in Durkheim's lectures on higher education (1938a; Pt II, chs 5-7). In their response to the impetus and success of the Protestant Reformation, the Jesuits, who helped to restore the morale and domain of the Catholic Church, broke the monopoly of higher education which had been centred solely in the universities. The Catholic Church needed to enter into close and influential relations with the growing intellectual classes. This demanded educational and social ability on the part of the Church and for the emergence of a system which would be designed to train people for specific tasks and occupations in society. The Jesuits, realizing the need, saw that it could be met only by mingling with the world and being open to its dominant ideas, even assimilating them, but at the same time using them for the ultimate good of the Church. This meant a new type of religious order which would be prepared to enter every important social area of life, to break out of the rigidity of the old communities and orders, and at the same time to be maintained and strengthened by firm self-discipline. In seeking to influence the young and operate a new type of education, the Jesuits held that it was necessary to harness Renaissance thought, which could lead so easily to Protestantism; this meant making full use of classical learning, to the point of trying to control it and demonstrate its theoretical importance for the Church. One outcome was that their students had to speak Latin in everyday conversation. So successful were the colleges founded by the Jesuits that for a time the very existence of the universities was threatened. In overlooking some of the common accusations made against the Jesuits for example, their rigidity of goal coupled with flexibility of means, bordering on the immoral – Durkheim stated that 'Jesuit education played the major part in the formation of our national genius, and gave it the distinctive features which it exhibits in the period of its full maturity' (1938a/

1969f:274/t.1977a:239). The Jesuits emphasized written exercises amongst their students, something unknown in the age of scholasticism; and eloquence or rhetoric was looked on as a superior art. On the other hand, little or no place was given to understanding classical civilization set in a historical context. Further, the classics were so taught that profane or pagan though they were, they were used as eulogies for the faith, and in so doing the Jesuits deliberately 'denatured the ancient world' (ibid.:287/250; see also ibid.:293/255). They turned classical literature, which was so popular at the time and which was basically non-Christian, into a form which was held to be inspired by Christianity. With the Jesuits the love of learning for its own sake was lost. But here Durkheim seemed to praise the Jesuits for giving to education a specific purpose, that of making pupils faithful Catholics (ibid.:291/254), for Durkheim himself saw education in utilitarian terms because all knowledge and learning were for men's avocations in life (ibid.:265/230). Jesuit education, however, was crammed, intensive and highly competitive to the point of endangering the mind in the demand for written work and a lack of thoug-htfulness on the part of students. On the other hand, Jesuits laid it down as axiomatic that there must be a close and personal link between the teacher and the pupil—something absent in medieval universities. The pupil was never left to his own ingenuity or by himself. The aim was as much to help the student as to prevent misconduct.

Durkheim concluded that the Jesuit system was well grounded in the conditions of the sixteenth century, but that the Jesuits applied their principles too rigidly. In coming too close to the student, they inhibited all freedom of movement, so that in the end their method became what we should today call counterproductive (ibid.:302-3/264).

But, by and large, compared with Protestantism. Durkheim saw in Catholicism in the nineteenth century a more rigorous, robust church capable of resisting profaning influences such as the intrusion of science and freedom of thought (1907c:51; see the following chapter).

Durkheim's attitude towards the Catholic Church was, however, ambivalent and he tempered words of praise with those of condemnation. He had a strong dislike of large, powerful bodies exercising control that can border on the despotic. This clearly emerges in his lectures on higher education in France where he writes:

> When a body in authority, any body in authority, is fired by a love of regimentation, when it has a tendency to make everything conform to a single unique norm, it experiences an instinctive horror for everything which is the result of whim and imagination. Anything which might disturb the established order takes on the appearance of a scandal which must be avoided; and since elective affinities are necessarily incompatible with programmes which have been decreed..every effort is made to suppress them by restricting freedom. (1938a/1969f: 141/t.1977a:121)

Such sentiments are associated with a similar dislike of a rigid hierarchy. Richter has said:

> As for his refusal to recognize bureaucracy as part of a normal society, he identified bureaucracy with hierarchy, and hierarchy with the Roman Catholic Church. As a survival' from an earlier stage, this type of organization was obsolete. (1960:203)

Thus, it was the nature of the structure of the Roman Catholic Church that Durkheim found quite unacceptable.

It was at an academic colloquium held in Paris in 1905 on the Separation of Church and State that Durkheim, speaking as a leading sociologist, caused uneasiness among his fellow discussants by referring to the Catholic Church as a 'sociological monstrosity'. The relevant part of the discussion reads:

> DURKHEIM:I shall only give you an impression: I believe the mistrust of the bishops [towards lay associations] is not without foundation. The law [of Separation], in the measure to which it will give more autonomy to lay people, will remove the Catholic Church from the abnormal position it is in now. The Church, from a sociological point of view, is a monstrosity.
>
> [Desjardins said that the Roman Catholic Church was not so much a monstrosity as miraculous.]

> DURKHEIM: It is the same thing. . . It is abnormal that an association so vast and diffuse, which itself links up complex moral groups where, as a consequence, so many causes of differentiation are bound to be at work – should be subject to such an absolute intellectual and moral homogeneity. (1905e:370)

Durkheim's very sinister word *'un monstre'* was such a forceful one that not only did it electrify the colloquium, it caused one of its members, Abbé Hemmer, to refer to it in a subsequent article in which he inverted the implication of the phrase:

> DURKHEIM has well said that the ancient institution of Christ is a sociological monstrosity. On this acceptable verification is founded in apologetics one of the proofs of the divinity of the Church ('Reflexions sur la situation de l'Église en France au début du XXe siécle', *La Quinzaine,* 1(3),1905, p.4).

So Durkheim, in Hemmer's eyes, did stalwart service for the Catholic Church!

Were there other sources that made Durkheim openly hostile to Roman Catholicism? Lukes has made the point, and it is a common enough one, that Durkheim was 'a good anti-clerical' (1972:534). Such an accusation has to be concretely related to the specific historical situation of the day in which the clergy were able to control the political attitudes of their flocks. This was particularly obnoxious to Durkheim, as the prevailing clerical outlook was frequently royalist or right wing. The Dreyfus affair witnessed an upsurge in French Catholicism in the direction of hierarchical authoritarianism. As an ardent Dreyfusard, Durkheim saw that large sections of the Catholic Church, sustained by the local clergy, rallied to the cause of nationalistic triumphalism. It is little wonder therefore that Durkheim's anti-clericalism was all the more confirmed by the events of the affair.

As Durkheim was ambivalent towards modern Catholicism, so there were some sections of the Catholic population similarly disposed towards him. Durkheim's contention that from available statistics suicide rates were lower in Catholic areas than in Protestant ones (see the following section of this chapter) carried ideological consequences and clearly pleased some Catholic apologists, particularly, as Richard noted, German Catholic clergy (1923:136/t.1975:240). It can also be argued in another direction that there exists common ground between Durkheim and Catholic theologians in so far as they both give a prominent place to institutional forms, and see that truth is located in rationality rather than in human consciousness or religious experience, as was common with many Protestants at the time.

These considerations apart, there was considerable objection from Catholic intellectuals to Durkheim's thought.[1] No Catholic apologist finding comfort in what Durkheim said about suicide would be equally pleased when he uncritically stated what Guyau had written: 'It is often the most Catholic countries which provide most criminals' (1887b:303/t.1975a:29). But other points of contention were much more serious: they related to Durkheim's assumptions about the nature of religion studied sociologically, his denial of the truth-claims of all religion, not least those of Christianity, that all religion is man-made, that the most important element of religion is its social component. These points we have already considered in detail in previous chapters. Nevertheless, Catholic opposition to Durkheim in the main was weak because the Church possessed no sociological thinker of his stature, comparable, let us say, with the Protestant sociologist, Gaston Richard (see the following section). Opposition tended to be more vociferous after Durkheim died, for it was aroused by the attempt of the Durkheimian, Paul Lapie, the French government's director of primary education, to introduce Durkheimian sociology into teacher training colleges (see ch. 27.3). While Durkheim was alive, the only serious academic opposition came from the French-speaking Belgian Simon Deploige (1905-7 and 1911; see ch. 4.1). But as Durkheim noted, not only had Deploige misunderstood elements of his thought, but he had very little to offer sociology save a return to Thomism (1907b and 1913a(ii) (15)). In the period after Durkheim's death, no comparable attack was launched by Catholics, and it has been said that they were not unhappy to support the arguments of Gaston Richard, not least because of his standing as a professor of sociology at the University of Bordeaux. This 'accidental' ecumenical venture was later strengthened when Richard was asked to contribute to a series 'Actualités scientifiques et industruelles' edited by

Jacques Chevalier in the 1930s. Chevalier was a right-wing Catholic, an 'integrist' who later served in the Petain government. He was a firm admirer of Richard and had been influenced by Le Play and Bergson.

After the Second World War one sees a remarkable change amongst certain liberally inclined Catholics. No longer is sociology seen to be an enemy of the Church, but now it is a handmaid. By its examination of the facts it can show the Church the inner workings of its institutions and is therefore to be welcomed. In the vanguard of the movement was the revered Catholic medieval historian and sociologist, Gabriel Le Bras, who became the patron of Catholic 'religious sociology' (see ch. 27.1 n.1). Influenced by Durkheim and his nephew, Marcel Mauss, Le Bras was convinced of the academic value of sociology in the study of religious phenomena and supported the contention of certain clerics that the application of sociology to the Church at the present time would equip the clergy with a means of combating the decline of religious institutions in France, which had occurred for over a century.

4. Protestantism: did Durkheim understand it?

Durkheim's attitude towards Protestantism was tepid, if not cold. He showed little of the ambivalence he had for Catholicism.

References to Protestantism are thinly scattered and, as readers might guess, it is in *Suicide* that most of his writings on the subject are to be found. As is well known, in searching for causal factors contributing to suicide, he attempted to discover whether various forms of religion had any bearing on rates of suicide and he found that, particularly in Switzerland, suicide tended to be higher amongst Protestants than amongst Catholics (1897a:bk III, ch. II). In his search to explain such a social fact – his methodological procedure need not detain us - he compared what he held were the social characteristics of Protestantism with those of Catholicism, which had significance in relation to suicide. Protestants, he noted, have fewer common beliefs and practices than have Catholics, the believer relies on his own conscience about his faith, and therefore his approach to religion is individualistic. The result is that the Protestant churches tend to be loosely integrated, for they exert very little control, nor do they inculcate a sense of religious loyalty and devotion as does the Catholic Church. Protestantism admits to a great deal of free inquiry, and for this and for other reasons there is to be found within it a strong desire for education. Amongst many variable factors, which are themselves interrelated, he holds that one provides the clue for tendencies towards suicide. It is the tendency to free inquiry. Yet it was something about which Durkheim was ambivalent. On the one hand, he strongly favoured it, but, on the other, he was aware that it weakens moral life. Towards the end of *Suicide,* he concludes that religion, therefore, modifies the inclination to suicide only to the extent it prevents men from thinking freely' (1897a:430/t.1951a:375). Catholics in the past have been able to do this, and Protestants to a less extent, but no religion today is able to exert sufficient control over individuals to prevent free inquiry, not even Catholicism. He adds, perhaps hinting at liberal Protestantism:

> When religion is merely a symbolic idealism, a traditional philosophy, subject to discussion and more or less a stranger to our daily occupation, it can hardly have much influence on us. (ibid. :431/376)

Durkheim always saw ritual as a key element of religion (see part IV of this book). Protestantism was particularly vulnerable here, for Durkheim said in his lectures on moral education that the autonomy of morality in Protestantism is further accentuated by the fact that ritual is minimized. The moral function of divinity thus becomes its sole *raison d'étre* (1925a:8/t.1961a:7/r.1975:195). As its specifically religious characteristics become eroded, spiritualistic philosophy, argued Durkheim, takes over from Protestantism, and in this sense Protestantism itself stands close to the long-standing evolution of history towards secularization (see the following chapter).

This is no occasion to challenge point by point Durkheim's assessment of Protestantism in relation to suicide. Some Protestant thinkers, for example, Gaston Richard, were fully aware of its implications and were therefore hostile towards him. However, it could be well argued that Durkheim wrote very much as an outsider and that his generalizations about Protestantism were far from accurate. Certainly some of the things he said hardly applied to the Calvinists in France, amongst whom there existed at the time he wrote, and still exists, a great sense of community and integration, in part engendered by years of persecution. L'Église Réformée as a minority group has striven to maintain its own identity and has thus created relatively close ties between its members. Durkheim admits such characteristics of small religious groups (1897a: 155/t.1951a:156/t. 1975:44). All the arguments to explain high suicide rates amongst Protestants could be applied to Jews, but, as Durkheim noted, their rates were particularly low. Durkheim was thus forced to find reasons which applied to Jews, but which did not apply to Protestants. This shifting of ground greatly weakens Durkheim's attempt to find a scientific explanation of the phenomenon he had unearthed.

The generalizations he tried to make about Protestantism raise the question of the value of such a term as Protestantism within sociological explanation. Protestantism exists within so many forms from small sects like the Mennonites, to established churches such as the Lutheran Church that it becomes very difficult to make universal statements about Protestantism which have a general significance. This difficulty is compounded by the fact that with the inroads of liberal thought into many Protestant churches there is to be found, on the one hand, dogma as rigidly held as that in the Roman Catholic Church, and, on the other, sets of beliefs which are little differentiated from humanism. The attempt to speak in broad terms is a failure that is to be seen also in Max Weber. Generalizations usually flounder when the Church of England is taken into consideration. Durkheim noted this to be the case in examining rates of suicide and found that amongst Protestant countries England had the lowest rates (ibid.:160ff./160ff./48ff.). Yet England is the country most famous for its individualism and for freedom of speech! Durkheim is thus forced to offer various lame reasons for the exception to his 'rule' the Anglican Church is more integrated than Protestant churches; there are more clergy per capita in England than in any other Protestant country; there exists a hierarchical form of church government; and there are national laws relating to the observance of Sunday. Perhaps Anglicanism was to him something of a theological and a sociological mystery, as it is to many continental thinkers.

In his lectures, *L'Évolution pédagogique en France,* Durkheim did not give the Protestant churches much credit for the development of education in his country. But he noted that at the time of the Reformation amongst the Anglo-Saxon and Germanic peoples, humanism was very rapidly curbed (1938a:314/ t.1977a:274). In fact Lutheranism was basically indifferent towards humanism and the advocacy by Luther for a study of the classics had the sole object of equipping preachers adequately for their task (ibid.:326/285). In this respect Luther, together with Melanchthon, were far removed from the outlook of Erasmus and the leaders of the Renaissance in Latin countries. Durkheim wrote: 'The fact is that Protestantism had a feeling for secular society and its temporal interests which Catholicism neither possessed nor could possess' (ibid. :327/285). The result was that humanism never made the headway in Germany that it did in France in the sixteenth century.

To be fair, Durkheim did point to some qualities in Protestantism with which he was sympathetic – the notion of free inquiry, an emphasis on morality, and perhaps a minimizing of ritual. And he also admitted that in the change in educational theory towards a concern for nature and science that came at the time of the French Revolution, Protestant countries were of service in fostering the new pedagogy, because the religion was already sensitive to the non-clerical *[laique]* side of society' (1938a/1969f:334-5/t. 1977a:292).

Initially, it seemed that much in Durkheim's *Suicide* attracted some Protestant ministers, as well as German Catholic priests, although obviously for different reasons. Gaston Richard commented that they were 'too ingenuous' (1923:136/1.1975:240).

Gaston Richard (1860-1945), to whom many references have been made, was an early collaborator with Durkheim and worked with him on the *Année sociologique* (see ch. 2.4; Pickering 1975:343-59; 1979b). Having been brought up as a Catholic and having rejected the faith and spent a short time as a non-believer while he was at the École Normale Supérieure, he became a Protestant and remained a strong supporter of the Église Réformée to his dying day. Until his withdrawal, Richard was the sole Protestant in the Année Sociologique group, and perhaps the only member committed to any traditional religion (see ch. 27.2). Whilst at the École he became a friend of Durkheim and although he was never a member of the closest circle around Durkheim, he was, because of his early writings and doctorat d'état, a senior member of the *équipe* (see various articles in *RFS*, XX, 1979). In 1907, after ten years of co-operation with Durkheim, he withdrew from the group. Earlier, when Durkheim left the University of Bordeaux in 1902, Richard followed him as lecturer in sociology, and became a professor in 1906. There he remained until he died. Cut off from Durkheim's group, he became for a while an isolated figure. He was known to be the most outspoken critic of Durkheim and was frequently referred to as 'le vieil adversaire de Durkheim'. One of the causes for the rift and then hostility to Durkheim and his followers was over the question of religion. As we have seen, he held that in many respects Durkheim failed in his work to live up to the goal he had set himself, namely, a scientific approach to social phenomena. He in fact made metaphysical statements about religion and therefore ceased to be scientific. Durkheim also, he argued, denied the freedom of the individual and his contribution to the development of religion. It is evident that behind much of Richard's criticism there is implied Durkheim's failure to understand Protestantism and indeed Christianity as well (see chs 27 and 28).

Another outspoken critic from the Protestant ranks was Marc Boegner (b. 1881), who became an outstanding leader of the Église Réformée and a member of the Académie Fransaise. At the conference of the Union of Free Thinkers and Free Believers held in 1914, it was his questions which Durkheim chose to answer in writing (see 1919b/t.1975a; also Poulat 1970). His questions on the whole tended to be critical and raised such issues as studying religion in its most primitive forms, the place of Australian Aboriginals amongst primitive peoples, the role of individual leaders in the evolution of religion and the relation between higher religions and those of a more primitive form (1919b:142-3/t.1975a:187-9; ch. 10.2).

5. A liberal or a medievalist?

In this chapter we have tried to demonstrate that Durkheim had considerable respect for Christianity. He pointed to its doctrines as being crucial in understanding the emergence of modern western society, for the Europe of his day had grown out of a Christendom based on strong religious beliefs. It is also clear that Durkheim held dear some of the values embedded in Christianity, notably its doctrine of man and its demand for discipline and self-control. He seemed to reject much of Protestantism, because he saw that it was far too individualistic and tended to encourage egoism. What clearly appealed to Durkheim most were the humanistic qualities that he saw in Christianity a willingness to suffer for other people which is inherent in its doctrine of God and in the story of Jesus Christ dying for mankind. Christians were commanded to love their neighbours, to be concerned for the things of the spirit which ultimately leads to a concern for the individual. In all this speaks the honest liberal humanist. who does not condemn Christianity as being an evil that has to be eliminated, or a force which has done little good for society. Its contribution to culture has been crucial and its doctrine of man, expressed in orthodox terms has elements that are to be commended and which could be said to form part of the *raison d'étre of* secular humanism

That Durkheim was a convinced liberal and an ardent supporter of the Third Republic, no one can deny. But there is lurking behind this conviction not only the need for strict discipline, but a harking back to the ideals of the high Middle Ages. Dedicated though he was to the hopes of an emerging society based on democracy and free thought, Durkheim nevertheless, in his exploration of the history of Christianity, saw in the medieval period a most desirable combination of Christian belief, academic excellence and an integration of thought and action - something like praxis. Now it has been lost. He wrote in his lectures on higher education in France:

> Nothing could be further from the truth than this view of the Middle Ages [that the Middle Ages was a sort of interval], and consequently nothing is more inappropriate than the name which we give to this epoch. Far from its being a mere

> period of transition without any originality of its own between civilizations which were brilliantly original it is rather the period of gestation for the fertile seeds of an entirely new civilization. (1938a/1969f:39/t. 1977a:31)

Again, when Durkheim points to Abelard as the most representative figure of the medieval period, does he not indicate that there are in him virtues of the highest order? He had a:

> brilliant dialectic, faith grounded in reason, and that curious mixture of religious fervour and a passion for knowledge which was a distinguishing mark of this great era. (ibid. :85/70; see also 84/69)

When speaking of scholastic philosophy, he notes that its characteristic is the mutual interpenetration of 'reason and faith within a single system of ideas which renders them inseparable from one another' (ibid.:112-13/96). Here it seems we have that perfect combination of faith and reason that Durkheim the rationalist sees to be ultimately desirable. Such unity, which existed in the medieval period, projected an ideal for which he strove in the twentieth century. Whilst he was unflinching in his support for *La Nation* and for liberal democracy, and whilst he rejected traditional Christian morality, though retaining a great deal of it, there is nevertheless beneath such externalities a secret longing for the ideals and aspirations of a much earlier period than his own.

Durkheim's respect for traditional western religion was basically a respect for something in the past, for a dying social force. The claims of that religion which had helped to found Europe could no longer be accepted by thoughtful people such as himself. For centuries in fact, longer than anyone had realized, that force had been diminishing and was now virtually spent. But for what reasons? It was a question to which Durkheim frequently addressed himself.

Chapter-2

SECULARISATION: THE HISTORY OF MANKIND

Chapter-2

1. The inevitability of religious change

Although Durkheim had something approaching an innate warmness towards all religions, and in particular, as we have shown, towards Christianity, he did not believe that traditional religions would persist in Europe, nor did he think it desirable that they should. It was patently evident to him, as to many intellectuals of his day in France and elsewhere, that Christian belief and practice had reached their last days. It was no surprise to him that it should be so. In a frequently quoted sentence, he wrote: 'Les anciens dieux vieillissent ou meurent, et d'autres ne sont pas nés' – 'The old gods are growing old or are dying and other gods have not been born' (6l0-11/427/156). No gospel is immortal and that of the Christians is no exception. Every religion thus faces death. But some observers would note that, if traditional Christianity was on its death bed at the turn of the century, it has proved to be a long time dying. Religions are much more resilient than is often imagined.

Religious change is very much part of Durkheim's sociology. Although he wrote nothing systematic on it, especially in relation to the modern period, there are many references to it in his earliest writings as well as in his last.

There are, of course, two distinct issues – one is religious change *per se,* and the other is religious change implying a decline or weakening of religion within society, especially in its institutional forms. It is the latter issue that is associated with the contentious term secularisation. Durkheim generally has at the back of his mind such a term. In some respects he saw secularisation in far more radical terms than do many modern sociologists. Nevertheless, he had a paradoxical approach to the subject: religion is dying and society is becoming secular; yet, on the other hand, religion is alive and will always be a component of social life.

2. Words used by Durkheim relating to religious change and secularisation

To describe the diminution of religious institutions, Durkheim did not use a French word which has a root in common with the English word secularisation. The term secularisation in its modern context is basically Anglo-Saxon. Rather, he employed several words, *déclin, affaiblissement, régression.* For example, he spoke about a weakening *(affaiblissement)* of religion in the *Rules* (1895a: 162/t. 1938b: 132) and God progressively withdrawing' *(déclin)* from his relationships with man in the *Division of Labour* (1893b/1902b:144/t.1933b:169). At first sight, these are acceptable terms. For example, no one would object to the word decline *(déclin).* But reflection on the term regression *(regression)* suggests an ideological component, for it implies a reversion to a less developed form' *(Oxford English Dictionary),* and the same idea is indicated in the French. Gaston Richard attacks Durkheim precisely at this point. He holds that Durkheim is not sympathetic towards the claims and social facts of religion (1923:126/t.1975:229). This is evident, if nowhere else, in Durkheim's adoption of the word *regression.* Sarcastically, Richard writes:

> Even before it was scientifically constituted, the history of religions had its inescapable law. The law was that the evolution of religion is regression or rather dissolution. (ibid. :133/236)

It is undeniable that for Durkheim the development of social institutions in the history of mankind has been accompanied by a regression of religion. He stated this in his first and last books, *Division of Labour* (1893b/1902b:144/t.1933b:169) and *The Elementary Forms of the Religious Life* (613/429/158).

Durkheim was being merely descriptive when he said that religion had now lost most of its sovereign power *(son Empire)* (1897a:283/t.1951a:255; see also 1900a(47)). One clear indication of its weakened state was its failure to control men's minds *(consciences).* This is evident if one compares a primitive society with a modern society: a primitive society is dominated by religion and, indeed, one can go so far as to say that one of the characteristics of primitiveness is religious domination.

For a society to become intensely religious means going back to the starting-point, that is, to becoming primitive. As Durkheim wrote:

> Unless the great societies today helplessly crumble and we return to little social groups of long ago, that is, unless humanity returns to its starting point, religion will no longer be able to exert very deep or wide sway over consciences. (1897a:430-1/t.1951a:375).

Thus, for Durkheim, regression would seem to be an unfortunate word to describe the decline in religious institutions unless it is used in a paradoxical sense. Durkheim would make it mean a loss of religious control, implying that it stands for a state in society in which traditional religion is outside the concern of man. Yet, as Richard rightly says, it means a return to a former state, and in Durkheim's terms this means society's return to religious domination. Hence two opposite meanings are contained in the one word. However, Durkheim envisages regression not just in terms of what might be called institutional religion. There is, over a wide historical sweep, a decline in the use of penal law, which Durkheim associates with religious law, and also a decrease in the number of 'proverbs, adages, dicta, etc. as societies develop' (1893b/1902b: 144/t. 1933b: 170; see also 1901a(i)/t.1973b). This, he holds, is another proof in showing that collective *representations* move towards generality and indeterminism, for in the 'fundamental conditions of the development of societies..there is a decreasing number of collective beliefs and sentiments which are both collective enough and strong enough to take on a religious character' (1893b/1902b:144/t.1933b:170).

The ambiguity that Durkheim exhibits about the term regression persists throughout his approach to secularisation (this is also noted by Gluckman 1962:19-20). The ambiguity is based on his own ambivalence towards religion itself – a denial of its truth-claims, on the one hand, and a worship of its practical effects, on the other.

Disregarding for the present the ambiguities in the use of the word regression, we shall assume that in speaking of the decline of contemporary religion we refer only to its weakened institutional condition.

For analytical purposes, *déclin,* and the associated words just mentioned, must be separated from *séculier* (secular) and *laïque* (lay), which possess distinctive French connotations.[1] Their association with anti-clericalism and the separation of church and state has had a long history. It would be wrong to assume that a church forced to become 'secularized' or 'laicized' in the French sense, and therefore shorn of clerical, episcopal or papal domination, would suffer a priori a loss in respect or in allegiance. Nevertheless to Durkheim and others, such a loss of power within society would mean a loss of control and a weakened position as an agent of socialization. To be *laïque* or *séculier* is to be shorn of social power. Hence in the last analysis, *sécularisation* may mean secularisation in the English sense. Whereas Durkheim may claim to be a scientific observer of the decline of traditional religion, he is also someone who lends support to its continual weakening, as for example in welcoming the separation of church and state (1905e) and, as we shall show, by propagating his scientific theories of religion.

3. Age-long secularisation

Durkheim sees the decline of religious institutions occurring along two time-scales. First, over a wide historical spectrum, in which secularisation has been in progress for millennia. Second, in more recent times, in which there has been an acceleration of the process due to particular circumstances in western society. We shall deal with each idea separately.

For Durkheim the waning of religious institutions is not something new. It did not begin in the so-called modern period. Rather, it has been a continual process from the time that man's civilization began to develop. One could almost say that it is the story of man's social evolution, or at least a large part of it. Such a position logically emerges from Durkheim's notion that in the beginning everything was religious (see, for example, 1897e; ch.14.3). The passage of time has meant that from a position of being encased in religion, societies have been able to dislodge most, if not all, social areas from religious domination. By man's discoveries and changes in his thought and values, areas of social life have been able to discard their religious ideology and become autonomous. In the history of secularisation, ethics, art, philosophy, science and so, on have eliminated all their original religious premises. The process has been at work throughout history: man's history is the history of his secularisation.

Such thinking goes back to the first of Durkheim's books. Here lie took a stand from which he never moved and to which he frequently alluded. The well-known passage is in *The Division of Labour:*

> If there is one truth that history teaches us beyond doubt, it is that religion tends to embrace a smaller and smaller portion of social life, originally, it pervades everything; everything social is religious; the two words are synonymous. Then little by little, political, economic, scientific functions free themselves from the religious function, constitute themselves apart and take on a more and more acknowledged temporal character. God, who was at first present in all human relations, progressively withdraws from them; he abandons the world to men and their disputes. At least, if he continues to dominate it, it is from on high and at a distance. and the force which he exercises, becoming more general and more indeterminate, leaves more place to the free play of human forces. (1893b/1902b: 143/t. 1933b: 169)

He reiterated the same point in lectures given a little later in 1895-6 entitled L'Histoire du socialisme:

> But in fact, as one advances in history, from inferior society to the city, from city to Christian peoples, one observes consistently that religion withdraws more and more from public life. (1928a:326/t. 1958b:225)

The phenomenon of decline is linked in *The Division of Labour* with the contrast Durkheim made between societies marked by mechanical solidarity and those characterized by organic solidarity. The former are segmental, in which social life is regimented: empirically such societies are associated with primitive peoples. By comparison, societies marked by organic solidarity allow greater individual freedom, in which social life is more differentiated, and such societies are identified with those in the modern western world. Durkheim sees religion as being a dominant agent for control in societies characterized by mechanical solidarity; whereas in those typified by organic solidarity it is far less influential. Thus there is a regression of religion as societies change from possessing one type of solidarity to another. The movement appears to be inevitable and means a virtual devolution of religion. Little wonder, then, that Richard, in referring to ideas in the *Division of Labour,* wrote: 'It [religion] is a form of solidarity condemned to retrogression or disintegration by the very laws of its formation and development' (1923:233/t. 1975:244-5).

In extending his thesis about organic solidarity, Durkheim saw one outcome of what we call secularisation was that as social life becomes free from religious control, so religious thought turns to personal life. Unable to control public affairs, religion's only hope is to gain control and influence over followers in their personal lives. Thus the history of religion is the history of the development of its privatization. Bẹlot pointed to privatization as being a key characteristic of western religion in his day (1909:37), and it would appear that such an idea was fairly common amongst French intellectuals at the turn of the century. More recently it has been emphasized by Berger (1967:133).

4. Recent secularisation

Although the secularizing process has been with man for the length of his history, it has not proceeded uniformly and there have been fluctuations and accelerations, certainly in the western world in recent epochs. Such secularisation, so much the stock in trade of modern sociologists of religion, became apparent, it is said, in the late eighteenth and early nineteenth centuries. It is often associated with the rise of industrialization. But Durkheim, in company with Max Weber, does not locate recent secularisation either within that epoch or with its associated social characteristics (see the section below). He would make its point of emergence earlier, around the fifteenth and sixteenth centuries at the time of the Renaissance and Reformation, arising out of the breakup of medieval religion (1907c:51). A shift in thought occurred then that was in the direction of individualism. In the revival of Greek and Roman studies, which was at the heart of the Renaissance, man, not God, became the centre of the universe (see 1938a; chs. 15 and 17). At the Reformation, there was a different movement afoot, but the result was much the same. Authority in religious matters was seen by the reformers to be located no longer in an institution exercising temporal power, but in the individual and in his interpretation of the Bible. The basis for religious truth thus shifts from public to private authority (see ch. 23.4).

So it is that Protestantism, by changing the seat of religious authority from the Church to the individual helps to bring about a loss of religious power and control in society, and with it an overall diminution of religious institutions. Also, the right of the individual to choose in matters of religious truth must inevitably give rise to a pluralist society, which itself accelerates secularisation. In locating the origins of recent secularisation in the Renaissance and Reformation, Durkheim's position is but a logical development of his all-embracing theory of secularisation.

As Durkheim was to say many times, religion does not have the same role in society today that it had in the past. Since it is 'a primordial phenomenon, it must yield more and more to the new social forms which it has engendered' (1899a(i):iv/ t.1960c:352-3). He saw no need to substantiate such a proposition about contemporary secularisation, because for him it was wellnigh self-evident. In contrast to his study on suicide, a more precise analysis of the contemporary religious scene by way of statistics, say of church membership or attendance, was quite unnecessary. Indeed, in the review of a book on the subject, he doubted the value that could be derived from such analyses, not least that for religious rites of passage (1903(ii)(57)). Although there was a decline in the baptisms and marriages solemnized in church in Paris in the late nineteenth century, Durkheim held that such evidence in itself was a poor indicator of the state of religious belief (ibid.). (There is implied here a primacy of belief over ritual (see ch.

20).) He held that other indicators, much more conclusive about the state of contemporary religion, were available and these did not at the same time require the use of statistics or surveys. That modern religion was in a state of decline or going through a process of secularisation could be shown, in Durkheim's eyes, in the following ways.

1. The loss of the temporal power of the Church, especially the Roman Catholic Church, is to be seen in the separation of Church and State which has taken place in so many countries in recent times. What the Church has to offer is not openly supported by rulers: it may even be rejected The modern state has no desire to be aligned with the beliefs and practices of any particular brand of Christianity, indeed with Christianity at all. Witness the separation of the Church and State in France in 1905 when the anti-clerical Third Republic was strong enough to overcome such ecclesiastical opposition as was then offered. The Church is given no option of assuming or rejecting an alliance with the state. Forced by its weakened condition, it has to assume a private role in society and, as we have said, to influence individuals as best it can. The truth of the matter is that the Church has now become a voluntary society.

2. Religion today allows itself to be the subject of scientific inquiry and of objective historical research. Formerly, until perhaps the eighteenth century, such an approach, especially in the Catholic Church, would have been unthinkable. It would have constituted an anathema and be seen as the work of heretics. That religion can now do no other than allow the scientist to pass through its doors and examine it as he does other phenomena means that it has lost control over its own affairs. The sacred of which it has been guardian, whether it be the sacred of some relic, the Bible, or the sacraments, is rendered profane by the possibility of uncovering what is believed to be the *raison d'etre* of the sacred (1893b/1902b:270/ t.1933b:285; 1907c; 1909a(1):517-8; and see following chapter).

3. In a similar way, Durkheim measured the secularized state of society in terms of the inability of religious institutions to enforce rules relating to sacrilege. A truly religious society is one where sacrilege is severely punished. As Durkheim

wrote: 'A religion which tolerates acts of sacrilege abdicates any sway over men's minds' (1898c: 12/t.1969d:27/r. 1975:69). In religious societies schisms are also unknown or, if known, are not tolerated. Today, these criteria no longer exist. Sacrilege against the Church is not severely dealt with - hardly even considered. Indeed, can sacrilege be said to exist at all? Those who defame the Church, flout its rules, criticize its beliefs and deride its rituals, all go about their business unpunished, unmolested, and are looked upon as acceptable citizens.

4. The institutional weakness of the Church is paralleled by its inability to control the lives of individuals, although that sphere is the one that alone remains to it. By way of example, Durkheim pointed to suicide. As we have seen, men in the past held to religious beliefs and were subject to religious disciplines in such a way as to prevent them committing suicide: this is no longer the case (see ch. 23.3-23.4). Also, that there was not more opposition towards the separation of Church and State was evidence of the weakened state of religion at the time (1907c:51).

5. Durkheim rejected the doctrines of traditional religion, but so did the vast majority of his colleagues in the universities. This probably was an indicator to Durkheim that most of the intellectual world was composed of non-believers. If the Church thus failed to hold the most intelligent members of society, its position as an intellectually respectable force is seriously open to question. In the matter of truth, science is to be followed rather than religion (see ch. 25.2). In his lectures, published as *Moral Education,* he wrote:

> All religious ideas are social in Origin; and, on the other hand, they still remain the preeminent form of public and private thought for the vast majority of men. Today, it is true, among more advanced thinkers science has replaced religion. (1925a:79/t. 1961a:69)

Elsewhere, with apparent approval, he quotes an idea from Guyau to the effect that all those of superior intelligence (meaning men), can do without religion, but not so the masses, women and children (1887b:303/t.1975a:29) That women as distinct from men need religion is implied in his *Suicide*

(1897a:231/t.1951a:215). The woman's more 'natural' religiosity is seen to be a ready protection against the tendency to suicide.

So much for the evidence that Durkheim gives for modern secularisation. But is he fooling us or is his thinking muddled? He seems to imply that religion remains very much part and parcel of many people's lives, even in the late nineteenth century. He is ready enough to admit the persistence of religion, despite his references to growing secularisation. Where does he stand? The answer is that he is completely convinced about an accelerating secularisation of traditional religions. This is to be seen in the loss of the social and political power of the churches, and also in the wide acceptance of science amongst intellectuals as a truth system to replace that of religion. And even in the populace at large, although the people still might be called religious and be associated with the churches, the influence of religion over their public and private lives, especially the former, is very much less marked than in previous centuries.

5. The effects of secularisation on society

In considering the effects of secularisation on society, Durkheim adopted what now appears a romantic position, based at least on an admiration of the medieval church. Here he follows in the path of Auguste Comte. In a discussion of his book, *Les Formes élémentaires,* at a meeting of the Société Française de Philosophic in 1913, he observed that when nations lost their religious faith they quickly fell into moral and social decay (1913b:69). He said:

> Since the gods are only personified collective ideals a fact to which every weakening of faith bears witness the collective ideal obviously becomes weakened itself; and it can only become weaker if the social vitality is itself damaged. In a word, if the gods are only the nations conceived symbolically, it is inevitable that the nations die when the gods die. The believer himself cannot fail to recognise this important sociological factor.

The fact that when religion decays the nation also decays was a contention that Durkheim knew was made often enough by others. For himself, however, he was firmly convinced of its truth, not through casual observation but by reason of his own theorizing, as is seen above. The onslaught of decadence, which comes as a direct result of a declining religion, was not due to the gods taking their vengeance on a disbelieving people (ibid.), but through ensuing moral poverty. This is a logical extension of Durkheim's assertion that the *representations* of a society, which include moral directives and goals, stand at the heart of religion. The *representations* of a society correspond to the *representations* of its religion. If the second lose their power, so must the first.

Along similar lines Durkheim argued that a society could exist only when its members were within a certain intellectual and moral community' (1898c: l0/t. 1969d:25/1975a:66;see also 1886a:69/t.1975a:22). Human beings can only live together when there exists a set of commonly held beliefs. That, Durkheim thought, was a sociological truism (ibid.). It follows, therefore, that the more demanding and the more widely adhered to are the common beliefs, the greater will be the social cohesion amongst members of a society (see ch. 16). Durkheim wrote in *Suicide:*

> Now, a religious society cannot exist without a collective *credo* and the more extensive the *credo* the more unified and strong is the society. (1897a: 158/t. 195 la: 159/r. 1975a:47)

If this notion applies to a religious society, it applies equally to society in general. Since a secularized society implies a lack of universally held religious beliefs, and since on Durkheim's own confession, religious *representations* are closely identified with the collective *representations* of society, a secularized society prima facie must be less firmly integrated than one that is religious. A decline of religion in a society must have a weakening effect on the social cohesion of that society itself. In this way, secularisation thus becomes an instrument for the erosion of social life. But is the matter in fact as simple as this?

6. Religious change, not secularisation?

Although a diminution of religion spelt moral decay in a society, and although Europe was in a state approaching that of anomy, Durkheim did not hold that the end of religion had come. God is not dead: a new god is taking his place. This is both a social fact and is also logically necessary for a society to continue to exist. In brief, at the present time, it is not so much a question of secularisation, of society reaching a state of secularity where religion is completely eliminated, but one of religious metamorphosis. He wrote:

> For if it is true that religion is, in a sense indispensable, it is no less certain that religions change, that yesterday's religion could not be that of tomorrow. (1898c: 10/t. 1969d:25/ r.1975a:66)

What is at stake therefore is religious movement and the problem is to account for the decline of the old and the emergence of the new. This means in sociological terms that religious change is to be seen as part of social change, and Durkheim's alleged failure to produce a theory of social change is to return to a monotonous chorus.

We will have an occasion to show that in place of a theory of change, Durkheim offered the concept of collective effervescence seen in its creative mode, which is derived from religious activity and which could itself be seen as a religious phenomenon. Although this irrational' explosive mechanism accounts for revival and the emergence of new ideas, it can hardly account for a decline or reversal. There is no 'negative' effervescence to show how the old is discarded. The old merely seems to 'fade away'. Apart therefore from the phenomenon of effervescence, Durkheim suggests that religion changes as the society in which it is set changes. He wrote in an early review: History teaches us that religions have evolved and changed with the very societies which gave birth to them' (1887b:307/ t.1975a:33). Here Durkheim stresses the social component of religion and its close relation to society. In an important footnote in one of his early writings, he said, having stated some of the timeless functions performed by religion:

> But it must be understood that the importance we thus attribute to the sociology of religion does not in the least imply that religion must play the same role in present-day societies that it has played at other times. In a sense, the contrary conclusion would be more sound. Precisely because religion is a primordial phenomenon, it must yield more and more to the new social forms which it has engendered. (1899a(i):v n./t.1960c:352 n.6)

But what precisely these forms are is not stipulated. And when he says that religion embraces a smaller and smaller portion of social life', he makes an obvious assertion and one that was commonly held at the time. What is needed is explanation: not the rehearsal of facts already known. Here, Durkheim seems to be in the muddle that he was in when he tried to explain suicide in his book of 1897. There are a number of factors at work which appear to be related but which cannot be easily separated.

7. Some suggested explanations

In one place Durkheim attributes the decline of traditional religions to inevitable events. 'The communion of minds,' he says, can no longer form around particular rites and prejudices since rites and prejudices have been swept away *in the natural course of things'* (1898c: 1 l/t. 1969d:26/r. 1975:67; our italics). So the scientific Durkheim, without any clearly enunciated reason appeals to nature'—the course of events—a mysterious force over which man has no control—to explain secularisation. It is hardly necessary to be reminded that the whole of *The Rules of Sociological Method* was a cry against such imprecision and such 'mysticism'.

In a somewhat similar vein, he wrote in lectures on moral education that:

> But gradually things change. Gradually, human duties are multiplied, become more precise, and pass to the first rank of importance; while others on the contrary tend to become attenuated. (1925a:7/t. 196la:6/r.1975:194)

One of the few places where Durkheim differentiates ritual from belief in his reference to contemporary secularisation is here in these lectures. Usually he speaks of religion in this context as a blanket term. He went on to say:

> Although there are religious duties—rites addressed only to divinity—the place they occupy and the importance attributed to them continue to diminish. (ibid.)

Durkheim implies elsewhere that religious practice and indeed certain religious beliefs go by the board on the grounds that there are now more demands made by society on people's lives. This, in turn, suggests changes in values and, somehow or other, religious values diminish in importance compared with other values. It was in his lectures on custom and law, given also at the turn of the century, that Durkheim put forward these ideas about the effect of the tempo of modern life. It is the enemy of religious practices: they are abandoned quite simply because there are other things to do. He said: 'The demands of a busier life tended to reduce the importance of ritual formalities' (1950a:227/t.1957a:194). Beyond this not very profound observation, Durkheim offers no further explanation.

At the 1913-14 Conference of the Union de Libres Penseurs et de Libres Croyants, Durkheim suggested that contemporary religious life was languishing and that revivals were short-lived, not because people had turned away from confessional formulae but 'because our power for creating ideals has weakened...because our societies are undergoing a phase of profound agitation' (1919b: 103-4/t. 1975a: 186). The enthusiasm of our forefathers for religion has therefore disappeared. Religion no longer thrills us, because many of its aspects 'have passed into common usage to such a degree that we are no longer conscious of them, or because they do not meet our current aspirations' (610/427/156). Hence changes in society, not changes in religion itself, bring about secularisation. It is the general state of society which is the cause and it is here that we encounter difficulty and confusion. Durkheim spoke of several characteristics of the age in which he lived:

1 In *Suicide* (1897a) and in his comments on anti-Semitism (1899d), he said that modern man was living in 'decadent

times', or in a period of agitation. This is indicated by social and political crises, such as those in 1848 with the European revolutions, in 1870-1 with the Franco-Prussian war and the Commune, and in 1894 and for a while thereafter with the Dreyfus affair (see ch. 1.4).

2 Another characteristic of the period of transition which Durkheim felt society was going through was marked by a loss of ideals and divinities 'which do not meet the requirements of the new aspirations which have come to the fore'(1919b:103-4/t.1975a:186).

3 The period is also characterized by 'moral coldness' which implies a moral mediocrity (610/427/156). Men are indifferent to constraints and virtues projected and imposed by religious and civil authorities.

4 Along with these characteristics, and indeed contained within them, there stands Durkheim's concept of anomy. It is impossible to consider this subject in detail here, other than to say that it is a state of society that Durkheim described as disaggregated *(désagrégé),* or in a state of disintegration (1897a:326/t.1951a:289). As a synonym for anomy, Durkheim also used *déréglement*—a disordered state or dissoluteness (ibid.:281/253). For the individual, it is the malady of infinite aspirations' as men and women reject the moral norms of society or have not been satisfactorily socialized in them.

Durkheim sees these as characteristics of modern society; they are close to characteristics which were described earlier on and can be seen to be the result of secularisation. There obviously exists a correlation between them and the decline of traditional religion. Which is cause and which is effect is not established. Often Durkheim is little more than descriptive. Something much more decisive is needed to get beyond mere description and the possibility of circularity of argument. For Durkheim, it is science which both breaks the old and creates the new.

The importance Durkheim attaches to science in our understanding of modern society, and in particular of religious change, is considered in the following chapter, at the end of which Durkheim's approach to secularisation will be assessed.

Chapter-3

The Invasion of Religion by Science

Chapter-3

1. Science, the real cause of secularisation

Running through all Durkheim's writings, even from the earliest, there is an unbroken strand which states simply and categorically that religion, both in the early days of man and now, has suffered a persistent decline due to one fact and one fact alone, the continual advance and acceptance of scientific thought and practice. At the turn of the century, he spoke of the triumph of science' over religion (1901h). Another sociologist, Herbert Spencer, held a similar view (1886a), while the philosopher, J. M. Guyau vigorously maintained that science was in the process of taking over religion (1887b). Triumph implies competition, if not hostility, between science and religion. The clash was obvious in the case of pagan religions, which in Durkheim's day were held to be shot through with superstitious practices and beliefs. These were the very antithesis of science. But Christianity, despite its sophisticated and philosophically based theology (as, for example, in the system of Aquinas), was not exempt. It, too, had to face the challenge of science with its certain knowledge about the world of physical phenomena. Science had advanced through being given its own autonomy and that autonomy meant complete freedom to use whatever methods it wished. Antagonism between science and religion was inevitable, because many religions in the past made assertions of truth in areas of experience which had now become the province of science. The conclusions which science has reached are very different from the truths proclaimed by the churches. Antagonism or the possible accommodation on the part of religion are thus the only possible outcomes.

For obvious reasons, religions, especially those of the West, have always been afraid that their claim to knowledge should be undermined by a rival authority, even though that authority might be some other religion. Reason and freedom of thought, which Durkheim axiomatically allied with science, can also be seen as two further enemies (see ch. 9.2). Speaking about the scholastic period of the Middle Ages. Durkheim wrote:

> For the moment one introduces reason, criticism and the spirit of reflectiveness into a set of ideas which up to that time has appeared unchallengeable it is the end: the enemy has gained a foothold. (1938a/1969f:87/t. 1977a:73)

Every time a new science was founded, the Christian Church rose in arms to oppose it (1893b/1902b:270/t.1933b:285). At first the clash was with the natural sciences in their study of the physical world. Then, in the late nineteenth century, the enemy came even closer to the 'City of God': the human and social sciences, psychology and sociology, went so far as to take as their subject man's behaviour in his innermost being and in the very society in which he lives. In 1893 Durkheim wrote:

> Christianity itself, although it instantly gave individual reflection a larger place than any other religion, could not escape this law. To be sure, the opposition was less acute as long as scholars limited their researches to the material world since it was originally abandoned to the disputes of men. Yet, as this surrender was never complete, as the Christian God does not entirely ignore things of this world, it necessarily happened that, on more than one point, the natural sciences themselves found an obstacle in faith. But it is especially when man became an object of science that the resistance became fierce. The believer, indeed, cannot but find repugnant the idea that man is to be studied as a natural being, analogous to others, and moral facts as facts of nature. (ibid.)

Here Durkheim appears as an early proclaimer of the notion that Christianity has become its own grave-digger - an idea that has recently become popular, not least through the writings of Peter Berger (for example, 1967). Indeed, in speaking of religious changes in the direction of secularisation, Durkheim openly declares that 'Christianity itself has contributed most to the acceleration' (1925a:7/t.1961a:6/r.1975:194). The reason is that Christianity has, by some form of dialectical process, given rise to ideas and institutions, which, once they have established their independence, turn round and deal deathly blows to the source of their origin. One *fact,* in particular, has been responsible for the decline of Christian thought - the insistence on the part of Christians to assert the truth about God, the world and man. This has given rise to science, which now denies the truths that Christianity originally put forward. If religions assert doctrines about reality which can be studied by science, the religions cannot deny or forbid critical analysis. From a scientific point of view, the doctrines may well be heresies (1890a/t.1973a:37).

The very action of science in investigating areas of experience which are held dear by religion can be, and nearly always is, sufficient to destroy the religious interpretation of the phenomena in question (see chs 16.8 and 28.3). The alternative explanation put forward in the name of science is convincing enough for people to reject religious explanation and doctrine. Offering a scientific explanation for what was once held to be a distinctly religious phenomenon is thus in itself a destructive process. In a review of Fouillée's *Les Elements sociologiques de la morale,* Durkheim wrote, concerning the religious character of moral phenomena -and what he said also applies to religion - that the very fact of treating them scientifically has the effect of profaning them' (1907a(3):355). And later in *The Elementary Forms* he stated:

> Once science came into being, it assumed a profane character, especially in the eyes of the Christian religion; consequently as it emerged it could not be applied to sacred things. (53 n.1/ 39 n.1/162 n.11)

But the opposition on the part of the Church to science entering the temple, examining holy books, analysing the psychological qualities of religious individuals, can no longer be sustained. The defensive walls have been breached. Durkheim said:

> the fact that the scientific spirit attacks it [religion] and questions it with the same freedom of thought that it applies to other natural phenomena goes to prove that it has lost its ascendancy which enabled it to be protected from profane thought. (1907c)

Thus, religion is impotent to prevent science undertaking its work and its work is such as to erode religion.

Interestingly enough, although Durkheim was thoroughly convinced that science profaned religion, he rejected the idea that it profaned morality. In 1906 he said:

> I wish to stress the fact that this science [sociology] permits the empirical study of moral facts, while at the same time not destroying the *sui generis* religious character which is inherent in them and which distinguishes them from all other human phenomena. (1906b/ 1924a:89/t. 1953b:62)

Durkheim felt that such a position prevented the adoption of utilitarian empiricism (ibid.). But he also wanted to protect, at least theoretically. what he saw as the religion of the future from being profaned by the intrusion of science (see ch. 26). To sustain his position he was forced to differentiate between religious phenomena and moral phenomena, and to maintain that morality is not above criticism and is therefore subject to reason and argument, whereas religion is held to be beyond modification by science. The sacred in religion is founded on dogmatism not discussion, which it does not admit (ibid.:70/49). He constantly speaks of the close relation between religion and morality. He once saw law and morality as being almost identical to religious belief, although the first two were not based on obligatory beliefs as was religion (1899a(ii):19/t.1975a:73; see ch. 9.3). The logic of his position is that there must be two kinds of the sacred. One operates in religion and is fragile: the other in morality, which admits examination but which is immune from the deleterious effects of criticism. Science in this case does not undermine the validity of morality. Such differentiation is unwarrantable.

The attack of science is on religious belief, not on religious action. Durkheim is a rationalist to the extent that he believes that once a person's faith has been undermined, he will cease to be involved in the ritual. He wrote at the conclusion of *The Elementary Forms:*

> Men cannot take part in ceremonies which seem to have no point, nor accept a faith which is totally incomprehensible to them. In order to extend religion or simply keep it alive, its justification is necessary, that is to say, there has to be a theory about it. (615/430/160)

Yet Durkheim will not go the whole hog: he will not admit that the decline of traditional religions has been brought about by science and science *alone*. Religion is resilient and an attack on its beliefs will not necessarily destroy it especially if religious sentiments are strong. He wrote in one of his early books:

> Faith is not uprooted by dialectic proof; it must already be deeply shaken by other causes to be unable to withstand the shock of argument. (1897a:171/t.1951a:169/r.197555)

Infuriatingly Durkheim does not spell out what these other causes are.

2. The superiority of science as a source of knowledge

In those areas of experience or reality where science legitimately enters - and what area can it not or will it not enter? - science rather than religion, Durkheim held, discovers the truth (see chs 11.8 and 15.1). He sees the superiority of science over religion, not least in the sociological fact that amongst intellectuals of his day - amongst more advanced thinkers' -science has superseded religion, and even taken its place (1925a:59/t.1961a:69). His adulation of science virtually turned science into a religion. Science is in fact liberation. We liberate ourselves through understanding', there is no other way (ibid.:132-3/116). And what provides understanding? Science. It is the well spring of our autonomy' (ibid.).

He was opposed to every religion which claimed to dogmatize about objective knowledge and reality. Christianity did not proclaim truth and it had no right to pretend it did. In the conclusion of *The Elementary Forms* he wrote:

> There is but one point at issue between science and religion: it is not the right of religion to exist, it is its right to dogmatize about the nature of things, and the special competence religion claims for itself to know about man and the world. (614/430/159)

Such a claim by Durkheim means that the adherents of religion should accept the findings of science and attempt to change their own views and doctrines accordingly. He hinted at this even in an early review (1887b:311/t.1975a:38) and was just as outspoken at the 1913-14 conference, where he said that free believers should not dogmatize, and that they should overlook their denominational formulae in order to have an openness of mind in seeing religion objectively (1919b:75/t. 1975a: 184; see also 1909a: (1): 60). His position implies that any allegedly scientific statement has precedence over a religious one on the same subject. Religion in its cognitive element has no alternative but to bow before science and rational thought. Thus, when a religion proclaims that the object of worship is to adore the divinity, such an activity cannot form a legitimate objective study, since God for the scientist does not exist. Further, theology can never be a scientific study, since it does not deal with reality.

The truth science proclaims is certain, although it is always open to challenge by the scientist. And when successfully challenged, it is forced to change. In this sense there is a steadfastness in scientific knowledge which places it above all other knowledge, for example, metaphysical knowledge. No other discipline has given man knowledge to such a degree as science and, further more, it is a knowledge that can be applied to everyday life.

> Once the authority of science is established, it must be taken into consideration. We can go beyond science because of the pressures of necessity; however, it must be our starting point. We can affirm nothing it denies, deny nothing it affirms, and establish nothing which directly or indirectly contradicts the principles on which it depends. (616/430/160)

The threat of science to religion was amply demonstrated in Durkheim's eyes by the fact that religious leaders themselves on so many occasions tend to oppose the conclusions of science. That they should even attempt to do this proclaims how they fear the discoveries and conclusions of science, which are in direct Opposition to their own proclamations of truth.

In his debate on science and religion, he observed that while science could proclaim no privileged position (surely with a note of sarcasm), religion did not have a science of itself, that is, it did not really know what it was doing (1909a(1):60). He later wrote in *Les Formes:*

> It is certain that they [religions] are mistaken in regard to the real nature of things: science has proved it. The modes of action which they counsel or prescribe to men can therefore rarely have useful effects: it is not by lustrations that the sick are cured nor by sacrifices and chants that the crops are made to grow. (117/83)

It is the task of science, not theology to reveal all and to discover the truth of religion. It and it alone is competent to do this. Thus, the assumption is that all down the ages religion has been living in a perpetual world of darkness (614/430/159)

For this reason, therefore, the enlightened religious person should welcome, not revile, science for its work in establishing truth. He wrote at an early date:

> Let those who view anxiously and sadly the ruins of ancient beliefs, who feel all the difficulties of these critical times, not ascribe to science an evil it has not caused but rather which it tries to cure! Beware of treating it as an enemy! (1897a:170/t.1951a:169/r.1975:56)

The evil which science, and here Durkheim means sociology, is trying to cure is the morally weakened state of society brought about by the decline of traditional beliefs, which in turn have been weakened by science!

There is no logical reason why religion should not judge science, and indeed there have been many theologians who have done this. But to Durkheim such a counter-attack will not be successful. And it will not be successful because religion has lost once and for all its ability to speak truth, truth about man, truth about the world.

> From now on, faith no longer exercises over the system of *representations,* which we can call religious, the same hegemony as before. Confronting it stands a rival power [science], its offspring which will subject it to its own criticism and control. All the signs indicate that this control will continually increase and be ever more effective, while no limit can possibly be fixed on its future influence. (616/431/160-1)

As we have indicated, the most recent and serious challenge

to religion from the sciences is now the social sciences, and in particular sociology. His oft-repeated chorus is that sociology, as he defines and expounds it, is every whit a science and comparable with say, biology or physics (see 1895a). By extension, it is possible to argue, as Deploige does (1911/t.1938:373), that the sociology of religion as a science is now directly replacing religious faith and thus is becoming a new kind of theology offering a reasonable account of faith, and even comparable to that of the great theological systems of previous ages. In this sense, Durk-heim's *sociologie religieuse* is the faith of today and tomorrow and the years to come (see chs 27 and 28). This 'new theology' would be:

> bound to depend upon the different sciences as soon as they come into existence; the social sciences first, because religious faith has its origins in society; psychology, because society is a synthesis of human *consciences;* finally, the natural sciences because man and society are functions of the universe and can only be artificially separated from it. (615/431/160)

These are the words with which he ends the two sections on religion in the conclusion of his great book on the subject.

3. Science is not god!

Yet, Durkheim was no naive rationalist who believed that ideas in isolation, or contained in a vacuum, could bring about social change. Traditional religion, in fact, is not at the point of dissolution just through the discoveries of science. In one of his early reviews, that on Guyau's *L'Irréligion de l'avenir,* he takes up this position by saying that:

> If the only mistake that religions had ever made was to be in disagreement with scientific truths, they would still be in a healthy state today. (1887b:301/t. 1975a:37)

He states that if society needs religion, religion would either modify its own doctrine in order to embrace new ideas or else would deny science altogether. We might add that this kind of movement, of religion absorbing some of the findings of science, was visible in the churches of his day among liberal Christians of both Catholic and Protestant persuasions. On the other hand, it is also clear that traditionalists, faced with the threat of science, hardened their dogmas and veered towards fundamentalism, either papal or biblical. Unaided science, however, does not bring about secularisation, and for two reasons- The first relates to the nature of religion; the second, to the nature of science.

The force of logic, reason and argument will not 'stamp out faith': 'logic can just as easily be used to defend as to attack it, and the theologian can reason just as well in order to prove it as the free thinker to refute it' (ibid.). Durkheim openly declared that 'religion could not be erased at the stroke of a pen' (1901h). The point is that the scientific, rational refutation of a particular religious belief would not automatically cause people to give up their practice of religion. It is not so much a question of specific beliefs but the general inclination to belief. An overall attitude towards belief is at the heart of every religious person. Preachers, Durkheim said, were aware of this. He wrote:

> they devote much less attention to establishing directly and by methodical proofs the truth of any particular proposition of the utility of such and such an observance, than to awakening or reawakening the sentiment of the moral comfort attained by the regular celebration of the cult. Thus they create a predisposition to belief, which precedes proofs, which leads the mind to overlook the insufficiency of the logical reasons, and which thus prepares it for the proposition whose acceptance is desired. This favourable prejudice, this impulse towards believing, is just what constitutes faith. (514/360)

Similarly, a rational or scientific attack on a particular ritual may not have much effect:

> the true justification of religious practices does not lie in the apparent ends which they pursue, but rather in the invisible action which they exercise over the mind and in the way in which they affect our mental status. (ibid.)

But much the same thing applies to a 'belief' in science. It is not the existence of scientific ideas and truths which is necessary, but the general acceptance of science by society at large (298/

208/ 127). For the populace to be aware of scientific achievements and thinking, there is the need to teach and preach science as well as practise it. There is nothing automatic in the propagation of scientific ideas.

What has just been said confirms the fact that Durkheim saw the growth of new ideas as issuing from some haphazard and non-rational process, as distinct from the rationality of the ideas themselves. It is well known that the general acceptance of the findings of science has often been slow. And secularisation, although it has been continuous, has at the same time been far from uniform. Nor are religion and free thought to be inversely correlated according to some precise mathematical formula. The relationship between them is complex. The growth of scientific ideas in society as a whole depends very much on the *conscience collective,* on the common outlook of society itself. Although Durkheim sees religion and free thought as being closely related in an inverse fashion, he is cautious about a more precise relationship.

> Religion, the eminent form of the common conscience, originally absorbs all representative functions with practical functions. The first are not dissociated from the second until philosophy appears. But this is possible only when religion has lost something of its hold. This new way of representing things clashes with collective opinion which resists it. It has sometimes been said that free thought makes religious beliefs regress, but that supposes, in its turn, a preliminary regression of these same beliefs. It can arise only if the common faith permit. (1893b/1902b:269-70/t.1933b:285)

And Durkheim goes even as far as to suggest that religion itself has been of great value to science by holding before it the fact that it is not God! He wrote in an early review:

> The great service which it has rendered to science has been to remind it constantly of its limits and that is why it has lasted. Some day might not this sentiment about the limits of our knowledge, confirmed as it is by long experience, permeate science itself and become an integral element of scientific thought? (1887b:311/t. 1975a:38)

4. Only a partial take-over?

From what has just been said, it is evident that Durkheim did not believe that science would suddenly supplant religion, or that it could act as a surrogate religion. Complete victory was not envisaged. His approach was more subtle. He wrote: 'For in asking that religion become an object of science, I do not mean at all that it should be swallowed up by science' (1909a(1):58).

It has already been observed that Durkheim, like so many others, divided religious phenomena into two distinct compartments - belief and practice (see ch. 17). Religion makes statements about the world and man's experience of it, as well as about an alleged world which is beyond the senses. At the same time religion demands that man makes a response in terms of action, be that action ritualistic or ethical.

Durkheim's analysis of contemporary secularisation and the future of religion is based on the contention that science has virtually taken over the cognitive or speculative function of religion (see ch. 16). As Durkheim was to write towards the end of his life: 'Born of religion, science is tending to substitute itself for religion in everything that concerns the cognitive and intellectual functions' (613/429/159; see also 1909a(1):58). This is what in fact is happening and the cosmological component of theology, for example, is now little in evidence (1909a(1):58).

Yet science is not in a position to engineer a complete take-over. The affective function - the ritual component - cannot be controlled by the new empire-builder. This remains in the hands of religion. Although science is responsible for changing man's beliefs by changing the content of one function, it can never be a substitute for religion and can never be a religion in itself. That there is no *complete* demise of religion even within the speculative sphere is not due so much to the nature of religion as to the nature of science. Science is never fully realized in so far as its work is never finished. 'It is fragmentary, incomplete' (615/431/ 160). It advances slowly, deliberately, but is sure of every step it takes. Its knowledge to date, therefore, is only partial. This fact has certain practical consequences and one is that religion is thus entitled to claim some area in which it can speculate, but not be certain about. He wrote:

> Even the most rational and laicized religions cannot and never will be able to do without some special form of speculation which, although it has the same object as science itself, nevertheless is not really scientific. In these religions the obscure intuitions of sensations and sentiment often take the place of logical reasoning. (615-16/431/160)

Religion, in terms of its claim to knowledge, is allowed a certain autonomy, but it is much smaller than it used to be and must continue to diminish as science progresses. If 'God' is allowed any place at all, he is of necessity a 'god of the gaps'.

That science moves slowly and that man cannot wait for it to complete its knowledge has a practical outcome of another kind (1904a(5):383/t.1979a:32). In everyday living man has to act. For this he needs knowledge, but if there is no scientific knowledge available, he must act with what knowledge' he possesses in hope and faith. This is true in the realm of morality as well as in other areas of life. In directing action, religion has a full part to play. It is still required to perform some controlling function over man's instinctual and social behaviour, although its power in this respect is considerably weaker than once it was (1886a:68/t.1975a:21). It is therefore legitimate for religion to proceed as a social necessity, provided of course that it realizes its limited sphere of influence.

5. Resultant confusion

To point to religion in the future as a necessary element in society forced Durkheim into an extremely difficult position. As we have just seen, religion today ceases to be for the most part, although not entirely, a vehicle for explaining human experience. But since its claims to knowledge are now assumed by science, sacred knowledge becomes profane knowledge . As we have had occasion to remark before, Durkheim's attempt to differentiate religion from science was full of difficulty and the position he gave in his theory to religion in the future does not solve the problem: rather, it compounds it. That the two components of religion can be readily dealt with in such a way that one component almost disappears and the remaining one can proceed virtually unharmed and so continue to maintain its identity is an extraordinary piece of surgery. Even the most extreme functionalist today would have hesitations at this point.

But this raises an important theoretical problem. It is Durkheim's failure to explicate the cognitive component of religion. The following are some of the aspects which are involved in mental activity associated with religion:

1 explanation of events by positing a cause;
2 statements about gods, spirits their existence, their characteristics;
3 the origins of the universe;
4 doctrine of man, anthropology'-his nature and place in the universe;
5 statements about moral behaviour;
6 directives about ritual action.

All these elements may be, or are, contained within the myths of a religion or in its doctrines or theology. The point to note is their diversity. When Durkheim speaks of a take-over by science, he has in mind the explanation of natural events. And he would certainly add that since truth was the object of science, that element of the cognitive function of religion relating to the existence of gods and spirits and that relating to the origins and development of the universe would also be superseded by scientific knowledge. But on this all now agree that science has to be agnostic. The other aspects are clearly outside the realm of science itself, although as we have indicated, he associates science with a certain doctrine of man and a humanistic moral system. Nevertheless, in the face of the complex nature of the cognitive element of religion, it is difficult to see how Durkheim can maintain that scientific thought is a more perfect form of religious thought (613/429/158). There is no unbridgeable gulf between the two: they differ only in the matter of degree (Lenoir 1918:588). One would like to suggest that, with a slight stretching of the point, it would be safe to conclude from Durkheim's thought that the man who is devoted to science is indeed a religious' man. Durkheim would hardly allow the equation to be reversed, however!

His former teacher, Boutroux, attacked Durkheim for claiming too much for science. According to Boutroux, science has no right to determine reality or to weaken' it by references to the normative, and its sole task is that of ordering and systematizing reality (Durkheim 1909a(l): 60). But Durkheim used science in a different way. 'Science for him [Durkheim] explains things rationally, that is, it causes them to emerge from a given principle in accordance with a logical necessity' (ibid.). In practice, with reference to religion, it meant looking at religion in exclusively objective terms. Thus, for Durkheim, science when applied to religion meant more than an open, empirical analysis, and despite protests to the contrary, Durkheim's approach contains rationalist overtones.

The most serious weakness of Durkheim's position, then, stems from the fact that he means so many different things by science observation, experimentation, logical reasoning, freedom of thought, individualism. Further, religion itself, having given birth to science, is not adequately differentiated from science. In an important article on *Suicide,* Nye and Ashworth observed that Durkheim found it problematic in separating, by way of definition, science from religion. They observed that he did not make the usual nominalistic separation by stating that science treated as 'useful' what religion considered was 'real' (Nye and Ashworth 1971:137).

The position is further muddled by Durkheim's equation that totemism is primitive science (see ch. 6.3). The assertion is also strengthened by the contention that science has been born out of religion and is hence basically of the same nature (see 342/239/143-4). Religion is thus the mother: science the daughter. There must therefore be mother-daughter similarities. Confusion reigns, as Belot says, because the process of parturition is not clearly defined (1913a:374). Durkheim fails to separate social knowledge from knowledge about the physical universe. Since he cannot differentiate religious knowledge from that derived from science, his epistemology is dominated by confusion.

It was always a point of surprise to Richard that Durkheim, in nailing his flag to the mast of science, could so blatantly disregard the basic assumptions of science. Richard follows the colossus of Enlightenment philosophy, Kant, whose system of thought enabled scientific analysis to proceed unchecked by metaphysical speculation, although such speculation found a place elsewhere within his system. Durkheim himself, as Richard knew, was a neo-Kantian who, one assumes perhaps falsely, accepted many of the basic ideas of Kant in the matter of science and philosophical speculation. Richard wrote in 1911 that it was remarkable:

> how he [Durkheim] has been able to believe that with the wings of a sociologist he has flown over the abyss created by Kant, the abyss between science and morality, between knowledge and religion, between the world of facts and the world of values, how he has been able to confuse the applicability of a technical knowledge with a prescription of *conscience* and finally to draw from a precarious ethnographical induction on the forms of savage or primitive cults, a judgment on the value of the deepest religious experiences. (1911a(i):332)

Richard could not understand how Durkheim had confused two very different sets of ideas. First, sociology as a science in the very limited sense of the word, as a study concerned with social phenomena and social relationships; and second, metaphysical speculation, which appeals to this science..and tries to resolve general problems of morality, religious philosophy, and theory of knowledge' (ibid.:331). Richard concluded: the two endeavours seem to me not only different but contradictory' (ibid.).

Another aspect of the epistemological confusion relates to religious belief in the future. It will be very severely restricted since man has very little area in which to speculate. But what will be the content? Perhaps more than Durkheim realized, if Richard's logical development of Durkheim's position is accepted–

> If the most clearly defined religion which has the most social form, totemism, is the very science of primitive peoples, the intellectual equivalent of our religion is not faith in God, it is our science, on condition that it is widened to include not only the group—mathematics, physics, biology—but the sociology of religion, including the theory of collective understanding. (Richard 1923:240/t. 1975:251)

Again, if, as Durkheim maintains, the speculative and rational elements of religion are fast disappearing, though a small remnant will always remain, what is left to religion? Little more than the activist function. But on what is this based? Nothing more than a collective emotion, nothing more than an irrational way of life (Richard hints at this, ibid. :233/245). It is like suggesting that a man with his head cut off or with vital organs missing can function almost as well as he did before such losses. By depriving religion of its intellectual dimension it becomes emasculated and such a vestigial and irrational form must quickly give way to the complete demise of religion itself. But this is contrary to what Durkheim wants!

6. Appraisal of Durkheim's analysis of secularisation

Before some attempt is made to assess Durkheim's approach to secularisation, two issues raised earlier have to be briefly reviewed that the process of secularisation has been afoot throughout man's history and that modern industrialization in western Europe is not a significant factor in that process.

The thesis that the whole of history is the history of secularisation can be accepted only within such a wide framework that its value as a proposition becomes extremely questionable. Durkheim's position rests on two assumptions: first, that in the beginning 'all was religious'; and second, since then, there has been a continual and gradual, but none the less apparent, diminution of the control of religion over social life. The first seems very much like Auguste Comte's notion of a theological stage. Indeed, openly critical though Durkheim was of Comte, there is much in his treatment of religion that is reminiscent of Comtean thought, more especially in the matter of religious change (see Richard 1943). The first of the propositions is extremely difficult to prove, not least because we know nothing about the history of preliterate societies. What kinds of lives people lived in such societies before they were discovered by western man is lost to knowledge for ever, or at least, is difficult to reconstruct with certainty. Also, our anthropological understanding of preliterate societies shows no certainty that the totality of life within such societies has been dominated by religion to the extent Durkheim would have us believe. Mary

Douglas has forcibly argued that different levels of religious commitment are to be found between tribe and tribe, and that virtually secular primitive societies are now known to exist (1970:chs 1 and 7).

The second proposition which needs to be supported by precise historical knowledge is a far from easy task, as sociologists and historians have discovered, Only rough indicators can be found to measure levels of religious dominance or commitment, but even if broad indicators are used, religion, when it often seems to be on the decline, suddenly receives strength through revival. This is most apparent in western society over the past two hundred years, where the levels of religion and secularisation present a highly complex picture. 'Little by little' is Durkheim's phrase about the growth of secularisation, but the uniformity suggested by it can hardly be substantiated. Durkheim's statements about religion in general do not allow for revivals or changes through external pressure, as in the cases of armed conquest or aggressive evangelization. Marc Boegner was quick to criticize Durkheim for this in response to Belot's exposition of *Les Formes* in 1914 (Boegner 1919:139). The notion of general secularisation as a historical process which has occurred from the beginning of man's social existence cannot be supported, or, if it is accepted in very broad terms, adds up to little.

Another problem is that of explaining the process of autonomy — a point on which Durkheim remains silent. If all social institutions have been born in the womb of religion, how have they become separated? How have they cut themselves off from their mother? Apart from referring to the growth of science, the nearest Durkheim comes to offering even a clue is to be seen in the changes that societies undergo when they move from those characterized by mechanical solidarity to those marked by organic solidarity. In the second type, beliefs and sentiments of a collective kind are relatively weak: hence in a society of organic qualities, individualism based on private ideals and beliefs is more prominent than in societies labelled mechanical. But, once again, whence comes the change? Durkheim is strong on indicators, for example, changes in types of law and religion itself could be an indicator, but weak on causal factors. As is commonly known, the nearest he comes to positing reasons for change in this particular context is in the increase in population, bringing with it an increase in moral density which causes the former type of society—segmentary societ—to break up. The inadequacy of this theory of change has been criticized enough to make further comment unnecessary . But it hardly accounts for the emergence of the autonomy of institutions, freed from religious control. How does science that is religious become non-religious? What makes it proceed in such a direction?

It is at first surprising that in seeking for causes which might be said to contribute to recent secularisation, Durkheim, unlike many sociologists before and after him, pays scant attention to factors under the general heading of industrialization. He makes but a passing reference to Spencer's theory that secularisation is the result of the popularization of scientific knowledge, which has been brought about by industrial progress (1886a:64/ t.1975a:16). According to Spencer, what has been eroded in religion is the fundamental belief in supernatural causation. The agent has been science, propagated by the handmaid of industry. Further, Spencer believed that religion had acquired a more moral and spiritual content by the growth of free inquiry and the 'sentiment of independence', with which Durkheim agrees (1909a(l):5), but disagrees with him in that such qualities have been precipitated, 'awoken and fostered' by the development of industrial societies (1886a:67/t.1975a:20). In this connection, the nearest that Durkheim comes to mentioning industrialization - and this is but the vaguest hint - is in his *Professional Ethics,* when he refers to a weakening of religious formalities occurring as life becomes busier (1950a:227/t.1957a:193).

The reason why Durkheim almost completely disregards industrialization as a key factor in the recent decline of religious institutions is simply that he rejects morphological factors and embraces those relating to ideas. It is not the effects of industrialization, of work habits, of repetitive labour, of the growth of areas of poverty and distress which adversely affect traditional religion. Rather, it is changes in ideas and values about the world, the supernatural, man's relationships with man, that determine changes in the direction of secularisation. The key is in collective *representations* and changes here are not to be attributed to the industrial revolution but to earlier revolutions, the Renaissance and the Reformation. Durkheim does not consider the possibility that the industrial revolution has itself brought about changes in collective *representations.*

So how, then, is Durkheim's approach to secularisation to be assessed? We can readily accept the fact that in very general terms secularisation has been in process for a long time; that today western man lives in a society that is highly secularized in so far as religious institutions have lost their power; that man lives in a pluralist society; that there are certain elements in Christian theology that appear to have given rise to the recent secularisation; and that on the whole the process or processes are continuing in the direction they originally took, with no sign of reversal. All this, actually or latently found in Durkheim, is frequently commented on today and generally accepted. The indicators he used for the growth of secularisation are particularly convincing, in some ways more so than detailed statistics.

At the level of explanation and interpretation, Durkheim's analysis is extraordinarily neat. Using as a base the two prime functions of religion, he shows how the growth of science so operates as to explain secularizing tendencies but at the same time to allow the continued existence of some form of religion in the future. By logical ingenuity he is able to derive conclusions and explanations which suit his purposes admirably. It is brilliant but not convincing. Everything turns on the acceptance of the two functions and his theory of society. On both points, as we have seen, he is open to criticism. He is befogged by his adulation of science. No one would deny the growth of scientific thought as a factor of overwhelming importance in the process of secularisation. And Durkheim is to be praised in that he does not take a crudely rationalist position in the matter of the propagation of scientific knowledge. But in his hands science is seen both as a tool for destroying religion and also as an instrument for pointing to the conservation of religion. Religion, therefore, must continue. Durkheim's explanation fails because it is not radical enough.

Chapter-4

The New Religion: the cult of man or society?

Chapter-4

1. Prognostication and the characteristics of a future religion

That religion will persist in some form, Durkheim, as we have seen, was in no doubt. As religions are social phenomena, none is immortal; but 'neither is there any reason to believe that humanity will be incapable of inventing new ones in the future' (611/428/157). The process of such creativity is perpetual, for it is deep in man and society.

But what form will religion now take, as the traditional religions are dissolving? Durkheim was ambivalent about the sociological temptation to predict the outcome. On the one hand, he felt it was unwise to foretell the future:

> one would like to try to imagine the composition of a future religion, that is to say, a religion more conscious of its social Origins. Of course, one must be very cautious in doing this. It is quite pointless to try to guess in what precise form such a religion would be able to express itself. What one can foresee are the social forces which will give birth to it. (1919b:103/t. 1975a: 186)

This is very much the cautious Durkheim, trying not to damage the science he has been spawning by hazardous guesses which might easily prove to be wrong (see also 1907c). And again, in one of the first things he wrote (a review of Spencer's *Ecclesiastical Institutions),* he says:

> For so long as men live together, they will hold some belief in common. What one cannot foresee and what only the future will be able to decide, is the particular form in which this faith will be symbolized. (1886a:69/t.1975a:22-3; see also 1887c:311/t. 1975a:38)

There are, nevertheless, plenty of instances where scientific caution is thrown to the winds and where he is prepared to chance his arm about the new forms of religion. Marc Boegner did not hesitate to point out his inconsistencies (Boegner 1919:141) - his reluctance to prophesy as a scientist and yet a readiness to talk freely about the emergence of a new religion. Indeed, one might add, to state that there will be religion at all in the future is to play the role of prophet.

Obviously stemming from his conception of the relationship between science and religion (see the previous chapter), he stated that future religions would be basically rational.

> All that can be surmised is that they will continue to be further penetrated by rationality than even the most rational religions today, and that the social sense, which has always been the soul of religion, will be asserted more directly and more decisively than in the past, without being shrouded in myths and symbols. (1907c:51)

In *Suicide,* published some ten years before, Durkheim noted that any new religion would have to admit freedom of thought, the right of criticism and of individual initiative to a greater extent than that displayed amongst the liberal Protestants of his day (1897a:431/t.1951a:375). But he was also quick to comment that such a movement would mean that religion in the future would be able to limit suicide even less than traditional religions, since for him, freedom of thought and suicide were positively correlated.

In addition to freedom from prevailing myths and a greater place given to free thought, Durkheim seemed to imply that every man would carry out his religious inclinations as be wanted to. He wrote that the day would come 'when the only form of worship will be that which each of us will freely perform in his own heart' (63/46/122). Does this imply that all social characteristics of religion would disappear and individual manifestations be triumphant? If so, the sociology of religion would be out of business! Despite this somewhat obscure remark, Durkheim implied that the new religion would indeed have social characteristics, which like all else of the Third Republic would be 'laïque en apparence'. They were as follows.

1 It would express the unity of society and its most

sacred values.

2 It would hold periodic meetings when individuals would be given the opportunity of affirming the values of society by some ritualistic expression. Such meetings would also provide inspiration and new insight into social life (610/427/156).

3 The new form of religion would contain some references to 'objective knowledge' about the social and personal worlds in which people live. The degree of knowledge would be determined by science, which would increasingly control this aspect of religion. In the meantime, religion would continue to speculate in areas of experience so far not penetrated by science. As just stated, the new religion would have a faith or theory based on reason (612/428/157; 615/430/160).

4 The new religion would have justice as one of its basic themes. Durkheim said at the 1913-14 conference: 'We aspire to a higher justice than any of the existing formulae can express in a way that will satisfy us' (1919b:104/t.1975a:186-7)

Durkheim received encouragement about the possibility of a new form of religion emerging in western society from the fact that the French Revolution had produced, within recent memory, new religions and new collective *représentations*. He wrote:

> At that particular time, under the influence of general enthusiasm, things purely secular in nature were transformed into sacred things by public opinion, for example, the Motherland, Liberty, Reason. A religion was established which had its dogmas, its symbols, its altars, and its holy days. It was to these spontaneous aspirations that the cult of Reason and the Supreme Being attempted to give some form of official recognition. It is true that this religious revival lasted only a very short time because the patriotic enthusiasm which at first caught the imagination of the masses gradually waned. (305-6/214/132)

What had happened in the French Revolution was not only sociologically interesting, but it seemed to give him hope that the future religion, although not the same as that generated by the Revolution, would be of a similar kind. He saw that if men had created gods in response to those traumatic events, they could continue to make them in other similar situations. Thus, the means of creation, as always, would be in the effervescent gathering in which deities are born out of blind psycho-social forces (see ch. 22).

He realized, of course, that it was not sufficient that gods were thought to exist. They had to be present in people's minds 'with sufficient force so that the *representations* which they express are effective' (1913b:69). The gods must be believed in with a collective faith, for the faith of each can only be strong if it is shared by everyone' (ibid.). Interestingly enough, Durkheim's thought here bears strong resemblances to some kinds of Protestantism in so far as he stresses the importance of faith - faith which is held by the individual and with little reference to practice or cult.

2. The source of religious revival: the working classes

Religion is a product of man, it is derived from humanity, from society. Durkheim said: 'There is an idea that we absolutely have to get used to; it is that humanity is left on this earth to its own devices and can only count on itself to direct its own destiny' (1919b: 105/t. 1975a: 187). Humanity is a blanket-like term lacking sociological precision. Where in society or in what section of society will the new religious forms emerge?

As we have seen, Durkheim believed that at the time in which he lived, there existed a social languishing, a lack of nerve, moral mediocrity, a virtual state of anomy (see ch. 24.5) - a judgment doubted by Richard and others (1923:237/t.1975:248). For Durkheim, this 'state of uncertainty and confused agitation cannot last forever' (611/427/157). Therefore, the day will come when societies will experience 'creative effervescence' and from this, new ideals will be born and new formulations emerge which will for a time serve as a guide to humanity' (ibid.). So the religion of the future will come into existence.

Quite out of the blue, Durkheim locates the emergence of revival in the near future as arising within the working classes. This unheralded commitment to such a group was made at the 1913-14 Conference of Free Thinkers and Free Believers. He proclaimed:

> One can go further and say with some precision that it is among the working classes [*les classes populaires]* in particular that these new forces are in the course of formation. (1919b: 104/t. 1975a: 187)

The reason why Durkheim committed himself to this position was probably because he felt that *les classes populaires* had a collective warmth, an openness and enthusiasm, which by contrast were absent in the middle classes.

The reference to the working classes is surprising, for they are so seldom referred to in Durkheim's sociology. Indeed, the oft-repeated criticism against his sociology is that there is virtually no reference to social conflict, and it nowhere deals with class division or class antagonism. Here Durkheim appears to follow Auguste Comte in paying scant regard to the problem, although Comte tried to promulgate his church of humanity amongst the working classes. Durkheim saw that religion had a controlling and consoling function within the various classes of society (see ch. 16.5). When religion was an effective force, it warned masters and the rich that worldly interests were not the highest goals of life and had to be subordinated. To the workers, religion offered consolidation and contentment by holding before them compensatory justice in a world to come. This world was also seen to be created, sustained and controlled by God himself, complete with its class divisions (1897a:283/t. 195la:254-5).

One is tempted to conclude that in pointing to the working classes as the source of religious revival, Durkheim, like Comte again (who included the female sex), was indulging in bourgeois romanticism. And romantic ideas about the proletariat can also be found in Marx. Now that history has moved on, Durkheim's prophecies are seen to be false. The working classes in the West have not been the heralds or devotees of a new religion. The form of religion found amongst them at the present time is diffused, containing elements of superstition and simple beliefs. This is not to say that such folk religion is unimportant, but it is very far removed from that kind of religion Durkheim thought would emerge in the period in which we live (see Towler 1974:ch. 8). Religion in the West today, in either its traditional or humanistic forms, is located, if anywhere, mainly in the middle classes.

3. The emergence of an old French religion?

Throughout his academic career Durkheim never ceased to indicate that his own beliefs corresponded to those of the religion of the future. Referring to his position in what we would call the early period in the development of Durkheim's religious thought, Richard has written:

> In his correspondence and in open conversation which I had with him, Durkheim took delight in saying that we have no other religion than that [the inviolability of the person] and that was all he would retain of the religion of humanity, dear to Auguste Comte. The inviolability of the human person was for him only the transformation of the Roman concept of the Sacred and the Jewish notion of interdict. (1925(ii):361)

Thus here and throughout his writings, Durkheim is seen to join the ranks of others of his time in declaring that the religion-to-be will be a species which has been variously called the religion of humanity, individualism, the cult of man, the cult of personality, and so on. In this form of religion, man dethrones God and puts himself on it.

That man has become a god to himself is in recent times an idea of the Enlightenment, stemming philosophically from Kant and his *Critique of Pure Reason* (1781)—it will be recalled that Durkheim himself was a neo-Kantian. Nowhere was the notion of the man-god so practically worked out as in France, which became the seed-bed of humanized, lay religions, in part helped by the thought of J.J.Rousseau. The Revolution itself can be seen to be in some way a religious movement. As de Toqueville is reported to have said, it was 'a political revolution which had the effect of a religious revolution and in a way assumed the aspect of one'. An outcome of the failure of the 'religion' of the Revolution was Saint-Simon's *Nouveau Christianisme* (1823), the teaching of which was propagated by his disciples such as Bazard, Enfantin and others. In another direction his ideas were taken up and developed by Auguste Comte, in his highly theological and ritualized religion of humanity. The Third Republic gained the reputation for spawning governments which were overtly committed to humanism and its political counterpart, liberalism. In this it was supported by many middle-class intellectuals and academics. Needless to say, lay religion in France has been subject to a great deal of analysis (see Charlton 1963; Weill 1925). Durkheim's 'religious' outlook was in general very much that of the *ideologues* of the Third Republic, for he reflects in perhaps a more sophisticated way an idealism dominant in his day—that of a worship of science coupled with a self-assured belief in the progressive independence of men from the religious institutional oppression of previous generations. But he did not only reflect it, he proclaimed it and, as we have seen, he was one of the most outspoken upholders of the Republic (see chs 1 and 2).

However, for Durkheim, the point of origin of such a religion was not the French Revolution, the Reformation, the Renaissance, scholasticism, the decline of Greek and Roman polytheism, or the demise of oriental theocracies (1893b/1902b:146/t.1933b:171). The development of the cult of man corresponds to the growth of secularization (see ch. 24). Indeed the two are closely related: they are almost identical. Individualism has thus been in progress without cessation all through history (ibid.). In the beginning, 'society is everything, the individual nothing' (1897a:382/t.1951a:336). But the path has been in the direction of the individual and, like that of secularization, has not been 'straightforward' but nevertheless has proceeded 'without a break in continuity'. Granet (1930:291) observed that this important relationship is seen in a key passage in *The Division of Labour:*

> As all the other beliefs and the other practices take on a character which is less and less religious, the individual becomes the object of some kind of religion. We have a cult of the dignity of the person, which like every strong cult already has its superstitions. (1893b/1902b: 147/t. 1933b: 172)

Here is 'an inevitable law against which it would be idle to inveigh' (ibid.). Durkheim thus puts forward one of those laws which he thought sociology should attempt to produce in accordance with the guidelines he set out in the *Rules* (1895a). But he is silent about the inner workings of the law. Even if there is a correlation between the growth of secularization and the growth of individualism, how is it that one is related to the other? What is the causal connection? There is no answer. All that Durkheim can do is to point to certain historical periods and religions and show how they have accelerated the process. In this, Christianity is singled out as giving greater impetus to the movement than any other religion. Even to the Greeks and Romans, the cult of humanity as described by Durkheim was 'quite unknown' (1938a/1969f:372/t.1977a:325). As Christianity most assuredly cut the path of secularization, so it opened the door for science and freedom of thought, and hence the cult of man (1898c:11/t.1969d:261r.1975:68). The Renaissance constituted another surge in the same direction (1938a/1969f: chs 15 and 16). One is tempted to deduce that, according to Durkheim, the heritage *par excellence* of simple or primitive societies, and indeed that of Christianity itself, is human sacredness, the sentiment of personal dignity.

Thus, through historical processes, society has now reached a position where man has ascribed to human personality something of the transcendental. Durkheim wrote at the turn of the century:

> There remains nothing that man may love and honour in common, apart from himself. This is why man has become a god for men, and it is why he can no longer turn to other gods without being untrue to himself. (1898c:11/t.1969d:26/ r. 1975:67)

In transforming himself into god, man does not worship an individual man, but disregards the multitude of individual differences and posits universal qualities and characteristics. It is man in general whom he worships:

> The cult of which he is at once both object and follower does not address itself to the particular being that constitutes himself and carries his name, but to the human person, wherever it is to be found, and in whatever form it is incarnated. Impersonal and anonymous, such an end soars far above all particular consciences and can thus serve as a rallying-point for them. (ibid.:9/23/64)

Expressed in terms in keeping with Durkheim's definition of

religion, man has made himself sacred. In his lectures on moral education, Durkheim stated: 'Don't we say, casually, that the human person is sacred, that we must venerate him?' (1925a:8/ t.1961a:10/r.1975:197).

We have outlined the main tenets of Durkheim's version of religion centred on man. The immediate likeness to Comte's religion of humanity has already been suggested and was raised in an earlier chapter (ch. 13.4). To this issue we briefly return.

Scholars, including Richard, would agree that Comte's concept of the religion of humanity was by no means the same as that which Durkheim used. Comte's notion was much more general in seeing humanity as a universal, unitary concept covering the whole of mankind, past, present and future. Durkheim feared that such a concept bordered on the metaphysical. His own notion was more sociological. Man received his exalted place in certain societies: only in them is it legitimate to talk about the cult of the individual. Each society has different values just as each religion is different in the content of its beliefs. If the deification of man occurs in a society, it is because that society has brought about such sacralization. Should Durkheim claim any originality in connection with the cult of man, it would be in this kind of analysis, for there is no universal 'god' of man in Durkheim as there is in Comte. To be sure, Durkheim saw that the religion of the future in modern western society would be what we might loosely call humanism. He seemed to imply that such a religion would grow as western civilization expanded. But this is not what Comte meant by the religion of humanity, which involved a Catholic type of cult and theology and was missionary in outlook. Such characteristics and aims were anathema to Durkheim. For him, the new religion would arise from below, from the thought of academic liberals, who would allow each society to create its own 'gods' which would be closely tied to the *representations* each society developed. Richard overlooked these differences between Comte's religion of humanity and Durkheim's close association of society and divinity. He made a more sweeping condemnation of Comte's positivism and Durkheim's rationalism in so far as claims were made by both in the name of science but which were beyond scientific proof. Comte and Durkheim entered the realm of metaphysics in what they were asserting and they degraded the discipline, by committing a fundamental error about the nature of religion, stating that it is basically a collective phenomenon or a collective emotion (Richard 1943:136-7). Incidentally, Belot criticized Durkheim on historical grounds claiming that the idea of a god of humanity or simply a god of society was relatively late in the development of the notion of God. Divinities of nature, which were earlier, had little interest in the welfare of society (1909:17).

Saint-Simon was probably a greater influence on Durkheim than Comte and some of this is to be seen in those sections devoted to Saint-Simon in the course of lectures he gave on socialism (1928a). Durkheim indeed admitted that Saint-Simon - Comte was his secretary - was the more important of the two in the development of sociology. Certainly, in the realm of the analysis and theory of religion, Gurvitch is convinced that Durkheim was more influenced by Saint-Simon than by Comte (1965:24). But even here questions are to be raised. Durkheim held that Saint-Simon's *Nouveau Christianisme,* based on the unity of humanity, love and god, and extending from time to eternity, led very easily to pantheism which was clearly something Durkheim strongly rejected. Further, as in the case of the religion of humanity, its protagonists had a strong sense of mission (cf.1928a:276/t.1958b:190). And this, from a slightly different point of view, confirms what we have suggested already, namely, that both polytheism and pantheism ill fit Durkheim's association of the concepts of God and society.

4. The heresy of egoism

Durkheim never exclusively fixed on one term to describe the religion he was convinced was going to become dominant in the western world and which had been developing for centuries. He sometimes referred to it as individualism, or moral individualism, as the cult of man, or the cult of the individual, or, again, as the cult of the human personality. One term he certainly avoided was that of the religion of humanity because of its association with Auguste Comte. And the notion of personality, although sometimes used by Durkheim, was not extensively employed, perhaps not least because it could be associated with psychology, and Durkheim would keep that discipline at a safe distance from sociology. He realized the term individualism contained ambiguities which he wanted to avoid. Although the phrase the cult of man has strong religious connotations, and some might think contains irrational overtones, Durkheim had no qualms in using it. It seems on the whole to be a useful term to employ, especially when one considers what Durkheim was referring to.

All the traditional religions have had their heretics, who in the eyes of the orthodox are more dangerous than members of other religions. Durkheim believed that the cult of the individual was no exception and was capable of heretical exposition. His article 'Individualism and the intellectuals' (1898c) contains a clarification of what is meant by moral individualism or the cult of man and at the same time is a refutation of a similar but dangerous belief. But such calls to orthodoxy had already appeared in *Suicide* (1897a) and subsequently in an important article, 'Two laws of penal evolution' (1901a:(i)). The heresy that can spring from individualism is that of egoism, seen as the fulfilment, even saturation, of individual needs and sensory appetites. The egoistic man, as distinct from him who follows the cult of man, thinks only of himself and places himself as an individual at the pinnacle of his values. Egoism is thus anti-social; indeed, it is the enemy of society and, as such, has to be curbed by the practice of self-discipline and social controls. These are undermined, if egoism becomes dominant. English utilitarian egoism, such as that of Herbert Spencer, is an obvious example of the heresy, for it emphasizes 'the tangible, empirical individual as realized in each particular *conscience*' (1901a(i):89/t. 1973b:302). Durkheim employs Kant's arguments to reject such individualism and sees the value of extending the concept of human personality, in general, to humanity as a whole, to man as universal being, and thus abstracting him from concrete and particular forms (ibid.). If one's faith rests in this generalized form, the shortcomings and evils of egoism are nullified, for in this case the individual man is now seen to be part of man in general, and this means a concern for the state of others, as well as for the individual. In practical terms, it implies commitment to the liberty of others, to their rights, and to the notion of social and economic justice. It implies, as Durkheim says, the old adage: ' "do not unto others that which you would not wish done to you" ' (ibid.). Again, writing in 1906, he said:

> The human personality is a sacred thing; one dare not violate it nor infringe its bounds, while at the same time *the greatest good is in communion with others.* (1906b/1924a:51/ t.1953b:37; our italics)

Durkheim's 'Individualism and the intellectuals' was a defence against the heresy that he and other Dreyfusards were charged with; an individualism which undermined the well-being of society by the following of selfish, individual ends. Durkheim showed that the cult of man, which he followed, was indeed the very opposite of the heresy with which he was charged and that the form of individualism to which he subscribed was associated with that of Kant, in particular, as well as that of Rousseau. Like their doctrines, his own transcended the individual and showed that 'duty consists in averting our attention from what concerns us personally' (1898c: 8/t. 1969d :24/r. 1975:61). Put into more 'religious' and at the same time functionalist terms, Durkheim held that the person who admits his belief in individualism, as he defines it, performs the same useful action as the ancient Roman when he observed his traditional rites which upheld collective and national sentiments (ibid.:12/27-8/ 69; see also 1950a/t.1969g:94ff./ t. 1957a:58ff.).

5. But who is god? Man or society?

In rejecting the heresy of egoism, Durkheim unwittingly raised the fundamental question about the nature of the cult of man and its theological or philosophical substantiation. To posit grounds for rejecting egoism but at the same time to accept the cult of man tempts one to ask whether, in the eyes of Durkheim, man in fact represents the highest order of existence, or whether there is not something which transcends man himself. Is man, universal man, in fact the ultimate of Durkheim's system?

The issue at stake is but another facet of the problem which confronted Durkheim, namely, the relation of the individual to society. It is centred on such issues as the problem of socialization, of the individual adopting social norms and culture, of the problem of freedom and social absorption, of the relation of individual *répresentations* to collective *répresentations,* and now, once again, it turns up in the issue of the sacredness of the individual and the ultimate authority of society.

Although Durkheim refused to define religion in terms of divine being or beings, and went so far as to deny categorically their existence, he was willing enough to refer to man's nature as being in some sense divine, for he 'has something of that transcendental majesty which the churches have at all times given to their Gods' (1898c:8/t.1969d:21/r.1975:62). Again, 'man has become a god for men' and therefore 'we belong to no temporal being because we are kin to God' (1897a:379/t.1951a:334; see also 1906e:256). So if the gods do not exist, man does, and here we have an empirical reality they do not possess. But man has not always been sacred; how does he become so? Sacredness is not inherent in man. 'Society has consecrated the individual and made him preeminently worthy of respect' (ibid.:106/72). Again, 'It is society that instituted it [cult of the individual] and made of man the god whose servant it is' (ibid. :84-5/59).

In another context, as we have seen, Durkheim virtually deified society, as is witnessed in the distorted statement 'God is society'. No matter how ambiguous such a statement is, it does imply that society has associated with it *représentations* that are held to be divine. It is the mysterious transcendental 'other' before which men must bow. As Durkheim admitted, there is in reality only one force greater than man himself and that is society. In speaking of the emergence of a rational morality, he wrote:

> All that we needed was to substitute for the conception of a supernatural being the empirical idea of a directly observable being, which is society - provided we do not view society as an arithmetic sum of individuals, but as a new personality distinct from individual personalities. We have shown how society so conceived constrains us since it dominates us. (1925a: 199/t. 1961a: 104)

Durkheim saw that a rational morality was one that was 'demanded by society' (ibid. :103/90). Under these circumstances the collectivity takes unto itself the role of divinity. If society declares what and who God is, it must itself be God. He was caught in a paradox. Nationalist though he was, Durkheim also saw that nationalism had to be subject to the highest control of universal humanistic values (Schoffeleers and Meijers 1978:49). In this respect there exists a supra-national creed emanating from western society which will and should engulf the whole of humanity. Durkheim is never free from such ideology. The conclusion is inevitable: the subject is equated with the object.

Yet there is contrary evidence in Durkheim's writings, not only from passages that have already been given but also in a sentence he wrote in *Suicide.* 'But today he [man] has acquired a kind of personality which places him above himself as well as above society' (1897a:378/t.1951a:333). But how is it that man can be above society, when society makes him god?

Durkheim wants it both ways. He suggests that there now exists a cult of man in which man is god, but although god is without a limit, man is far from being so and must be subject to limitations because his instincts have to be controlled, and society as an entity *sui generis* exerts those controls. Since society is ultimate power, it must be god. And of course, as we have indicated (see ch. 13), in the last analysis society is made equivalent to *La Nation,* the country, a whole society (see, for example, 1925a: 123/t. 1961a: 107). *La Patrie* is very much the incarnation of humanity (Mitchell 1931:104; and see ch. 1.6). But if it is a case of 'my country right or wrong', is this not likely to conflict with universal concepts of humanity? Durkheim's position assumes that *La Patrie* is a manifestation of humanistic ideals as he envisaged them. What if a society does not possess them? Further, in the West, consensus values are minimal (see Lane 1981:225ff.). Where in such diversity stands 'God'? Can Durkheim really maintain that his god—humanity—is found in society—in *La Patrie?* Would he acknowledge it in the so-called civil religion of the United States (see Warner 1962; Cole and Hammond 1974; Schoffeleers and Meijers 1978; Gehrig 1981)? The old problem emerges - how does one differentiate national values, which may be seen to be sacred, from the cult of man; again, from the state itself, and also from churches? Durkheim's enthusiasm for the concept of humanity blinds him to these issues.

Durkheim was never able to explain satisfactorily the relation between the individual and society. The introduction of the cult of man in no way helps the problem; indeed, it aggravates it. Nor does a dialectical juggling with the terms provide a way out, for example, in the merging of the two entities. Despite the canonization of man proposed by Durkheim, it remains a historical fact that the individual is often in conflict with society. Indeed, it could well be argued that he has gained his rights, achieved justice and freedom of thought, not by co-operation with society but by fighting against it. Man has triumphed, not through the agency of society but in spite of it. If therefore there exists conflict between the individual and society, which of them can be labelled god or the ultimate?

It is a matter of debate whether or not the cult of man is a point of difference in Marxist and Durkheimian thought. Marx would abolish religion in order to make man man: Durkheim would make man god. Here Durkheim's ideas more nearly resemble Feuerbach's; for example, when Durkheim writes 'Man has become a god for men' (1897a:378/t.1951a:334). In his speech in 1914 to the Conference of Free Thinkers and Free Believers, Durkheim makes the following point which may refer to a Marxist, whose name is unknown:

> A short time ago, an orator, gesticulating prophetically towards the heavens, told us they were emptying and urged us to turn our eyes towards the earth, that is to say, to occupy ourselves above all with pursuing our economic interests to the best of our ability. This formula has been called impious. From my position one can say it is false. No, there is no need to fear that the heavens will ever become finally depopulated, for we ourselves populate them. (1919b:103/t.1975a:186).

6. Can the cult be justified? Its theology and ritual

Durkheim's conviction that a new religion was emerging brought upon him a great deal of criticism both during his life and afterwards. Needless to say, attacks came from many quarters, from committed Christians, be they Catholic or Protestant. Obviously there were those who, as agnostics or atheists, openly rejected the possibility or desirability of some future religion. For them, the whole movement of humanism was one of liberation from religion in any form. Also, there were those who felt that Durkheim's theoretical position was wrong, in so far as it demanded the persistence of religion. Amongst these van Gennep. He wrote in his review of *The Elementary Forms:*

> the progress of humanity has consisted in the growing secularization of all mental and practical activities, and in the proportional disintegration and destruction of religion. As for replacing religion with another sociological imperative, I do not see the point of it, nor do I consider even its possibility. (1913:91/t. 1975:208)

A few years earlier Belot disagreed with Durkheim and seriously doubted the value of trying to create or uphold any form of religion in the present day (1909). He advocated that religion should be allowed to die and morality alone take its place. For him, unlike Durkheim, morality is of a different and an independent source from that of religion. Not surprisingly, such criticism still persists. In a recent book dealing with Durkheim's concept of morality and the religion of the individual, Wallwork wrote:

> But Durkheim is less than convincing when he predicts, on evolutionary grounds, that traditional religions are destined to be replaced by the new cult of man because they conflict with the modern scientific *weltanschauung*. (1972:149)

There is limited value in quoting similar words of criticism from other sociologists, philosophers and theologians. We need to turn to a more detailed examination of his concept of the religion of individualism.

Durkheim wrote: 'This cult of man has for its first dogma the autonomy of reason and for its first rite freedom of thought' (1898c:10t.1969d:24/1975:65). On what grounds does Durkheim assert these and similar doctrinal utterances? Unlike Comte's religion of humanity, Durkheim's cult of the individual, and indeed the creed of humanism in general, has never been officially or authoritatively formulated. To suggest as Durkheim does that reason is its prime doctrine is hardly a reason for justifying it! Since Durkheim rejects revelation, he feels he must find some equivalent. The foundation of the religion, as we have seen, is the ideological enthronement of man. Durkheim attempts to show this as a movement which has been evolving over a long period of time. There is also a theólogical reason for accepting the religion. As he writes;

> We know indeed that the sacred character which still marks the individual today is founded in reality; it is no more than the expression of the very high value that has accrued to individual personality through the conscience and dignity it is invested with. (1950a/1969g:199/t. 1957a: 172)

Durkheim holds that his doctrine of man, having some affinity with that of Christianity (see ch. 23.3-23.4) is at the basis of the new religion. 'The most significant part of our being,' he said, which we call the soul, comes from Him [God] and expresses Him through us' (1925a:119/t.1961a:104). Using Christian language Durkheim, as it has been repeatedly said, closely associates God with society. What is divine in man is the social (1913b; 1914a; ch. 8). 'We all carry the imprint of divinity' (1925a:119/t.1961a:104).

Because the cult of man does not exist in a form that is instantly recognized, Durkheim was forced to argue for its existence. And as well as pointing to what he held were historical facts, many of his arguments are reminiscent of the theologian trying to prove the existence of God, and sometimes one sees in him the scholastic philosopher arguing ontologically. For example, in 'Individualism and the intellectuals', after he has presented with approval Kant's concept of morality based on man *in abstracto,* he goes on to assume that from this, as we have noted, the human person is sacred and has something about him of the transcendental which churches have always bestowed upon their gods (1898c:8/ t.1969d:21/r.1975:62). So man is a divine being by deduction! And, with his customary logic, Durkheim sees that as man treated his gods in the past, so he treats man now, offering him respect and worship. Since man must never profane his gods, so man today must never profane man. He wrote:

> Whoever makes an attempt on a man's life, on a man's liberty, on a man's honour inspires us with a feeling of horror, in every way analogous to that which the believer experiences when he sees his idol profaned. Such morality is therefore

> not simply a hygienic discipline or a wise principle of economy. It is a religion of which man is, at the same time, both believer and god. (ibid.:8/21-2/62)

On these grounds alone man should not commit suicide (as he argued in his book on the subject, see 1897a:383/t.1951a:337), and we might add that such a reason should prevent him going to war or committing murder or other violent crimes! However, the question of crime in Durkheim is problematic and ambivalent -something that has been carefully pointed out by Richard (see Richard 1925(ii):361). Durkheim's argument for the existence of his religion is very much like the moral argument for the existence of God. Man is a moral creature, but a moral system does not have authority unless there is a moral being superior to man: since a moral system exists, a moral being exists. Similarly, for Durkheim, man is a moral creature, whose moral system needs to be undergirded by some authority superior to himself, that is, a religion: therefore the religion exists. And he goes so far as to admit this in his *Suicide,* when he wrote that the cult of human personality is that on which all our morality rests (1897a:379/ t.1951a.334). Time and time again, Durkheim admitted that an ethical system needs an authority above itself and therefore a humanistic ethic requires a humanistic religion (see 1908a(2); 1909a(2)/t.1979a). One may well ask the question whether any person is persuaded not to commit suicide or murder because he worships man? Empirical evidence is certainly required if Durkheim's position is to be substantiated. There can be no doubt that at the time Durkheim wrote there were a large number of middle-class intellectuals, especially French liberals, who held views which were in some way in keeping with those of Durkheim. Within the working classes, from whom Durkheim hoped a religious revival would spring, little that would pass for the cult of man has ever existed or exists today. This we have already noted. Durkheim made no attempt to try to prove his case, undertook no empirical research to strengthen his position, other than pointing to changes of thought in the intellectual climate of society. Yet those who are highly committed to humanism today are most reluctant to use the kind of terminology that Durkheim felt to be so important in delineating the religion of the future.

One of the most severe problems that faces all liberal humanists is that of suffering. Humanism contains an essentially optimistic ethic. How does such an ethic or religion cope with violence, national disasters, war or concentration camps? Durkheim may say that man worships man, but man does not hesitate to slaughter his fellow beings. Humanistic appeals do not assuage evil, only force does that. Durkheim himself was shattered by the holocaust of the First World War, which decimated his own select body of students. One wonders if, as a result of the war, he did not abandon his faith in the religion of the future which, just before the declaration of war, he had so much praised (see 1919b). The loss of his son André hastened his death: but had not his own faith in the future also died ?

In his essay 'The dualism of human nature', Durkheim comes to the brink of considering questions of theodicy, where he attempts to show how idealism and monism cannot incorporate notions of sin and suffering (1914a; see also 1913b). He admits that these are accommodated in various kinds of dualistic systems. However, the notions of sin and suffering have no place in the creed of the religion of the future. He openly rejects those traditional religions which have placed suffering at the centre of their beliefs. He wrote:

> The great religions of modern man are those which insist the most on the existence of the contradictions in the midst of which we struggle. These continue to depict us as tormented and suffering. (1914a:213/t.1960c:331-2)

And then, in approving primitive religions, he adds, 'the crude cults of inferior societies breathe forth and inspire a joyful confidence' (ibid.). It is evident that Durkheim—on the eve of the outbreak of war, let it be noted once again—would solve the problems of suffering and evil by repressing them and throwing up a smoke-screen of self-generated happiness. (The relation of theodicy to sociology was considered by Richard towards the end of his life (1943).)

Can man, can society make man sacred? In one sense, of course, it is possible. As we saw earlier, anything can be designated sacred by society. But to make man sacred is not to achieve something of the same order as saying that gods exist who are sacred. The first is visible to the naked eye; the second is not: the first is not surrounded by mystery; the second is. Man is never hidden, existing beyond human sight. He does not have to be revealed in some non-rational way. He can never be sacred in the same way as the gods are (1906b/1924a:93/t.1953b:71).

To say that the cult of man has 'as its first rite freedom of thought' is to make one doubt whether Durkheim in stating this was totally oblivious to his analysis of ritual, for it bears little relation to his early ideas on the subject and certainly to what he was to write on it in *The Elementary Forms.* Was he unaware that the cult of man is a cult without a cultus?

As it is generally understood, humanism is essentially antiritualistic. To humanists religious ritual - ritual in any form -speaks of either superstition or irrationality. And Durkheim's own ambivalence is apparent, on the one hand, in an intellectual realization of the need of ritual within a religion and, on the other, a personal distaste for it. Of ritual in the modern context, Durkheim wrote in a way that almost contradicts what he said in *The Elementary Forms* :

> For we know today that a religion does not necessarily imply symbols and rites in the full sense, or temples and priests. All this external apparatus is merely its superficial aspect. Essentially it is nothing more than a system of collective beliefs and practices which have special authority. (1898c:10/t.1969d:25/r.1975:66)

However, what are these practices, which are supported by a special authority, and which are associated with the cult of man? From other contexts we may deduce that they are great national observances such as Bastille Day. But such occasions are social, they do not relate to the sacredness of the person, and there are no rites which openly declare such a faith. Once again, on this evidence alone, one may ask whether the god at the back of Durkheim's mind is society rather than man. Gluckman, referring to the *Division of Labour,* observed that Durkheim emphasized that as religious formalism began to decline the god of humanity began to emerge (1962:19ff.). Gluckman also noted that in primitive societies social relations are ritualized, but not so in modern societies. Ritual becomes more general as it turns itself into congregational worship, and then vanishes almost entirely. Thus, ritual in western industrial society seems destined to extinction despite any ascendancy in human values.

Comte's religion of humanity had more logic in it than Durkheim's cult of man. Comte fully understood the necessity of ritual for a religion; and with that firmly in his mind took it as his task to introduce in great detail a sophisticated ritual, in part borrowed from rites of the Roman Catholic Church, but which had humanity as its object of worship. (Russian leaders seem to follow Comte rather than Durkheim in recent attempts to strengthen civic ritual in Russia (see Lane 1981).)

In many respects Durkheim felt that what historical religions had done in the past for society, the cult of man could achieve in the future. For Durkheim the most important characteristic was the force that a religion exerted over the individual *conscience;* by this means a religion was able to influence people in their moral behaviour and to call forth acts of self-denial and asceticism. The major issue turns on whether a self-consciously generated and internalized ideal can gain not only respect and following but can be raised to a transcendental status which is necessary for a religion to exist. Here it would appear that there is at least one internal inconsistency. In his lectures which covered Bazard's development of Saint-Simon's *Nouveau Christianisme,* he attacked both Bazard and Saint-Simon for proposing a religious system which in opposite ways led to pantheism, where all that exists, be it material or non-material, is divine (1928a/1971d:260/t.1958b:234-5). Such a system, in addition to other weaknesses, was not able, argued Durkheim, to restrain egoism and psychological drives and demands. It makes no call for self-sacrifice. Unchecked liberty would give rise to social chaos, not harmony. There must be an appeal from outside the system for man to be loyal and obedient to the system's demands. It must have an authority greater than that of the individual. Christianity had been successful in this respect, because its god was over and above the world and called for men to be obedient to the demands of control (ibid. :258/232). Apart from the issue of pantheism, the criticism which Durkheim levels against *Nouveau Chrtstianisme* is equally applicable to what he saw as the religion of the future. The new religion, however, is no different from Saint-Simon's. Witness his platitudinous attitude to the cult of the individual, written at the time of the Dreyfus affair:

> This religion of humanity has all that is required to speak to its believers in a tone that is no less imperative than the religions it replaces. Far from confining itself to indulging our instincts, it offers us an ideal which infinitely surpasses nature. (1898c:9/t.1969d:23/r. 1975:63-4)

But above all, in contrast to Comte once again, Durkheim can point to no church, no organization by which men assemble and jointly express their faith and practice. Its controlling force over society is minimal. Evans-Pritchard was wrong in stating that Durkheim envisaged a secularist church of the kind that arose out of the French Revolution (1962:32). One response in defence of Durkheim is to suggest that membership of the religion is identical to that of society, since the society's beliefs would correspond to those of its members. But such a condition would mean that the society was characterized by mechanical solidarity and this flatly contradicts Durkheim's own thinking about the emergence of the cult of man. Again, it is difficult to say that society equals the Church in a pluralistic world, for such a proposition is clearly a failure to be realistic.

In the light of what has been said, the question arises as to whether what Durkheim was proclaiming constituted a religion, as he claimed it was. The answer is clearly in the negative. The cult of man, as we have observed, is without a ritual and without a church. As such, and in accordance with Durkheim's own definition of what constitutes a religion, it cannot in any way be so designated. The basic elements are missing and therefore the proclamation that the cult of the individual is a religion is unconvincing (see, for example, 1898c:8/t.1969d:21/ r. 1975:62; see also 1950a/1969g: 104/t. 1957a:69)

Another reason for saying this was that Durkheim never claimed to be, nor was he in fact, a founder of a secular religion. If Durkheim had a strictly religious task, it was as a theologian of a religion that he claimed was already in existence. Richard calls Durkheim's cult of man the daughter of Comte's religion of humanity which he saw as a systematic combination of positivism and humanism, but this was not really the case (1935:19; 1943;). It may be true, as Richard also stated, that Durkheim's concept of the religion of the future was one facet of his *sociologie religieuse* . However, Durkheim did not want to turn his sociology into a religion as Comte had done (611/427/156). He claimed that in the first place his task was merely to point to what in fact was happening in the course of history, and unlike Comte, he did not seek to propagate the faith or encourage the practice in terms of ritual, or again to create a church. He did not see himself as a preacher, evangelist or missionary for a *religion.* But at the same time it can be justifiably said that he attempted to give some scientific basis to the religion which stemmed from his theory of society, where divinity is society symbolically transformed (Goblet d'Alviella 1913:220).

7. Basically a system of morality

Durkheim was firmly convinced that his analysis of what he thought was the religion of the future was both academically and politically acceptable. He seemed sure that in emphasizing a reverence for science and a reverence for man and bringing them together he had breached the gap between religion and science, which many intellectuals, both believers and non-believers, had for a long time seen as being a great, if not unbridgeable gulf (see Aron 1967b, 2:41). From now on, thanks to him, the scientist and the fair-minded (that is, the liberal) theologian can meet on common ground. Since Durkheim's time, the relation between religion and science has gone through many phases of rapprochement and hostility. Certainly the dream he had has never materialized. The 'best' of science and the 'best' of religion cannot in fact dwell happily in the same bed. Contrary to what Durkheim hoped, one cannot have it both ways.

In the broad sweep, however, Durkheim was right on two counts. First, there has been a continual decline of traditional western religions. Second, and more in keeping with this chapter, there has been a growth in the acceptance of the ideals of humanism, defined in the widest terms, and to be found particularly amongst intellectuals. The notion of Kantian man remains triumphant and, in the absence of God, man continues to think of himself as a self-legitimating being. This needs to be carefully documented for present-day society, but one can immediately point to the Charter of the United Nations, to Charter 77 and to the speeches of leading politicians in the West. The most 'sacrilegious' attitude a person may take today is to be anti-humanistic, to be racialist, or an opponent of Charter 77. Further, this humanistic outlook has in recent years become dominant in the churches themselves, both Protestant and Catholic, where the classical themes of salvation and redemption based on the work of Christ and the theology of St Paul have fallen into the background in the face of the dominant concern with personal relations, the ethic of love, and social justice.

We have stated that Durkheim was no founder of the cult of man and that, despite his proclamation to the contrary, he was dealing with hardly a religion at all. More precisely, he was advocating what we might call a functional alternative to a traditional religion, as when he wrote:

> This cult, moreover, has all that is required to take the place of the religious cults of former times. (1950a/1969g:104/t. 1957a:69)

But the alternative is not another religion; it is in fact a moral system. Such is the conclusion of many scholars (for example, Giddens 1978:99). This striving for a secular morality—some form of Christian ethic, shorn of theological dogma, ritual and a church —was clearly evident not only in Durkheim but also in such thinkers and political leaders of his time as Renouvier, Guyau, Desjardins, Barrés, Buisson and Péguy before his conversion to Catholicism.

Durkheim was optimistic about this morality, which was at the foundation of the Third Republic. Apart from the question of its 'truth', he was convinced that such a morality would stand firm in the face of scientific inquiry and rational criticism, for they both had given rise to it. Such a morality would be free from the undermining forces of scientific investigation. One wonders whether the events of history and subsequent changes in society which occurred after his death would have shaken his optimism -we might point to the final stages of the First World

War , the rise of Hitler, the growth of communism, and the development of a permissive morality. Durkheim's unshakeable hope was based very largely on the legacy of Christianity, as he himself admitted. He was living in an immediate post-Christian age, which was still relying on the capital and goodwill of Christian ideology and structures. These have continued to be eaten away and the capital expended. What price his optimism today?

Chapter-5
The Protestant Ethic Thesis

S.N. EISENSTADT

Chapter-5

Weber's famous 'Protestant Ethic' thesis – the thesis published originally by him as 'Die Protestantische Ethik und der Geist des Kapitalismus' in *Archiv für Sozialwissenschaft in Sozialpolitik*, in 1901-02 (vol.20) and reprinted in his *Gesammelte Aufsätz für Religionssoziologie*, in 1920 (see also Weber, 1930) – which has allegedly attributed the rise of modern, as distinct from pre-modern, types of capitalism[1] to the influence of Protestantism and especially of Calvinism, has provided – probably more than any other single specific thesis in the social sciences – a continuous of focus scientific controversy.

This controversy has burst aflame a new in each decade, each generation of scholars seeing in it a continuos challenge. Although in each generation there were those, like Robertson (1933) in the twenties, Fanfani (1934) in the thirties, and Samuelson (1961) in the fifties, who denied it any validity, yet somehow even such denials had to be stressed anew, each generation having to grapple with the fact that so many still attributed to this thesis some central importance in the social sciences in general and in the understanding of modernity in particular.

In the last fifteen years or so, with the upsurge of the great interest in development and modernization beyond Europe, interest in this thesis has arisen once more. Many seek in the existence or non-existence of some equivalent to the Protestant ethic the key in the understanding of the successful or unsuccessful modernization of non-European countries.

In order to be able to understand what it is in this thesis that may be of such critical importance it will be worth while in survey very briefly some of the major stages of the controversy

Excerpts from S.N. Eisenstadt, 'The Protestant ethc thesis in analytical and comparative cntext'. Diogenes, no.59 (1967), pp. 25-46. (Reprinted in Eisentadt, ed., The Protestant Ethic and Modernization)

around it, even if it would of course be impossible to present here a complete history of this controversy.

We may very broadly distinguish between two types of controversial arguments with regard to the Weberian thesis, corresponding to some extent, but not entirely, to chronological stages in the development.

The first stage of this controversy, best summarized in Dischoff (1944) article and in Baerling's (1946) book (see also Tawney 1956; Elton, 1963, pp.312 ff.), has mostly, although not entirely dealt with the analysis of the alleged direct causal connexion between the Protestant-Calvinist ethic on the one hand, and the development of capitalism on the other. At this stage the Weberian thesis was attacked at almost all the quotients of the assumed equation. Some have stressed that most of the initial Calvinist communities – be it Calvin's Geneva itself, the earlier Calvinist communities in the Netherlands, in Scotland or in this Palatinate – did not favor the development of new, more autonomous economic orientations or organizations, that in this manifest attitudes to economic activities they did not go much beyond the more severe medieval Catholic orientations, and that in some respects they were even more conservative and restrictive towards such activities, mainly because of their predilection for the extreme, totalistic religious regulation of all aspects of which made them take all these matters more seriously than medieval Catholicism.

On the other end of the equation it was often stressed that the first great upsurges of capitalism developed in pre-Reformation catholic Europe – be it in Italy, Belgium or Germany – and that they were much more 'developed' than those in the first Protestant of Calivinist countries. On the contrary, economic regression or retardation very often set in many of these communities, as for instance in Calvin's Geneva, to no small degree due to the restrictive orientation of the Protestant communities mentioned above.

Others have cast doubt on the specific 'mechanism' through which, according to Weber, Calvinist belief became transformed into or linked to motivation for this-worldly economic activities namely the psychological derivatives of the idea of predestination, the great anxiety which this idea created among believers, urging them to undertake in a compulsive way this-worldly activities to prove their being of the elect.

While some tended to cast doubt on the very relevance of any aspect of Calvinist religious orientation for the development of modern frameworks and activities, other like Hudson (1949, 1961) and lately the Georges (1958,1961) have tended to point in other orientations in the Calvinist Weltanschauung, such as the emphasis on individual responsibility, on the general orientation in 'this world' (as against the 'other-worldly' orientation of many other religions), as well as the general shattering of the traditional Weltanschauung, as possible ways or mechanisms through which the Protestant, calvinist Puritan or Denominational outlook could facilitate the development of modernity.[2]

Others who admitted the 'predilection' of Protestantism for various aspects of the 'modern' world – be it economic, scientific or modern politics activities – tended to attribute this predilection to structural situations and exigencies within which protestantism was put as a result of the wars of religion or the counter-Reformation, to its being in a minority position in these countries, or to indirect impact of Protestantism on the over-all institutional structure of these countries in the direction of growing pluralism and tolerance. They often did stress that the tendency of many Protestant groups – Huguenots in France or in exile, Protestant sects in Holland and England – to participate more actively than their Catholic or even Lutheran nieghbors in modern capitalistic activities developed, usually later, in the seventeenth to eighteenth centuries, and that it was very often due in reasons which had but little to do with the original calvinist belief emigration and exile and denial of possibilities of participation in central politics and cultural spheres.

Still others tended o emphasize that the tendencies of Protestants to participate in these activities were later developments, but necessarily typical of the mainstream of Calvinism or Protestantism, but more characteristic of its transition into a more pluralistic, tolerant, semi-secularized world and of the decline for its strong religious commitments than of its own initial inherent religious tendencies. For these writers it was often the *weakening* of the original totalistic religious impulses of the Puritans that provides the basic link between Protestants and modernity.

Tawney's (1926) classical study, which was intended as a sympathetic defense of Weber's thesis against many of the earlier critics like Robertson, was basically a detailed study of exactly such processes of the continous change of the motivational orientations of Puritan groups in the direction of secularization of growing emphasis on economic motives and activities within a society which became more and more 'tolerant' and secular.

In almost all criticism of this type or at this stage we can thus find an ambivalent attitude to Weber's thesis. On the one hand we find a critique of the direct casual relationship between the rise of Protestantism and the development of economic activities which has allegedly been explained by Weber in the concrete European or American setting. But on the other hand, most of these critics with the exception of the extreme negativists, do admit that despite all this there was indeed 'something' in the Weber an thesis. In one or another they acknowledge the existence of some 'insight' or Kernel of truth in Weber's thesis without however, defining exactly what this kernel may indeed in outside some the very broad, general terms mentioned above.

II

In order to be able to understand more fully this 'kernel' is in necessary to go to the second type of argument, or to the second phase of controversy. This type of argument can already be found in the earlier works of Troeltsch (1912,1931) and Holl (1927,1959). Although these two scholars were in a way in seemingly opposing camps – Troeltsch supporting Weber's thesis and Holl at least partially denying it – yet they did to a large extent have something in common. Neither Troeltsch not Holl was mainly concerned with the analysis of the mechanisms of the alleged direct casual relation between Protestantism and capitalism activity. Troeltsch fully acknowledged that the initial impetus of Calvinism was what would be nowadays called a totalistic own an attempt to establish a new civilization totally regulated by religious precepts.

But for him the major problem was not whether these initial orientation did promote or even facilitate the various type of such modern activities but rather what their influence was once they did not succeed in establishing the first totalistic impulses. Holl's major concern or polemic against both Weber and Troeltsch was mostly in defense of Lutheranism, which as often term depicted as the more conservative force in the Reformation, and but new transformative powers, against the more dynamic revolutionary Calvinism. Against this view Holl claimed that, from abroad comparative point of view (a view which in his includes the analysis, transformative tendency of its own which, while differing from that of Calvinism, being more centered the individual and less on the religious community, could yet, given appropriate conditions, contribute greatly to the formation forms of modern life and cutlture.[3]

But this type of approach to Weber's thesis had been largely neglected since then and only recently has it been taken up again, often without any reference to these earlier studies, in different ways by various scholars. Of these a brief discussion of the work of Trevor-Roper, Luethy and Walzer[4] can best serve for the pursues of our analysis.

Luethy, and to some extent Trevor-Roper denies the correctness of Weber's thesis in the economic field proper. They claim that economic development in Europe was independent of the specific direct impact of Protestantism. They show, for instance, as others still before them, that the first initial impact of Protestantism on economic life was, as Calvin's Geneva shows, a restrictive one. But they admit, indeed they stress, that especially England, the Netherlands, and to some extent the Scandinavian countries were more successful, after the Counter-Reformation, in developing viable, continous, flexible modern institutions, whether in the economic, political or scientific fields, than most of the Catholic countries like Spain, Italy or even France which were the first to develop many modern institutional frameworks.

At one level of argument it seems as if to them, as to some of their precursors, this was mostly due to the structural implications or exigencies of the victory of Protestatism and necessarily to anything inherent in the religious orientation in Protestantism in general or of Calvinism and Puritanism in particular.

But at another level of argument the picture is already somewhat different. This, for instance, Luethy transposes Weber's theory almost entirely to the political field. For him the main impact of Protestantism on European history has been in the political field. This impact was effected, according to him, through the direct reference to the Bible as a source for new basis of legitimation of authority as well as through the new structural impetus to the development of pluralistic settings which developed through the outcome of the Counter-Reformation or the Wars of Religion.

In principle the type of criticism the Luethy directs against Weber could easily be directed against his own thesis, it could easily be shown that the original political impulse of either Lutheranism or Calvinism was not in 'liberal' or democratic direction but rather in a more 'totalistic' one. But whatever the correctness of such criticism of details, it would be largely misdirected, because Luethy's analysis does not deal with the direct economic or political impact or 'results' of the activities of certain religious groups or beliefs but rather, as has already been the case by Troeltsch and Holl, with its transformative effects.

From this point of view Luethy's more specific work (1959-61 esp. vol. 2, p.786) on the Protestant Bank is very significant here he shows how the ultimate difference between 'Catholic' finance and 'Protestant Banks' was based on the degree to which the latter were not tied to the given political order but were conceived as an autonomous sphere of organized activity, supported by the legitimation of economic calculus. This legitimation could be derived from the Calvinist ethic, but it developed in Geneva after the downfall of the initial totalistic-religious regime in Geneva, while in France the reliance of the monarchs on the mostly foreign) Protestant banks also developed only after the impulsion of the Huguenots on the one hand and the bankruptcies of the Royal ('traditional Catholic') finances, on the other hand. Parallel indications have been developed even more fully by Weber's independent analysis of the two groups instrumental in shaping of Puritanism in England, the intelligentsia (ministers, students and lay intellectuals) and the gentry. He shows that originally the impulses of Calvinism were directed not in the economic field, but in the political one and that in this field they are also initially mostly totalistic.[5] But then he continues to show, very detailed analysis, how, after the initial failure of these totalistic orientations, when the Puritans became a persecuted minority, and especially an *exiled* minority of 'intellectuals', here took place a transformation of their orientations in the direction of the reconstruction of new rules, organizations, new patterns of human connexions and new society and polity.

III

Thus Luethy's work on the bank and Walzer's analysis of the Britain intelligentsia indeed contain very important indications are the full re-examination of the Weberian thesis in its broadest analytical and comparative applications.

The crux of this re-examination lies in shifting the course of the argument from an examination of the alegedly direct, causal relation between Protestantism and capitalism (or other aspects of th modern world) to that of the transforamtive capacities of protestantism.

It is of course true that originally the Reformation was not 'modernizing' movement. It did not have very strong modernization impulses; it did not have very strong modernizing impulses; it did indeed aim at the establishment of a new, purer 'medieval' socio-political religious order. Originally Protestantism was indeed a religious movement aiming at the religious reconstructing of the world. It was just because of these strong 'this worldly' religious impulses that from the very beginning they were caught up with, and in, the major socio-political economic and cultural trends of change which European time especially Western and Central European) society was undergoing from the end of the seventeenth century on ; the development of capitalism, the development of Renaissance absolutism and the consequent 'general' crisis of the seventeenth century, the crisis between 'state' and 'society', the development of a secular outlook and science (Trevor-Roper, 1965b.)

The Reformtion did not directly cause any of these developments, although in many indirect ways it did of course contribution to the weakening of the traditional framework of European society. Many of these crises or developments stemmed from the same broad roots as the Reformation from the crisis of Catholic civilization in general and the Catholic Church in particular, But their specific cause, as well as the groups which fostered them. Whether the humanistic like Erasmus, the new international merchants like the Fuggers, did on the whole differ from the reformers, although sometimes overlapping and often very much-serving as important mutual reference groups. But however strong the concrete interrelationships between these various groups and the various 'crises' which they fostered, neither was a direct cause of the other.

The significance of the Reformation and Protestantism is to be found not in the fact that it directly caused or gave rise in new types of economic, political or scientific activities, but its contribution to the restructuring of European society, a structuring which developed as a result of all these crises but which came, in the post – counter-Reformation period, to a full fruition in the protestant than in the catholic countries, because of some of the transformative potential of Protestantism as it developed in these settings. This crucial impact of Protestantism in the direction of modernity came after the failure of is initial totalistic socio-religious orientations.

Thus the special importance, from a broad comparative point of view, of Protestantism could be seen in that, for a variety reasons to be a shortly examined, it did contain within itself the of such transformation, and that in its specific setting these could bear fruit and greatly influence the course of European civilization on the way to modernity[..]

IV

This shift of the locus of the discussion and controversy about the Weberian thesis from the analysis of the direct-causal links between Protestantism and capitalism (or other types of modern institutions) to the analysis of the broader transformative powers or tendencies of Puritanism or Calvinism puts this discussion, to begin with, in a broader perspective of the totality of Weber's work. As Mommsen has recently put it very succinctly.

In Max Weber the exemplar among such religious movements that change the world' was Puritan. Although the investigated other variants of Christianity and other great world religions from the standpoint of the social consequences of their teaching, none in his opinion had influenced the course of human development in quite such a revolutionary manner as had Puritanical religiosity (Mommesen, 1965, p.31.)

But beyond this it puts this discussion in a broader general comparative and analytical perspective.

Already in Weber's general work on sociology of religion the major economic behavior but on the more general 'Wirtschaftsehik' of each religion, i.e. on those broader types of orientations inherent motivation and activities.

But the shift to the analysis of the transformative capacities of different religions contains an additional element, namely the possibly that, under certain conditions, different religions may new types of activities which go beyond the original direct 'wirtchaftsethik', i.e. there may take place a transformation of the original religious impulses which may in turn lead to the transformation of social reality.[6]

This shift does necessitate a reformulation of the problems for comparative analysis in general, for the consequent re-examination of the Weberian thesis, even within the context of Weber's over all work, in particular. In addition to asking about the Wirtschaftsethik' of orientation of different religions, or of the religious orientations of different social groups,[7] it is necessary to ask about the *transformative* capacity of different religions (or, for that matter, of secular ideologies), i.e. their capacity for internal transformation which may then facilitate the development of social institutions and individual motivations in directions different from their original impulses and aims.

Here several problems stand out. The first problem is what

it is within any given religion (or ideology) that creates or account for the existence of such transformative capacities. The second question is in what directions such transformative capacities may develop. Last comes the question, what are the conditions in the society within such religious or ideological groups developing which facilitate or impede the institutionalization of such transformative capacities or orientations?

With regard to all these questions only very tentative and preliminary answers can be given both with regard to Protestantism and even more with regard to other religions. But even such preliminary answers perhaps may indicate some of the possibilities of such an analytical and comparative approach.

V

With regard to the first question, what it is in the nature of Protestantism that creates such transformative potential or capacity, to a large extent the answer has been given by many scholars although it probably needs further elaboration and systematization.

All of them seem to agree that this potential or capacity does not seem to be connected to any single tenet of the Protestant faith, but rather in several aspects of its basic religious and value orientations.

The most important of these are its strong combination of 'this-worldiness' and transcendentalism, a combination which orients individual behaviour to activities within this world but at the same time does not ritually sanctify any of them, either a mystic union or any ritual act, as the final point of religious consummation or worthiness. Second is the strong emphasis on individual activism and responsibility. Third is the orientated, direct relation of the individual to the sacred and to sacred tradition, an attitude which, while strongly emphasizing the importance and direct relevance of the sacred and of tradition, yet minimizes the extent to which this relation and individual commitment can be mediated by any institution, organization or textual exegesis.[8] Hence it opens up the possibility of continous re-definition and re-formulation of the nature and of this tradition, a possibility which is further enhanced in the strong transcedental attitude which minimizes the sacred of any 'here and now'.

These religious orientations of Protestantism and Protestants especially Calvinists) were not, however, confined only to the realm of the sacred. They were closely related to and evident two major orientations in most Protestant groups' conception the social reality and of their own place in it, i.e. in what may called their status images and orientations (Pauck, 1961; Meluhar, 1959).

Most of the Protestant groups developed a combination of two of such orientations. First was their 'openess' towards the wider social structure, rooted in their 'this-worldly' orientation which was not limited only to the economic sphere but which also, as we shall see later, could encompass other social second, they were characterized by a certain autonomy and self-sufficiency from the point of view of their status orientation. They evinced but little dependence from the point of the view of the crystallization of their own status symbols and identity on the existing political and religious centers.

VI

With regard to the second question, namely that of the directions on which such transformative capacities can be effective, the picture is already much more complicated, certainly much more so than as presented by Weber himself.

The first such level of institutional aspect, probably least from with by Weber, which Protestantism tended to transform that of the Central political symbols, identities and institutions by the very nature of the totalistic reformatory impulses of Protestants these institutions constituted natural foci of the orientations and activities. The very basic theological term whether of Luther, Zwingli or Calvin, or whatever the marked differences between them in their attitudes to political institutions contained some very strong ingredients for the reformulation of the relation between state and 'society', between ruler and ruled, and redefinition of the scope and nature of the political community.

The initial failure of their totalistic attempts did not about nullify these impulses. On the contrary, the structural roots of the various crises of European society in the sixteenth and seventeenth centuries, and especially the crisis of state society as well as the political exigencies of protestant communities of various European states, facilitated and even reinforced continous orientation towards the political sphere and towards activities within it.

And indeed the Protestant Reformation did have a great impact on the central political sphere. Certainly this impact was not necessarily intended by the rulers who adopted Protestantism. Yet it did have important structural effects which greatly facilitated the further development of a more flexible and dynamics social system.

Of crucial importance here was the search of the rulers for new legitimation as well as their attempts to forge new symbols in collective identity.

On both these levels, that of legitimation of new patterns of authority and of forging new symbols of national identity, thus developed, through the initial religious impact of the major Protestant groups and especially through their transformation, the possibilities of the reformation of the relations between rulers and ruled, of patterns of political participation and of the scope and nature of the political community.[9]

These orientations also contained possibilities for the restructralization of the central legal-institutional and of four basic premises, centered around the idea of covenant and around the reformulation of many concepts of law which led to a much more differentiated view of the state and autonomy of voluntary business corporations, them from the more restricted view inherent in traditional law (Little, 1963). And indeed, in the first Protestant societies – England, Scandinavia, The Netherlands – and later in the United States, through the incorporation of Protestant and symbols, perhaps even before the full development of motivations to new types of economic or scientific activities there developed a transformation of the central symbollic and political sphere and of the basic interrelations between the political and social spheres. This not only reinforced the existing relative autonomy of these spheres but created new, more flexible types of political symbols, new bases of political obligation and more flexible political institutions.

Here the comparison with Catholic countries, especially during and after the counter–Reformation, is extremely instructive. The ingredients of almost all the elements–new bases of legitimation and new national symbols autonomy of religious institutions (as evident, for instance, in the Gallican Church) – existed in most of these countries on the eve of the Reformation and even to some extent throughout the Counter-Reformation. And yet in these countries, such as Spain and France or even earlier in the Italian states of the Renaissance where the very first types of modern statecraft developed, these potentially diversifying orientations were stifled in their development not only by various external exigencies (like the vicissitudes of warfare among the small Italian principalities and the deflection of trade routes from him) but also by the maintenance of the older, Catholic symbols of legitimation, of the traditional relations between Church and by viewing both of them as the natural or preordained mediators between man and community on the one hand and the sacred and natural orders on the other.[10]

VII

But the transformative effects of Protestantism were not limited only to the central institutions and symbols of society but also to other aspects of the institutional structure of modern societies and especially to the development of new types of roles, structure and role sets and to motivations to undertake and to form such roles. The essential core of Weber's Protestant thesis, as distinct from Weber's wider discussion of the transformative effects of Protestantism, focuses on one aspect of the problem – the development of the role of economic enterpreneur and of the specific setting within which the role become institutionalized.

Here again it is obvious that many of the basic ingredients of this role and of its new specific goals have of course existed before, and have even continued to develop, to some extents in Catholic countries. But it is true that in the period after this

Counter-Reformation these developments, even when quantitatively initially *not different* from the later developments in the Protestant countries, could not free themselves, as Luethy's work on the Bank shows, from their dependence on the political center, in terms both of their goal-orientation and legitimation. In the Catholic countries these frameworks could not attain such autonomy and could not foster the consequent continous impetus for further, more differentiated development. It was mention in Protestant countries, or among Protestant (Calvinist) communities that these roles acquired a new type of autonomous legitimation and were able to develop a relatively independence organizational framework.

It was also mostly among the Protestant communities that another crucial aspect of the crystallization of new roles took place namely the relatively intense development of motivation for the undertaking of such roles and goals and for identifying with them.

Thus we see that the transformative potential of Protestant could effect the development of new roles in three different directions: first, in the definition of specific new roles with new types of goals, defined in autonomous terms and not tied to existing frameworks; second, in the development of broader institutional organizational and legal normative settings which could both optimize such new roles and provide them with the necessary sources and frameworks to facilitate their continuous working; and last, in the development of new types of motivation,[11] of motivations for the understanding of such roles and for identifying them.

Although these three aspects of the development of new roles and role complexes are very closely interwoven and interrelated and were perhaps not fully distinguished by Weber), yet they are to be kept distinct, because to some degree at least they can develop to different degrees.

But whatever the exact aspects of such new roles, which tended develop under the impact of the transformative tendencies of protestantism, as has already been briefly mentioned above, they did not develop only in the economic sphere but in a much greater variety of institutional spheres. They could indeed develop in the political sphere, proper, giving rise to new types of active political participation and organizations in the form of parties, community organizations and public service (Scotland, The Netherlands, France) (Burrell, 1960). They could also develop in the natural and especially scientific and educational sphere.[12] In the economic sphere proper they could develop in other ways distinct from capitalist-mercantile or industrial entrepreneurship proper, for instance, in the transformation of the economic activities the gentry (Stone, 1965, p.10).

Here again in all these spheres the beginning and possibilities such new roles existed before Protestantism, but it was more the Protestant countries as against the Catholic ones that they developed in terms of organizational autonomy of goals, organizational structure and legitimation.

VIII

We may now pass very briefly to the third question, namely that the conditions under which such transformative capacities of Protestantism (or other religions) could indeed become 'absorbed' or institutionalised.

In very broad terms it seems that the possibility of such institutionalized is greater the stronger the seeds of the autonomy of the social, cultural and political orders are within any society. The existence of the autonomy of the cultural order facilitate the development of new symbolic realms which can support and legitimize central institution building while the autonomy of the sphere of social organization facilities the development of new organizational nuclei which help in the crystallization of some viable new institutions without disrupting the whole fabric of the pre-existing order, thus enabling the new order to build in some extent on some at least of the earlier forces.

It is indeed in the realm of European and especially Western European culture that we find the strongest tradition of autonomy of the major institutions of the cultural, political and social orders, and it is here indeed that the first and most continuous impetus to modernization did develop. But the course of modernization was not of course either even or continuos or the same in all, even Western and Central European, countries.

The specific transformative potentials of Protestantism can be seen in the fact that it look up these seeds of autonomy and pluralism and helped in recrystallizing them on a higher level of differentiation than in the Catholic countries, like Spain and France, where the potentially pluralistic impact of various modern trends, including Protestantism, was inhibited by the formation of the Catholic state during the Counter-Reformation.

But even with in the Protestant countries there existed great variations. The transformative orientation of Protestantism did not necessarily develop fully and in the same direction among all protestant groups in all countries, though to some minimal extent they probably occurred in most of them. The concrete development and institutionalization of such orientations depended to small degree on the interaction between the orientations and placement of the major Protestant groups on the one hand and the pre-existing social structure, and especially on the extent of 'openness' of the existing political and cultural centers, of the broader groups and strata and on their initial reaction to religious innovations. The exact scope of such institutionalization differed greatly according both of the nature of groups (i.e. aristocracy, urban participate, various 'middle' groups, urbanproletariat or pesantry) which were the bearers of protestantism on the one and their placement within the broader social structure in general and with regard to the political and cultural center in particular, on the other.

The transformative capacities of the Protestant groups were smallest in those cases where they attained full powers – when their more totalistic restrictive orientations could become dominant or in situations where they were downtrodden minorities.[13]

Contrariwise, both the scope of new institutional activities which different transformed Protestant groups developed, and the extent to which they were successful in transforming central spheres of the society were most far-reaching in those situations in which the various Protestant groups were in a position of what may be very broadly called 'secondary' élites, close to but not identified with, the central élites, and in so far as Protestant groups and orientations became integrated into wider national communities which developed on the basis of the prior autonomy of the Estates becoming the only bearers of such new political or national identity.[14]

The various interactions between different transformative potentialities and existing structural flexibility could give rise to paradoxically similar, or divergent, results. The influence of Lutheranism, allegedly more conservative than Calvinism, took a variety of forms for example. In the German principalities Lutheranism was indeed very restrictive, because the existing political framework was not an appropriate setting for the development of a new national identity and community or for the development of a new rational identity and community or for the development of more autonomous and flexible status orientations in the broader (see Drummond, 1951; MacNeill, 1954; Ritter, 1938, 1950, 3, esp. pp. 133-70; Adam, 1938). Here, the 'traditional' or autocratic rulers of the small principalities adopted the new religious orientations, and in this context the more conservative among these orientations became predominant, often restricting further institutional development.

But in the Scandinavian countries these religious orientations were integrated into new, wider national communities and developed on the basis of the prior autonomy of the Estates. While they certainly did not impede the development of an absulute state in sweden, they did help to make possible the subsequent development of these states in a more pluralistic direction (holmquist, 1922; Schrey, 1951; Schweiger, 1962, Ritter, 1950).

Similarly paradoxical results, also demonstrating the importance of restrictive prior situations or frameworks, are evident in the institutionalization of Calvinism. Of special importance has is the Prussian case, where the institutionalization of these orientations by the absolutist, autocratic Hohnezollerns did not facilitate the development of a flexible and pluralisitic political framework, though it did support development of more action collective political goals (Kayser, 1961).

***References*:**

Adam, A. (1938), 'Die nationale Kirche bei Luther,' *Archiv für Geschiche der Reformation*, vol. pp. 30-62.

Andreski ,S. 91964), 'Method and substantive theory in Max Weber'. *Brit. J. Soc.*, vol. 15, pp.1-8.

Baerling, R.F. (1946), *Protestantisme en kapitalisme, max Weber in die Critick,* Wolfers, Groningen-Batavia.

Bellah, R.N. (1963), 'Reflections on the Protestant ethic analogy in Asia', *J. Soc. Iss.*, vol. 19, pp. 52-60.

Brefuer, J.G. (1950), 'Puritan mysticism and the development of liberalism', *Church History*, vol. 17.

Burrell, S.A. (1960), 'Calvinism, capitalism, and the middle classes some after thought on an old patter', *J. mod. Hist.*, vol. 32, pp.129-41.

Castro, A. (1954), *The Structure of Spanish History*, Princeton University Press.

Daniel-Rops, N. (1961a), *The Protestant Reformation*, Dent.

Daniel-Rops, N. (1961b), *The Catholic Reformation*, Dent.

Drummond, A.L. (1951), *Protestantism Since Luther*, Epworth.

Elton, G.R. (1963), *Reformation Europe*, 1517-1559, Collins.

Fanfani, A. (1934), *Cattolicesimo e Protestantesimo nella Formazione del Capitalismo, Milano.* English translation, *Catholocism, Protestantism and Capitalism*, Sheed Ward 1935.

Feuer, L.S. (1963), *The Scientific Intellectual*, Basic Books.

Fischoff, E. (1944), 'The Protestant ethic and the spirit of capitalism *Social Research*, vol. 11, pp. 54-77.

George, C.H. (1958), 'Protestantism and capitalism in pre-revolutionary England', *Church History*, vol. 27, pp. 351-71.

George, C.H., and George, K. (1961), *The Protestant Mind of the English Reformation*, 1570-1640, Princeton University

Press.

Ghyl, P. (1960), *Noord en Zuid*, Utretch-Antwerpen.

Ghyl P. (1961), *The Netherlands in the 17th Century*, Benn.

Ghuen, R.W. (1959), *Protestantism and Capitalism*, Health.

Hunser, H. (1963), 'La modernité du XVIe siécle'. *Cahiers des Annales*, Vol. 21.

Hull, K. (1927), *Gesammelte Aufsätze zur Kirchengeschichte*, vols. 1 and 2.

Hull, K. (1959), *The Cultural Significance of the Reformation*, Meridian.

Hullmquist, H. (1922), 'Kirche und staat im evangelischen Schweden,' *Hugabe für karl Müller, Mohr, Tubingen*, pp.209-2077.

Hudson, W. (1949), 'Puritanism and the spirit of capitalism', *Church History*, vol. 18, pp.3-16.

Hudson, W. (1961), 'The Weber thesis re-examined', *Church History*, Vol. 30, pp.88-9.

Kayser, C.R. (1961), Calvinism and German political life, *unpublished* Ph.D, thesis, Radcliffe.

Karney, H.F. (1964), 'Puritanism, Capitalism and the scientific revolution, *Past and Present*, vol. 28, pp.81-101.

Kalakowski, L. 91965), 'la genése et la structure, dans I'étude des ideologies religieuses', in M. de Gandillac, L. Goldman and J. Piaget, ends., *Entretiens sur les Notions de Genése et la Structure*, Mouton, pp.307-23.

Kundsay, A.D. 91945), *The Modern Democratic State*, Oxford University Press.

Little, D. (1963), The Logic of order – an examination of the sources of Puritan –Anglican controversy and their relation to prevailing legal conceptions in the 16th and 7th centuries, unpublished Doctor of Theology Thesis, Harvard University.

Luethy, H. (1959-61), *La banque Protestante en France*, 2

vols., Sevpen, Paris.

Luethy, H. (1964), 'once again: Calvinism and Capitalism', *Encounter*, vol. 22, pp. 26-38. [Reprinted in Luethy (1965).]

Luethy, H. (1965), *Le Passé, Menace Présente*, Sevpen, Paris.

MacNeill, J.T. (1954), *The History and Character of Calvinism*, Oxford University Press.

Merton, R.K. (1938), 'Science, technology and society in Seventeenth century England', *Osiris*, vol. 4.

Mommsen, W. (1965), 'Max Weber's political sociology', *Int. soc. Scien J.*, vol.17.

Muller –Aarmack, A. (1959), *Religion and Wirtschaft*, Kohlhammer.

Nelson, B. (1965), 'Max Weber's sociology of religion,' *Amer. Soc. Rev.*, vol. 30, pp. 595-601.

Nebhur, H.R. (1959), *The Social Sources of Denominationalism* Meridian.

Pauck, W. (1961), *The Heritage of the Reformation*. Free Press of Glenque.

Rabb, K. (1962), 'Puritanism and the rise of experimental science in England, '*J. world Hist.*, vol.17.

Ritter, G. (1938), 'Das 16. Jahrhundert als weltgeschitliche Epoche *Archiv für Geschichte der Reformation*, vol. 35.

Ritter, G. (1950), *Die Neugestaltung Europeas in 16. Jahrhundert*, Druckhaus Tempelhof, Berlin.

Robertson, H.R. (1933), *Aspects of the Rise of Economic Individualism* century', Britain and the Netherlands, vol.2, pp. 109-33.

Roords, D.J. (1964), 'The ruling classes in Holland in the seventeenth centruy', Britain ad the Netherads, vo. 2, pp. 109-33.

Samuelson, K. (1961), *Religion and Economic Action*, Heinemann.

Schöffer, I. (1964a), *'De Nederlandse revolutie', Zeven Revolution, de Bussy, Amsterdam*, pp. 9-29.

Schoffer. I. (1964b), 'Protestantism in Flux during the revolt of the Netherlands'. in *J.S. Brombley and F.H. Kossman, eds., Britain ad the Netherlands*, vol.2, pp. 67-84.

Schrey, H.H. (1951), 'Geistliches und Weltliches Regiment in der Schwedischen Reformation', *Archiv für Geschechte der Reformation*, vol. 42, pp. 146-59.

Schweiger, G. (1962), *Die Reformation in den Nordischen Landern*, Kozel Verlag, Munich.

Scoville, W.C. 91950), 'The Huguentots and the diffusion of technology', J. *Polit. Econ.*, vol. 9, pp. 294-311.

Sholem, G. (1946), 'On the Sabbatean movement of the 17th century' *Major Trends in Jewish Mysticism*. [Reprinted 1956.]

Sholem, G. (1958), Shabbetai Tzui, 2 vols. (Hebrew).

Stone, L. 91965), 'Review of C. Hill's *Intellectual Origins of the English Revolution*,' *New York Review of Books*, August.

Tawney, R.H. (1926), *Religion and the Rise of Capitalism*, Harcourt, Brace.

Tawney, R.H. (1956), 'Religion and economic life', *Times Lit. Supp.*

Trevor-Roper, H.R. (1963), 'scotland and the Puritan Revolution', un H.Y. Bell and L. Ollard, eds., *Historical Essays 1600-1750; presented to David Ogg*, pp. 78-130.

Trevor-Roper, H.R. (1965a), 'Religion, the Reformation and Social change', *Hist. Stud.*, vol. 4, pp. 18-45.

Trevor-Roper, H.R. (1956b), 'The general crisis of the seventeenth century', and 'General crisis: a symposium,' in T. Ashton, ed., *Crisis in Europe*. Routledge, pp. 59-97 and 97-117.

Troeltsch, R. (1931), *The Social Teachings of the Christian Churches*, 2 vols., Allen & Unwin. (New edition 1956.)

Troeltsch, E. (1912), *Protestantism and Progress*, Williams and Norgans (new edition 1958.)

Van Der Sprenkel, B. (1964), 'Max Weber on China', *History and Theory*, vol. 3, pp. 348-70.

Van Gelder, H. (1961), The two Reformations in the Sixteenth Century, Nijhoff, The Hague.

Walzer, M. (1964), 'Puritanism as a revolutionary ideology', *History and Theory*, vol. 3, pp. 59-90.

Walzer M. (1965), *The Revolution of the Saints*. Harvard University press.

Wayne-nafziger, E. 91965), 'The Mennonite ethic in the Weberian framework,; *Explorations in Entrepreneurial History*, second series, vol.2.

Weber, M. (1930), Protestant ethic and the Spirit of Capitalism, trans. T. Parsons, allen & Unwin.

Weber, M. (1961), *General Economic History*, Collier.

Wong, C.K. (1964), 'Introduction' to max Weber, *The Religion of China*, Free Press.

NOTES

1. On Weber's distinction between pre-modern and modern capitalism weber (1961) p. 4.
2. In this vein, see also the older works of Hauser (1963). Several of the variant studies can be found in green (1959).
3. On these differentiations between Lutheranism and Calvinism , as also from the point of view of Weber's strong emphasis on Calvinism, Nelson (1965). See also Müller0Armack (1959). More recently a similar thesis with regard to Lutheranism has been taken up by Ritter (1938, 1950 pp. Ch.3.)
4. See Trevor-Roper (1965a), Luethy 91964) and Walzer (1964, 1965). The also Luethy (1965), pp. 58-99 where parts of his work on the Protestant most relevant from the point of view of a *general* discussion of the Protestant Ethic thesis,

have been reprinted.

5. See Walzer (1965). A similar emphasis on the political activities of same, especially French and Scottish Protestants, can be found in Burrell (1960) and Trevor-Roper (1963).

   The transformative potentials, in the political field, of the Puritan idea of covenant have been explored previously by many people. See among other, Hudson, (1949, 1961) and Breuer (1950).

6. One of the interesting analyses which deals explicity with such transformative capacities of religious movements after their initial failure is that of G. Scholem (1946, 1958.)

7. This is a central aspect of Weber's work which is analysed by Andeur (1964). See also Yong (1964) and van der sprenkel 91964).

8. This point has been analysed with great skill, with regard to the remains in the Netherlands and their potentially more revolutionary open orientations, by L. Kolakowski (1965).

9. One of the earlier expositions of this view can be found in Lind (1945.)

10. see for instance Castro (1954); and also, for a Catholic analysis, very interesting from this point of view, Daniel-Rops (1961a and b.)

11. on the importance of the relations between the motivational and the organizational aspects of the development of roles, see Bellah (1963).

12. The influence of Protestantism on Science has constituted another continuos focus of research and controversy derived from the Protestant thesis. See for instance, Merton (1938), Feuer (1963), van Gelder Rabb (1962) and Kearney (1964).

13. On their situations as minorities, see among other Scoville (1950) and Wayne-nafziger (1965).

14. Of special interest in this respect are the developments in

the Netherlands, the relation between Protestants and the development of the Dutch nation. See Geyl (1960, 1961), Schöffer (1964a and b) and Reoords 1964).

Chapter-6

Religion and Social Class in America

N. J. Demerath

Chapter-6

Two hallmarks of American religion are its susceptibility to non-religious factors and its resulting variety. In the absence of any state church, religion is particularly vulnerable to influences such as .social class. This has been a central theme in observations of American society since the beginning of the 19th century. In 1832 Alexis de Tocqueville (see 1954) commented that the nominational competition but saw it as contributing more hypocrisy than vitality, and she pointed an especially accusing finger at an unscrupulously tyrannical clergy. Contemporary observers have also agreed on the perception of diversity while disagreeing over its effects. On the one hand, Talcott Persons (1960, ch. 10) has urged that denominationalism provides in adaptable religious system to meet the needs of a variegated society. On the other hand, H. Richard Niebuhr (1929) deplored denominationalism as a fragmentation of the true religious spirit. While denominationalism is not our concern, it reflects the influence of social class, and this is very much to the point. It is no secret that class has had more than passing effect on American religion. Not only is this a theme among foreign journalists, social theorists and theologians, but it has also commanded the attention of empirical analysts. By now, it is almost *de rigueur*, and certainly a commonplace, to begin studies of American religious variation with a table showing the relation between social class and denominational affiliation. This study is no different, and Table It is drawn from data that originally appeared in the National Council of Churches' Information service.

Based on a national sample, the table orders the major United States religious groups by decreasing status. At the high-status extreme, nearly one-fourth of the Christian Scientists, Episcopalians, and Congregationalists are from the upper class ;

Excerpt from chapter I of N. J. Demerath, III, *Social Class in American Protestantism*, pp. 1-25.

Table 1

Social Class Profiles of American Religious Groups

	Class			
Deonomination	Upper	Middle	Lower	N
	%	%	%	
Christian Scientist	24.8	36.5	38.7	(137)
Episcopal	24.1	33.7	42.2	(590)
Congregational	23.9	42.6	33.5	(376)
Presbyterian	21.9	40.0	38.1	(961)
Jewish	21.8	32.0	46.2	(537)
Reformed	19.1	31.3	49.6	(131)
Methodist	12.7	35.6	51.7	(2100)
Lutheran	10.9	36.1	53.0	(723)
Christian	10.0	35.4	54.6	(370)
Protestant (Small bodies)	10.0	27.3	62.7	(884)
Roman Catholic	8.7	24.7	66.6	(2390)
Baptist	8.0	24.0	68.0	(1381)
Mormon	5.1	28.6	66.3	(1.75)
No Preference	13.3	26.0	60.7	(466)
Protestant (undes-ignated)	12.4	24.1	63.5	(460)
Atheist, Agnostic	33.3	46.7	20.0	(15)
No Answer or Don't Know	11.0	29.5	59.5	(319)

From Schneider (1952), appendix, p.228.

fewer than one-half are from the lower class. At the other end, fewer than one tenth of the Roman Catholics, Baptists and Mormons are from the upper class; roughly two-thirds are from the lower class.

Although their particulars of the relationship will vary over time and between different areas of the country, [1] Table1 is generally representative of myriad studies of local communities as well as of large national samples. There are, however, two important caveats which bear upon the present study. First, even though denominations can be ranked by status, there is no justification for converting relative ranking into absolute categorizations. Episcopalians may be *relatively* upper class, but more than 40 percent are from the lower class. Baptists may study for it may be relatively lower class, but they claim their Rockefellers as well. Status heterogeneity within denominations is crucial in this study, for it is less concerned with the subtler distinctions within them.

A second qualification concerns the difference between religious conference and religious involvement. These are not identical, and it is possible that their relations to social class may be more religiously involved than their more heralded upper-class co-members. At the same time, although the Baptists are generally lower class, the upper-class adherents may control the church organization.

But if research on actual religious involvement is more important for our purposes, it is also less common and less precise compared to studies of class and religious preference. Perhaps because of its relative sparseness, its neglect of denominational distinctions, its oversight of the differences between various kinds of involvement, and its general quality as a research inside', research on involvement has harbored an unexposed contradiction. The majority of studies find those of high status middle and upper class) more religiously involved. Yet an important minority report that those of low status (working and lower class) are more involved.

The Case for High-Status Religiosity

American religion, especially protestantism, has been widely held to be an activity of the middle and upper classes. The argument rests principally on three indicators of involvement church membership, attendance at church services, and participation in the church's formal activities. On each of these measures, persons of high status appear to be more deeply involved than those of low status.

Before moving to the actual studies, two comments are appropriate. First, although the empirical relations are relatively unambiguous, their meaning is open to question. Throughout I will try to show that the three measures do not exhaust, nor always illuminate, the concept of religious involvement. Rather than stop short at the data themselves, I will try to probe beneath them.

A second comment concerns my use of the term 'high status' to refer to the combined middle and upper classes. This is partly a reflection of my concern with the latent debate between those who see the greatest involvement among the middle and upper classes and those who see it among the working and lower classes. More important, however, is another conflict within the former camp alone. While all of the studies in this section agree that those of high status are more involved than those of low, they disagree on the relative involvement of the middle and upper classes themselves. Some have described a linear relation where involvement increases consistently with increasing status so that the lowest class is the least involved and the upper class is the most. Others, however, have reported a curvilinear pattern. Here there is a slight drop-off in involvement among the upper class, and the middle class is most involved, though both high status groups are more committed than those of low status. This is a minor but persistent inconsistency that I will deal with in the conclusion of this section. Until than I will note its occurrence but stress the larger difference between the high-and low-status groups over all.

Religious identification

It was not until the 1930s that social scientists began to examine variations in religious involvement or religiosity[2] empirically because information on church preference and membership was easily available from questionnaire surveys and from the churches themselves, this was one of the first measures explored. Because social class had already proved a potent explanatory factor, it was one of the first correlates examined.

Hadley Cantril (1943 ; see also Pope, 1953), a pioneer of the national poll, used data similar to those in Table 1. Pooling four surveys from the Office of Public Opinion research and Gallup's American Institute of Public Opinion, he went beyond the question of informal religious preference and investigated the more formal issue of actual membership. Cantril was especially concerned with the class differences between Protestants and

Catholics. He divided the aggregate sample into three categories: Protestant church members, catholic church members and non-members. Needless to say, he found that Protestant members had generally higher status, though the difference was not large in the South where Protestant fundamentalism is strong among the lower classes.

But the more important finding for our purposes concerns the non-members. Membership *Per se* was not Cantril's focus ; hence the lumped Jews into the non-member category. Yet, despite the high status of Jews generally, the non-members were still lower in status than the Protestant and Catholic members combined. In other words there was a generally positive or direct relation between membership and social class. Although the extreme upper class had a slightly lower rate of membership than the middle class, the two high-status groups combined had a higher rate than the lower classes. The finding, while curvilineasr, gave early support to the larger pattern of high-status religious involvement.

Subsequent support is available from the so-called community studies with which empirical sociology cut its teeth in the late thirties and forties. Lloyd Warner's (Lloyd Warner and Lunt, 1941) Yankee City series and Robert and Helen Lynd's (1929) celebrated study of Middletown confirmed the pattern described by Cantril. Although the upper classes were slightly less frequent church members than the middle classes, both had higher rates of membership than the lower classes.

Studies of other communities give still more support. Louis Bultena's (1949) analysis of Madison, Wisconsin, James West (1945) investigation of Plainville, Lee G. Burchinal's (1955) examination of a small midwestern farm community, Warner's (1949) analysis of the similarly midwestern Joneswille and Hollingshead's (1949, 1953) more sophisticated analysis of Elmtown (Warner's Jonesville) corroborate a higher rate of religious identification among the high-status townsfolk. Unlike the findings of Cantril, the Lynds and Warner in his work on Yankee City, however, the relations with class in these later studies are linear. Here the upper classes have the highest rate of church membership, with the middle classes next and the lower classes last. This difference between linearity and curvilinearity will be taken up later. Meanwhile, the larger and more consistent difference between the combined high-status groups and the lower classes is of paramount concern.

Table 2 presents Hollingshead's results for Elmtown. Although Hollingshead is better known for his focus on Elmtown's youth he also published material on the general

Table 2

Religious Affiliation and social Class in Elmtown

	Social Class			
	I and II	III	IV	V
% Members	97 %	94%	87%	71%
N	(35)	(158)	(312)	(230)

population of community which sought to refine Warner's technique of assessing social class. For each person, Warner relied upon class ratings from a select body of informants who were mostly upper-middle class housewives. Hollingshead also used ratings but, to avoid any bias, from informants scattered throught the class hiearchy. The table, then, is the product of a more reliable analysis classes I and II are upper and Upper-middle-classes, and these are combined because of the small number of cases. Class III, of course, is the solid ;middle class, class IV represents the skilled and working class and class V includes those of extremely low status, generally either unskilled laborers or unemployed . the relationship is clear and, in this case, linear. Fully 97 per cent of the topmost classes are church members; this declines consistently to only 71 per cent among the lower class.

Note that Hollingshead's percentages of identification are high for a nation in which the over-all level of formal church membership is under 65 per cent. of course, this is largely because of Hollingshead's inclusion of informal church membership. It is also because Hollingshead deals with a small town, and rates of religiosity and the size of the community are inversely related in our society. It is an accident that most American Protestantism has its strongest roots in a rural or frontier past.

From another view, however, these community studies raise more serious issues. It is true that each finds the lowest percentage of church members among the lower classes and the greatest proportion within the combined high-status group. But this alone does not insure an unambiguous interpretation. The studies also find social class to stand in a similar relation to every other type of voluntary association, whether social clubs, community service groups, political parties or the P.T.A. In very instance the lower classes are the most withdrawn. The conclusion is reinforced by Mather (1941), Komarovsky (1946) and Wright and Hyman (1958).

The question, then, is whether church affiliation has a religious significance beyond that of organizational affiliation in general. It is possible that church membership *per se* is a particularly nor measure of religiosity. Membership need not connote a commitment to religion. It may stake a status claim or serve as a vehicle for mobility as the cynics suggest and as Underwood (1957,esp pp. 246-50) observes. It may be a prerequisite for something as basic as credit or a job, as witnessed by Pope and Weber.[3] Or it may simply represent a penchant for formal associations. In fact, it can be argued that the churches have sought to capitalize upon all of these motives. Lloyd Warner and Lunt (1941), Robert Lee (1962) and Charles Page (1952) have all noted that churches increasingly recruit members through a network of activities that are more secular than sacred. The proliferation of church recreation leagues is the referent in Page's phrase, the 'basketballization' of American religion. William H. Whyte (1956, p.372) describes the appeal of age group social clubs in the churches of the middle-class organization men in Park Forest, Illinois. There, during 1955, a modern jazz concert and a folk sing were the most successful gatherings of one congregation. Finally, many persons have suggested that the churches function as ladders of social standing ; membership change in response to actual, anticipated and illusory mobility.

But, of course, church membership is not antithetical to religious commitment. Moreover, the foregoing does not explain the low membership rates of the lower classes. One possible explanation here, however, is that the churches engage in selective recruitment. While their doors are open to all, as Table

1 attests they may be especially keen on the higher-status member because of his ability to staff important positions of lay responsibility and because of his contribution to the congregation image in the community. and yet the lower classes are not simply the abject victims of neglect or discrimination. Many prefer a more spontaneous religion and pay little attention to actual membership or even to a consistent organizational allegiance. Neither of these are important to the celebrated lower-class revivals and 'storefront' sects. Here there is great turnover and, even when membership is tallied, there is little inclination (and few channels through which) to report it to the larger Protestant councils who add the summary totals.

As further evidence for religiosity among non-church members and further testimony of the gap between formal membership and informal preference, consider the aforementioned research of Bultena (1949) in Madison, Wisconsin. While Bultena found a slight positive relation between membership and social class, he also inspected the non-members on their own terms. Roughly one-fifth of the Madison adult population in 1940 were not church members. But of these, fully 60 per cent expressed both a specific denominational preference and a high degree of private religious concern. Clearly membership is not coterminous with religious feeling or personal commitment, not is it prequisite. It may represent only the most secular aspect of the high-status religious experience, and it may be irrelevant to such of lower-class religiosity. At best it is only one among many measures of involvement. At worst, it may harbor a systematic us that affects the lower classes for whom religion may be important while membership is not.

Church attendance

Since the early 1940s, church membership has given way to church attendance as the most prominent measure of religiosity. The question, 'How often have you attended church in the past month?' is not fully entrenched in the standard repertoire of survey items. It has been related to everything from political reference and academic success to sexual compatibility. Throughout there is the assumption that attendance is an accurate gauge of religious involvement generally ; indeed, for some researchers, the two are seen as identical. And yet here again the measure is from unassailable. Although all of the studies cited show that those of high status are more frequent attenders than those of low status, the question of meaning remains. As we shall see, a low rate of attendance is not tantamount to religion. Attendance, like membership, assesses only one part of the religious experience.

One of the first studies to examine the relationship between church attendance and social class was the Lynds' (1929) analysis of Middletown (Muncie, Indiana). Using a dichotomous distinction between the business (white collar) and working (blue collar) asses, the Lynds found that 55 per cent of the business-class adults attended church at least three times a month, but only 5 percent of the working class attended that frequently.

More recent community studies provide corroboration. Hollingshead's (1953) work in Elmtown uses more elaborate class distinctions as in Table 2 and finds a positive linear relationship between class and attendance that is similar to the relation between class and membership. Burchinal's (1959) findings for attendance are almost identical. Finally Gerhard Lenski's (1961, pp 102-3) recent analysis of *The Religious Factor* in Detroit shows that the middle classes have a higher percentage of regular attendance than the working class, using, a two-category class system similar to the Lynds'.

Further support comes from national polls. In 1951. The *Catholic Digest* (polls release) found that only 62 percent of the lower class attended church but some 75 per cent of the upper class did so. A 1955 poll by the American Institute of Public Opinion reports a similar if somewhat weaker relationship. Analysis of more recent data from the A.I.P.O. again supports a positive, linear relationship between class and attendance. Hence the relation was even stronger than that reported by the *Catholic Digest*.

Finally, two analyses of the actual members of single denominations have also examined the relation between class and attendance. Glock, Ringer and Babbie (1967, esp. ch. 5) inspect several measures of religiosity in their unpublished study of Episcopalians. So does Yoshio Fukuyama[4] in his study of urban

Congregationalists. Both studies are consistent with previous research in their findings that the lower classes have the lowest rate of attendance, although Glock and Ringer find a curvilinear relation in which the middle classes have the highest rate and upper-class members suffer a relative dip. Two thing are important here. First, the issue of linearity versus curvilinearity apparently confounds the research on attendance as well as the research on membership. Second, the class differences in attendance are generally smaller among those who are church members than among the general population. This last observation is a useful point from which to begin a critical assessment of the research on attendance.

I have already mentioned Burchinal's results concerning clubs and attendance for the community at large. But the most arresting feature of Burchinal's study is his simultaneous examination of status, attendance and church membership. Dividing line small-town sample into two groups, church members and non-members, he finds that there is only a very slight relationship between social class and attendance within the categories of members and non-members considered separately. Thus, although i have earlier indicated that membership is not the only criterion of religious involvement and may include some bias, it seems to be an important intervening[5] factor in the relation between and attendance. The implication is that attendance may not simply reflect personal religious need, but rather the extent to such one is subject to the pressure of the church as an organization. Certainly non-members are less exposed to these pressures. This may account for as much of their low attendance as does their low status. Here, then, is one reason for restricting the centralizability of research on attendance. Much of this research proves the factor of membership. Attendance may also reflect only a more formal and institutionalized aspect of religion and not the religious experience as a whole.

Church attendance is, of course, often pictured as pharisaical by those who are alienated from religion altogether. But without doing to such extremes, there is evidence to suggest that not all attendance is religiously motivated and that the non-attenders are not exclusively Godless. Consider again the Lynds' research of the church-going practices of Middletown. With their customary thoroughness, they report not only the statistics but also some of the reasons for the statistics as supplied by townscapable themselves. The business-class (high-status) attenders give several explanations of their behavior. Among them are the following :

> You can usually hear a good sermon when you go to church, and I really have more respect for myself when I do attend church. (or) Why, it just never occurred to me to question church-going ! (or) I would like to live in a community where there was no church. I must confess I am not as interested in church or in church work as a good many. Most of the time I am just plain bored by church, but feel I ought to go. (*or, finally*) I haven't any very definite beliefs, but feel about going to church pretty much the way I do about bringing up children ; I am afraid not to go for fear my child will be missing something valuable if she is not established in habits of going to church (Lynd and Lynd, 1929, pp. 366-7).

Note the major themes of unquestioned loyalty, boredom, external obligation, and the need for self-respect. By contrast, the working-class non-attenders seem less inhibited about resisting social convention. They explain their lack of attendance like this:

> I feel just awful and I'm ashamed, but we never go. The reason people don't go to church as much as they used to is lack of discipline in the home and lack of interest. Then there's other things : unless a person prominent in the church or socially, people in the church have no interest in her. (*or*) just never got interest in going to church, though I go to revivals and things like that. (*or*) There's too much dressing up for church these days; he used to go in his overalls just as good as anybody. But not it won't got the clothes for that. (*or, finally*) People are mostly hypocrites. If they really believed the things they say in church they would do something about all the things that are wrong. If all the people who have called themselves Christians for 2000 years have really believed in Jesus and his way of living, they'd 've made world a mighty different place from what it is now (Lynd and Lynd, 1925 pp. 362-6).

It is true that the Lynds had the ears of skeptics and I have picked selectively from their quotations. Nevertheless, these remarks suggest then possible independence of church attendance on the one hand and religious concern on the other. Attendance may play vastly different roles in the religious experience of different classes – or, indeed, no role at all. For some of the high status attenders, actual religious feeling is strikingly absent. At the same time, all of these lower-class non-attenders can hardly be classified as irreligious. There is one who enjoys revivals and another who is agitated over religious hypocrisy.

Actually most of the authors cited in this section make similar qualifications of the meaning of the relation between class and attendance. In addition to Burchinal and the Lynds, Hollingshead reports that social class bears no relation whatsoever to belief in God. Attendance and belief are both important facts of religiosity, however, and if social class is not consistently related to both, one must probe deeper for a more complicated relation between class and religiosity as a whole. As we shall be later , Glock and Ringer, and Fukuyama also report that has stands in different relation to other facets of involvement. Clearly attendance does not exhaust the domain. It is possible but, it like membership before and like parish activities to follow, reflects only the 'doing' dimension of religiosity and not the important aspect of religious 'feeling'. The relation with class seems dependent upon the distinction.

Parish activities

In moving from church attendance to activities within the organization, we are moving in a secular direction. I have already noted that the churches sponsor many groups which compete with the attractions of the non-church community. in addition to such common activities as the choir, the Sunday School staff and the ladies' aid, a parish will frequently sponsor a basketball team, a bowling league, a great-books discussion group and possibly a circle or two of group therapy. Moreover, every congregation relies upon its laymen to staff important positions of responsibility which keep the organizations going. These might include positions on the finance committee and the building committee, and the representatives of the denominational lay councils on a national level. Among these activities and responsibilities. However, persons of high status appear to dominate both.

Some of the earliest speculation on the relation between class and religion centers in this area. Max Weber's [6] comparative analysis of Confucianism, Hinduism, Judaism and emerging Protestantism makes the point that religious movements carry the near indelible stamp of the status group that founded them. For example, some Protestant groups such as the Episcopalians, Presbyterians and Congregationalists have their roots in a bourgeois reaction to catholicism and seem to have retained this high-status trademark. Extending Weber's argument, a corollary applies to more denominations that began as lower-class sects in the wake of the Reformation. Thus, within any religious movement, the highest-ranking status group will assume any leadership and dictate the religious mood. This would apply to the Baptists, the Methodists and the Lutherans, for example.

Weber's argument rests on the premise that parish activities are more than incidental to the religious spirit of the congregation. For one thing, they provide more intimate contact with the religious leadership and, thereby, an avenue of influence. For another, many of these activities are instrumental in getting things done. Laymen are often ascribed a knowledge of future and secular concerns that extends beyond the pastor's. the often have the opportunity to turn the church as an organization to their own designs.

Qualitative evidence that this has occurred is available in several historical analyses of developing churches and denominations. S. D. Clark's (1948) study of Canadian Methodism reveals the growing pressures of the high-status laity and the growing disaffection of the lower classes. Paul Harrison's (1950) more recent analysis of the American Baptist convention afford another instance of this. Although it began as a lower-class set the Baptist movement has taken on higher-status members who have exerted increasing influence towards modernization. According to Harrison, not only has much of Baptist fundamentalism been subdued, but its principle of local autonomy for each parish has been subverted. Bureaucratization has quietly gained sway the national level.

But apart from qualitative evidence of influence in strength spots, there is also quantitative evidence of greater high-status participation in activities generally. Glock, Ringer and (1967) find that the association between class and the parish activities is no different than that between class and membership or church attendance. While women are typically more active than men and the upper class is less involved than the middle class, it remains true that those of generally high status participate more than those of low status.

Although parish activity does not have the currency of attendance as a measure of religiosity, Glock and Ringer are not aim in their general findings. Fukuyama (1961) reports a general similar relation between class and activity among common communalists. Hollngshead's (1953) aforementioned study of cult religion in Elmtown confirms the lower classes as the least have in church organizations. Harold Kaufman (1953) has found the participation and lay leadership positively related to class in rural farm community in upper New York state. It might be noted, however, that these latter three studies differ from Glock 'and Ringer's work with urban Episcopalians in two respects., neither Fukuyama, hollingshead nor Kaufman reports a linear relation as do Glock and Ringer; in each case, the some Upper class is the most active and the association is connectly linear. Second, because Glock and Ringer as well as Fukuyama, are dealing with church members alone, the relation between class and activity is weaker than those reported in hollingshead's and Kaufman's studies of whole communities. Once more, membership seems to be an important factor in the relation between class and involvement.

But there is a more important qualification of the association. The membership and attendance, the meaning of parish activities is unclear. I have already mentioned the secular quality of most activities. This alone creates suspicion of attempts to use as measures of religious involvement as a whole. A more ..caveat can be inferred from Glock and ringer's study. This concern is not solely with religious involvement in itself, but also with involvement in the church versus involvement in the aspects of the community. now it is true that class is sensitively related to parish activity when other commitments are not considered. But if one compares high-and low-status differents on the proportion of sacred to secular activities, the differences reverse. Thus, the low-status parishioner spends a meagre amount of his organizational investment on the church does the high-status member. Kenneth Lutterman (1962, ch.8, pp.37-8) provides similar evidence for investment of a some literal sort in his study of financial giving to churches. Through the low-status church member may give less money to the church on absolute grounds, he gives a higher percentage of the income. In short, even a small donation or a single activity may be more salient for the lower-class member because it is less called by commitments of other sorts. Again, then, there are reasons for doubting the case for high-status religiosity.

Linearity v. curvilinearity

Although all of the studies cited agree that the higher classes generally are the most active, several dispute the linearity of that association. Warner and Lunt, Cantril, Bultena, and Glock and Ringer have all found that involvement is highest among the middle classes. This is at odds with the studies of Fukuyamn Hollingshead, West, Kaufman, Burchinal, the *Catholic Digest* and later reports of the American Institute of Public Opinion that find religiosity at its peak among the extreme upper classes.

Now survey research is subject to mytrs idiosyncracies which make comparisons among studies risky. It is possible, for example, that the discrepency between Cantrio, Warner, and Glock and Ringer, on the one hand, and Fukuyama, the *Catholic Digest*, and the American Institute of Public Opinion, on the other is adducible to different definitions of social class. The latter studies use a broader definition of upper class, and, thus include many of the highly involved middle-class types as well.

But the disparity in the remaining studies may reflect something else. All of the studies reporting the upper class most involved deal with predominantly farming communities of less than 6000 persons. By contrast, all of the studies that find the middle classes most involved deal with samples drawn largely from Urban areas with populations in excess of 50,000. There are, of course, considerable differences between America's Towns and Middletown. One particular differences seems crucial here. Most small towns do not observe a sharp demarcation between the middle and upper classes. Not only are rural upper classes 'less upper' than their urban counterparts, but they are also more visible and better integrated into the community as a whole. In fact, the small-town upper classes are the community leaders, and this is necessarily manifest in such key community institutions as the churches.

On the other hand, urban areas are better able to sustain a distinction. The upper class is more socially distant through pronounced educational and power advantages. It is also less visible since its members are usually ensconced in retreats such as the board of directors of a business firm, foreign travel, exclusive country clubs, and a self-sustaining social world that is frequently endogamous. The urban upper class may rule the productive community, but it tends to withdraw from the community's voluntary activities. As if filling a vacuum, the middle classes provide the leadership here and, again this is manifested in the churches.

Sinclair Lewis supplies a biting distinction between the upper and middle religious styles in his stereotype city of Zenith. The speaker is advising the Reverend Mr Gantry on the Local social clubs:

> Yet, but the owner of the Advocate, and the banker that's letting with Grant run on till he bankrupts, and the corporation counsel that all out of jail, you don't find those malefactors going to no such club and yipping about Service! You find 'em sitting at small at the old Union Club, and laughing themselves sick about Service.I couldn't get you into the Union Club, They wouldn't have any preacher that talks about vice – the kind of preacher that belongs to the Union talks about the new model cadillac and how hard it is to get genuine Eyetalian vermouth. But the Tonawanda – they might let you in. For respectability. To prove that they could'nt have gin they have got in their lockers in their lockers (Lewis, 1960, p.373).

This distinction between the populations of the discrepant studies is only speculative, but it does provide one possible reconciliation. Of course, the problem of the relative involvement of the upper and middle classes pales beside the larger issue of the religiosity of the lower classes versus the higher classes generally. Here, as we have seen, the statistics are clear enough, yet they are qualified by three major considerations. First, church membership, attendance and parish activity all relate to formal participation in the church as an organization and not necessarily to private religious feelings. Second, the relation of class to attendance (and possibly parish activity) is partially an artifact of differential exposure to organizational pressures rather than a simple reflection of personal religious needs. Finally, the same type of religiosity may mean one thing to high-status parishoners and quite another to those of low status. Thus, church membership may be irrelevant to the more spontaneous religion of the lower classes. Here revivals may supplant formal church attendance, and even a small amount of parish activity may be more meaningful since these people are less active in secular groups.

The Case for Low-Status Religiosity

All of the qualification is of high-status involvement would seem hollow indeed if there were no empirical support in the opposite direction. the present section suggests, however, that this has not been mere cavilling. Although studies reporting the lower classes most involved are in the minority, their spareseness is no measure of their significance. Accuracy rather than bulk is the final arbiter.

Actually some of the studies already mentioned include side remarks on low-status religiosity – remarks that are overwhelmed in the final tally. The Lynds, for example, divide their treatment of Middletwon religion into four chapters: dominant religious beliefs, where and when religious beliefs are carried on, leaders and particiapants in religious rites and, last, religious observances. The fourth of these is by far the most elaborate. It was cited in the last section for its description of the business class at the most frequent church-attenders and most likely church members. But the first chapter offers a contrast in dealing with religious beliefs. The Lynds summarize as follows:

> First, members of the working class show a disposition to believe their religion more ardently and to accumulate more emotionally charged values around their beliefs. Religion appears to operate more prominently as an active agency of support and encouragement among this section of the city. A second point is the shift in the status of certain religious beliefs during the past generation – notably the decline, *particularly among the business class*, in the emphasis upon Heaven and still, more upon Hell (Lynd and Lynd , 1929, p.239; Demerath's italics).

The Lynd's observe further that the secularization of Middletown religion has occurred at different rates for the two classes. When asked if 'it is wrong to go to the movies on Sunday', roughly a third of the working-class high scholars replied - yes' as compared with only a sixth of the business – class students.

A second research hat finds both positive and negative relations between status and religiousity is Gerhard Lenski's (1961) analysis of a small sample of Detroiters. The Study is concerned more with the effect of religiosity on status than vice versa, yet it reports not only that attendance is directly related to class but also that other forms of involvement are inversely related to class. Persons of middle-class occupations and college educations are slightly less likely to be doctrinally orthodox and devotionally active than those own working class occupations and without college educations.

Another study that harbors a discrepancy between high and low-status religiosity is Glock and Ringer's research with Episcopalians. In addition to church attendance and organizational activity, they used a third measure of involvement pertaining to the 'intellectual dimension'. This refers to the parishioner's knowledge of traditional doctrine and the extent to which he reads religious literature. Whereas church attendance and parish activity are at their lowest ebb among the lower classes, the situations is reserved for intellectual involvement. Among women, the lower class scores highest with 51 per cent intellectually involved, and this decreases to 41per cent among the lower-middle, 34 per cent among the upper-middle, and 28 per cent among the upper also. Among men, the percentages run in the same order from a peak of 32 per cent for those of low status to a depression of 17 per cent for those of extremely high status.

Conflicting relations with status also occur in Fukuyama's analysis of Congregationalists. Fukuyama delineates four types of religiosity which he labels the cultic, cognitive, creedal and devotional. The cultic is an amalgam of church attendance and organizational activity and its positive relation with class has already been reported. The cognitive represents the parishioner's knowledge of religious doctrine and the affairs of his congregation. The creedal signifies personal allegance to traditional doctrine, regardless of one's detailed knowledge. Finally, the devotional connotes personal prayer and reliance upon religion beyond the church itself.

Table 3 presents the relation between each of these facts and social class. As we learned previously, the cultic is positively related to class, and gives a range from 53 per cent involved among those of generally high status to only 35 per cent among those of low status. The relation is also positivefor

Table 3

Social Class and Four Types of Religiosity among Congregationalists

Four Dimensions	*Socioeconomic Status*		
% Highly Involved	High	Moderate	Low
	%	%	%
Cultic	53	43	31
Cognitive	28	24	15
Creedal	27	28	31
Devotional	16	23	32

Abstracted from Fukuyama (1961), p. 159

thecognitive dimension, although it is important to note that, unlike Glock and Ringer's intellectual commitment'; above this dimension refers only to knowledge itself and not to involvement in it. Moreover, it refers to knowledge of the congregation as well as to knowledge of the doctrine. That one *knows* the financial state of his parish does not mean that he will develop a deep-rooted attachment to the it. As with knowledge of most things, religious knowledge should increase with familiarity and with education. Since the high status parishoners are apt to be active in parish administration and well educated, they helped to account for their high score. However, the other two dimension of religiosity after contrasting relations with class. Both *creedal* and devotional *religiosity* increase among progressively lower-status groups, although this is only pronounced for the latter, Both refer to a more inward religiosity that is concerned less with the formal church and more with personal feelings. Fukuyama (1961, p.159- concludes that 'different social classes differ not so much in the degree to which they are religiously oriented but in the manner in which they give expression to their religious propensities.,'

A last study that finds the lower classes more religiously involved in my own survey in Winchester, Massachusetts (Demerath, 1958). Actually, in this area the individual's own status has less bearing upon his religiosity than does his parents' status – succor to the argument that one's religion is a product of one's rearing and changes little in substance thereafter. Nevertheless, both forms of status are negatively related to fundamentalism in religious beliefs,[7] and, in both cases, the lower classes are less tolerant of religious relativism. Roughly one-third of the high status group believe in either or both heaven and hell; this increases to more than two thirds among the low-status respondents. When asked their hypothetical reaction to their child's desire to change his religious affiliation, a similar pattern obtains. The lower class is apt to be reproachful, while the middle and upper classes are more permissive.[8] Finally, those of low status have a higher frequency of personal prayer and even perceive prayer differently. They see it as a spiritual dialogue and divine source of guidance. The higher-status respondents interpret it more as self-administered therapy in the secular psychiatric sense.[9]

And yet here, as with status religiosity, there are grounds for dispute. Although the Lynds, Lenski, Glock and Ringer,

Fukuyama and my own previous research suggest that the lower classes are more religious when religiosity is measured by personal belief and private practice, two final studies provide some doubt. One of these is Gerhard Lenski's (1953) early analysis of social class and 'religious interest' in a representative sample of the Indianapolis area. Certainly interest alone is more personal and less institutionalized than formal membership, attendance and parish activities. But when Lanski related interest to four separate measures of status, he found more ambiguity than consistency. When class is measured by occupational prestige. The family's total financial worth and the respondents education, the lower classes are slightly more interested than the middle and upper classes. When class is measured by the household's yearly income, the high-status respondents show more interest. Although one can argue that the differences are generally in the predicted inverse direction and no smaller than the differences that Lenski later accepted in Detroit, here he rejects all of the findings as statistically insignificant.

The second study which provides grounds for suspicion in Rodney Stark's[10] analysis of national polls in Great Britain and the United States. Surprisingly, Stark finds that both participation and belief are positively related to social class in each country. Thus, the higher one's status, the more one is likely to attend church regularly and the more one is likely to claim belief in God. The latter finding is, of course, the puzzle since its positive relationship is a blatant contradiction of the negative association described by other.

How can we explain these discrepancies? One tack is to point out the considerable difference between such nebulous items as 'belief in God' and 'religious interest'. On the one hand and more precise questions such as religious reading and the interpretation and extent of personal prayer, on the other. The former questions will elicit positive answers from all but the most confirmed atheists, and atheism has never been the vogue in American upper-class circles. The latter questions, however, provide more range. They allow the preacher to discriminate between the more traditional and the more secularized positions. It may be that the essential difference between classes lies at this more delicate level.

Another explanation for the disparity concerns the populations studied. Both Lenski and Stark examined samples that were designed to represent whole metropolitan areas and whole nations. By contrast, my own research in Winchester focused on a small town in new England where the Catholic church sets church of the religious tone for the lower classes. The Lynds asked at only a single small city where church membership was the norm in the 1920s. And Glock and Ringer and Fukuyama concerned only with affiliated Episcopalians and Congregationalists. The difference here points to an important hypothesis concerning lower-class religion in general. If a lower-class individual is committed to religion at all, his internal involvement likely to be higher than that of his higher status church fellows. On the other hand, there is a large segment of the lower that has no religious commitment whatsoever. Perhaps because these people have found functional alternatives to religion in political extremism,[11] trade unions of the extended family, they are markedly different and must be held apart in any assessment of the Church's importance to its members. Neither Clark nor Lenski compartmentalized the two lower-class groups and this resulted in a, low over-all rate of religiosity. My research in Winchester dealt with an anomalous town where the distinction may not have been so important. Glock and Ringer and Fukuyama focused only on those who had some religious commitment in the first place.

References

Bendix, R. (1960), *Max Weber: An Intelelctual Portrait*, Doubleday.

Bultena, L. (1949), 'Church membership and church attendance in Madison, Wisconsin,' *Amer. Soc. Rev.*, vol. 14, pp. 384-91.

Burchinal, L.G. (1959), 'Some social status criteria and church membership and church attendance, *J. soc., Psych.* vol. 49, pp. 53-64.

Cantril, H. (1943), 'Educational and economic composition of religious groups', *Amer. J. Soc.*, vol. 48, p. 574-9.

Clark, S.D. (1948), *Church and Sect in .Canada*, University of Toronto Press.

Demerath, N.J., III (1958), Religious participation, attitudes and belief in an adult sample, unpublished A.B. *honors thesis, Harvard College.*

De Tocqueville, A. (1954), *Democracy in America*, Vintage, vol.2.

Fukuyama, Y. (1961), 'The major dimensions of chruch membership'. *Rev. relig. Know.*, vol.2, pp. 154-61.

Glock, G., Ringer, B.B., and Babbie, E.R. (1967), *To Comfort and to challenge*, University of California Press.

Gurin, G., Veroff, J., and Feld, S. (1960), *Americans View their mental health,* Basic Books.

Harrison, P.M. (1959), *Authority and Power in the Free Church Tradition: A Social Case of the American Baptist Convention*, Princeton University Press.

Hollingshead, A. (1949), *Elmtown's Youth*, Yale University Press.

Hollingshead, A. (1953), 'Selected characteristics of classes in a Middle Western community', in R. Bendix and S.M. Lipset, eds., *class, Status and Power*, Free Press, pp. 213-24.

Kaufman, H. 91953), 'Prestige classes in a new York rural community in R. Bendix and S.M. Lipset, eds., *class, Status and Power*, Free press, pp. 190-203.

Komarovsky, M. (1946), 'The voluntary associations of urban dwellers', *amer. Soc. Rev.*, vol. 11 pp. 686-98.

Lee, R. (1962), 'The organizational dilemma in American Protestantism in H. Cleveland and H.D. Lasswell, eds.., *The Conference on Science, Philosophy and Religion: Ethics and Bugness*, Herper, pp. 187-211.

Lenski, G. (1953), 'Social correlates of religious interest', *Amer. Soc. Rev.,* vol. 18, pp.533-44.

Lenski, G. (1961), '*The Religious Factor: A Sociologist's Inquiry*, Doubleday.

Lewis, S. 91960), Elmer Gantry, Deu.

Lloyd Warner, W., and Lunt, P.S. (1941), *The Social System of a*

Modern Community, Yale University Press.

Lloyd Warner, W., *et al.* (1949), *Democracy in Jonesville*, Harper.

Lutterman, K.J. (1962), Giving to churches: a sociological study of the contributions to eight Catholic and Lutheran churches, *Unpublished Ph.D. dissertation, University of Wisconsin.*

Lynd, R. and Lynd, H. (1929), *Middletown*, Harcourt, brace.

Martineau, H. (1962), *Society in America*, Doubleday, Anchor.

Mather, W.A. (1941), 'Income and social participation', *Amer. Soc. Rev.*, vol. 6, pp. 380-83.

Niebuhr, H.R. (1929), *The Social Sources of Denominationalism*, Holt.

Nunn, C.Z. (1964), 'Child control through a "coalition with God", *Child Dev.*, vol. 35, pp. 417-32.

Page, C. (1952), 'Bureaucracy and the liberal church' *Rev. Relig.*, vol. 16, pp. 137-50.

Parsons, T. (1960), *Structure and Process in Modern Societies*, Free Press.

Pope, L. (1942), *Millhands and Preachers*, Yale University Press.

Pope, L. (1953), 'Religion and the class structure', in R. Bendix and S.M. Lipset, eds., *Class, Status and Power*, Free Press, pp. 316-23.

Schneinder, H. (1952), *Religion in 20th Century America*, Harvard University Press.

Underwood, K.W. (1957), *Protestant and Catholic: Religion and Social Interaction in an Industrial Community*, Beacon.

Weber, M. (1958), 'The Protestant sects and the spirit of capitalism; In H. Gerth and C. Wright Mills, eds., *From Max Weber, Essays in Sociology*, Oxford, Galaxy Books, pp. 302-22.

West, J. (1945), *Plainville, U.S.A.*, Columbia University Press.

Whyte, W.H. 91956), *The Organization Man*, Simon & Schuster.

Wright, C.R., and Hyman, H.H. (1958), 'Voluntary association membership of American adults: evidence from National Sample Surveys', *Amer. soc. Rev.*, vol. 23, pp. 284-94.

NOTES

1. Temporal variation in status composition is a theme as old as the sociology of religion itself. Religious groups frequently begin as lower-class splinter movements, but undergo upward mobility in the quest for stability and community influence. As one example of geographical variation, notice the contrast between the lower-class Methodism of Warner's Catholic dominated Yankee City (Newburyport, Massachusetts) and the middle-class Methodism in the South. In face, a number of southern Methodist are concerned about their 'exclusiveness' as a high-status church. While they may be guilty of a bit of status up-grading, a meeting of Methodists in Richmond, Virginia, recently recommended increased attention toward the lower classes. 'Methodists told church in danger of "class" label', *Richmond Times-Dispatch*, 14 July 1960.

2. The term 'religiosity' is a convenient shorthand for the phrase 'religious involvement'. The usage here, however, should not be confused with Harold Laski's where it is used to suggest hypocritical, self-centered religion at odds with 'pure' religious motive.

3. Pope (1942), pp. 322-5, provides a specific instance in which the churches served as clearing-houses for mill employees. Weber (1958), takes a similar point after his travels through the United States in 1904, when he visited relatives who were backwoods farmers in North Carolina.

4. See Fukuyama (1961). Actually, Fukuyama's study closely parallel much of the present research. It appeared after the present essay which conceived, however, and provides a form of independent replicating though its brevity precludes the kind of extensive exploration intended it the following.

5. Technically, the term 'intervening' has temporal connotations. An intervening factor occurs before either the inddeendent or thedependent enable and dictate the course of their relationship. In this case, it is difficult to make assertions regarding time order. Since membership is frequently inherited from one's parents, there are a number of persons for him it is indeed an intervening influence in the strict sense. On the other hand there will also be persons which begin by attending a given church only later join it. Here the term is imprecise. Without getting into difficulties, the over-all point is that membership has an effect on relationship between attendance and social class. Time order is less than the fact of multivariate interaction.

6. For a useful summary of Weber's work in this area, as well as a detailed bibliography, see Bendix (1960), pp. 71-265.

7. The doctrine of predestination provides an interesting exception among Catholics. High status Catholics are more frequent believers on this item alone when compared to low-status Catholics. But, of course, predestination is antithetical to traditional Catholic theology and the absence of belief among the lower classes reflects orthodoxy rather than apathy.

8. In this connexion, see Nunn (1964). Nunn finds that the coalition is most common among lower-class parents. This is oneo of the several unique measures of religiosity that might be added to the support for the argument that lower-class religious involvement is greater than middle-or upper class involvement. I am indebted to Warren O. Hagstrom for this reference.

9. Cf. Gurin, Veroff and feld (1960), pp. 372-6. Here it is reported that those of low status are more apt to resort to prayer in periods of emotional stress. Hence we have still another measure of religious involvement that indicates that the lower-class are far from alienated from religion altogether.

10. Rodney W. Stark, 'Class, radicalism and church attendance in Great Britain', a paper delivered at the meetings of the American Sociological Association, Washington, D.C., September 1962. This paper includes only apart of the results mentioned. [For subsequent publication details see p.454 of this book –Ed.]

11. It is important to note that some of the most militant anti-clerical and, indeed, anti-religious movements are both lower-class and politically to the left. The American Rationalist Federation, for example, has deep in European socialism. Many of its branches comprise lower-class European ethnics who rally around rationalism for an identity that is distinct from the persecuting state churches of their native countries. In Europe itself, the ties between organized free thought and left-wing politics are even stronger. For example. The west German 'freie Gemeinde' are particularly powerful but also particularly communistic in political collaboration . The author is currently beginning research on this end of the religious spectrum.

Chapter-7

A Typology of Sects

B.R.WILSON

Chapter-7

In spite of the work of J. M. Yinger and Peter Berger (to say noting of those who deal with religious movements in non-industrial societies) it is still too often claimed that the sect-church dichotomy (with the addition sometimes of the 'cult') is an adequate tool for analysis in the sociology of religion (Berger, 1954; Simpson, 1955, 1956; Sundkler, 1948; Yinger, 1946, 1957). Since Yinger established types of sects and types of churches, our work has in fact outgrown Troeltsch's dichotomy. We are now beginning to use categories which do not depend exclusively on the opposition between the conservative church and the perfectionist sect, types in which Troeltsch had seen 'a logical outcome of the Gospels...' (Troeltsch, 1931, p. 341). If the sociology of religion is to move forward, we must create categories which allow us to study comparatively the social functions and development of religious movements. As a consequence, such studies must shun categories dictated too specifically by the characteristics of a particular theological tradition. Obviously, the types we can use are still drawn mainly from the material at our disposal, especially from Christian movements. But is it imperative that we should try to enlarge their application, and, if needs to be, modify their formulation in the light of this extension of their meaning, so that we shall have a series of analytical instruments which will no longer be centered on a particular civilization and religion (in this case, Christian).

One of the principal obstacles to this development lies in the that the sociology of religion is a field in which sociological thinking and religious thinking are not always distinguished clearly. The interest which theologians take in this special field and the education they have received are likely to perpetuate the use of specific categories which are indifferent to sociologically significant distinctions. This not to say that the

B.R. Wilson, 'A typology of sects in a dynamic and comparative perspective,' *Archives de Sociologie de Religion*, vol. 16 (1963), pp. 49-63 Translated by the Jenny M. Robertson.

contribution of theologians to the field are without value. Sometimes they provide valuable insights: but they often also introduce elements of confusion. In one recent study, Martin E. Marty (1960) has characterized sects as oriented. This distinction is preeminently sociological. It is not a question of their conception of God, which is a distinction of a theological nature. Nevertheless, it seems to me we need a more refined typology of responses to the outside world. There are variations of positive or negative orientation which interest the sociologist.

Sects are ideological movements having as their explicit and declared aim the maintenance, and perhaps even the propagation of certain ideological positions. One must, therefore, admit that those whose interest lies above all in ideological questions (the source and credibility of ideas about God, and justification of practices in his name) have legitimate interest in the study of sects. But sociological distinctions are not simply based on the distinction of theological belief and practice, and certainly nor on the *odium theological* which tries to characterize sects as extremist. In a valuable contribution to our conception of the denomination as a type, D.A. Martin places the denomination in opposition to the sect, without always giving enough attention in the diversity among sects. He describes them as if they were always revolutionary or introversionist, perhaps using as his authority for this the classifications proposed by Troeltsch. Martin writes 'while the denomination is characterized by moderation, the sect is either communist or anarchist, revolutionary or quietest, or uniformed, ascetic or licentious, completely sacramental non-sacramental, worshipping in a wild communal rant, or like the seekers, utter silence' (Martin, 1962). Martin thus characterizes sectarian eschatology as adventist and sects as revolutionary except in the case where too great a disillusionment has made them quietist. It is always easy to criticize a typology by underlining the case which does not correspond to the proposed classifications; but Martin's is too gross. Sects are not easily marshalled into a few dichotomies. The brethren, Quakers and Christadelphians are neither communist nor anarchist; the different Darbyist groups, Jehovah's Witnesses, Church of God in British Isles and Overseas, the holiness movements do not worship in wild rant nor in total silence; the Assemblies of God are neither ascetic nor licentious. But who would deny that these are sects? In fact, this kind of analysis takes the part as the whole; over looks the way in which separate elements combine together, and almost completely ignores the various possibilities for the transformation of sects.

From the sociologist's point of view, there are three sorts of drawback to the theological or doctrinal classification of sects. First of all, such a classification limits the possibilities for the comparative study of sects within different religious traditions. In the second place, it prevents recognition of other significant suspects of the character of sects, for the doctrine may persist when the social organization and the orientation of the movement have changed. Thus, classification which grows from doctrinal description does not sufficiently take into account the organizational and dynamic aspects of sects. Thirdly, because it is theological, this kind of classification runs the risk of stigmatizing the sect and characterizing it in terms which are essentially normative.

The sociologist can use diverse principles of classification to study sects. The structural aspect has perhaps not been thoroughly explored, although it may perhaps not offer a wide enough view of the phenomenon. I wish here to develop a classification used in a previous study of the transformation of sects (Wilson, 1959), in the hope that this typology can be shown to be of use the analysis of sectarian movements in non-Christian and non-western environments. I also wish to attempt a first, tenative and only by way of experiment, in applying this typology to religious movements at the Fringes of Christianity. This classification takes as its central criterion the sect's response to the world. It is hoped that we shall find there an adequate principle of classification capable of advancing the comparative study of sects and also of sect development.

One clearly sees that our criterion of response to the outside world constitutes a variable influenced by doctrinal thought, though it is not perhaps determined by that alone. It recognizes ideological character of sects, without nevertheless neglecting the way of life of the sect's members, which also necessarily affect the manner in which they accept, reject, neglect or attempt the transcend, to improve or to transvaluate the opportunities which worldly society may offer. Here we have a factor which can effect change without producing specific doctrinal changes, in response simply to the social changes affecting the members of the sect. Of course, a certain specific type of response is more likely to be seen in certain age groups, in certain social classes, among people with particular educational backgrounds or in certain ecological contexts. It might also be more attractive to one sex than another it will suit better a rural situation, or an urban or a suburban one. And it may arise and develop at one stage rather than at another of the social and cultural history of the sect under review. In this article we shall not be able to examine all these variables individually. But we shall intimate certain relationships between different types of sects and different stages of cultural development.

I should now like to propose a seven-fold classification of sects. Four of these types have already been put froward ; but here distinguish characteristics is quite a different way from that which I adopted in my previous research. I define each type of terms of its response to the world, of the kind of reaction which dominates the customary practices and its members' beliefs. For each of these types is suggested the typical theological position in Christian sects, by giving a few specific examples of these movements. We define also the activities to which they typically devoted themselves and refer to the biblical texts which they favour. The reader will understand that I do not claim that all these texts hold the same importance in Christian tradition, but that I seek simply to illustrate the way in which sects attempt to integrate with this tradition. I have not tried, except very tentatively and where the evidence is perfectly clear, to suggest from which social groups these sects recruit.

The *conversionist* sect is the typical sect of 'evangelical', fundamentalist Christianity. Its reaction towards the outside world is to suggest that the latter is corrupted because man is corrupted because men can be changed then the world will be changed. This type of sect takes no interest in programmes of social reform or in the political solution of social problems and may even be actively hostile towards them.

Its judgement on man and events tends to be moralizing because it is believed that man is entirely responsible for his actions. Influence of environment on behaviour, or any other determinist explanation. Typical activities of this type of sects are revivialism and public preaching at mass meetings rather than door to door. The leaders of the sect mobilize the group and use techniques of mass persuasion in order to convert individuals. The dominant in the atmosphere of the group is of an emotional. But not nature, Among Christian sects, the texts regarded highly are those which encourage the preaching of the Gospel through the world. They attach great significance to the relationship between the individual and a personal saviour, a relationship expressed in direct emotional terms rather than in a symbolic or manner. They hold the total understanding of the doctrine to be less important than the profound feeling of the essential personal relationship. In the same way as they interpret the Scripture literally, the sect's members tend to take this relationship literally. For them the Saviour is a person, a sort of involvement and suffering Superman. The Salvation Army, in the first stages of its existence, the Assemblies of God and other movements, as well as independent evangelical sects, are examples of this type of sect.

One recognizes the *revolutionary* type in the eschatological movements of he Chritian tradition. its attitude towards the outside world is summed up in a desire to be rid of the present social world when the time is ripe – if necessary, by force and violence. Its members are awaiting a new order under God's direction. they will then become the holders of power as the friends and representatives of God. This type of sect is hostile at the same time to social reform and instantaneaous conversion. it is nt oppsed to causal explanations, in so far as one accepts its own assumptions of causal categories. It tends to explain the world in determinist terms, just as its tends to consider the fate of individual as pre-determined. In the Christian tradition, we have therefore a position which is more calvinist than . One meets here less tendency to moralize than among the Conversionists, for reproaches are out of place when one makes to consider all events as the accomplishment of a divine plan. The members of these sects occupy themselves actively in prophetic exegesis, in comparisons of inspired texts and between the predictions of the sect and contemporary events. They often have long-drawn-out internal debates elaborating prospects of that future. Conversion is considered to be an occassional and gradual occurrence, and comes about only when the stranger to the sect has familiarized himself completely with the complexity of sect belief and is convinced of its truth. Permission to belong is not given freely, and the revolutionary sect, when it is fully institutionalized seeks to maintain itself in a state of vigilance and doctrinal purity. Its meetings are matter-of-fact, unemotional occassions. These are occassions to praise God decently and without emotional excess, for speaking of one's calm certainty that the promises will be fulfilled. The biblical texts in favour in these circles are directly eschatological or else obscure visions from prophetic books which can be interpreted as relevant predictions for the present period. They see God as a divine autocrat, as a leader, a dictator whose impenetrable will imposes itself on the progress of the universe. One finds in these sects little feeling of a direct relationship with divinity. On the contrary, they members have the feeling that they are God's instruments, waiting for the decreed moment, agents of His work and will. Jehovah's Witnesses, Christadelphians and the Fifth Monarchy Men (England seventeenth century) are typical representatives of these ideas.

The pietist sects represent the introversionist type those response to the world is neither to convert the population nor to expect the world's overturn, but simply in retireing from it to enjoy the security gained by personal holiness. This type is completely indifferent to social reforms, to individual conversion and to social revolution. None of these elements seems significant to these sects in their view of their position and task on this earth. The introversionist sect may accept, especially in its early stages, some particular inspirational experiences and retain them for objective phenomena significant for the entire group on consider them as purely individual revelations which might help the growth of personal piety. These groups are concerned more with deepening than widening spiritual experience. One finds among them a certain disdain for those 'without holiness' and little or no desire to introduce them to it. These movements' meetings are 'assemblies of the saved' (gathered remnant). The community will support the individual and hold him in its bosom. Rather than push him to seek his mission in the outside world. These groups, if Christian, put great weight on biblical texts which exhort the faithful to be a law unto themselves and to live from the world. They conceive of a divinity of the type of the Holy Spirit rather than in a more personalized way. The real relationship in this case is less than between sinner and saviour, that between outporing vial and receiving vessel. Typical examples of this category of sects can be seen in certain 'holiness movements', as well as in European pietist movements of the eighteenth century.

Manipulationist sects, which I previously called gnostic, are those which insist especially on a particular and distinctive knowledge. They define themselves *vis-à-vis* the outside world essentially by accepting its goals. They frequently proclaim a more spituralized and ethereal version of the cultural ends of global society but do not reject them. These sects instead try of change the methods appropriate to attaining these ends. They sometimes claim that the only way of achieving this is to use the special knowledge taught by the movement. That is the only true and worthwhile way of acquiring health, wealth, happiness and social prestige. Although reinterpreting 'worldly' activities, these sects offer special techniques and verbal modes of assurances which justify the pursuit and attainment of cultural goals. These movements are thus of the type sometimes called 'cults', and which marty[1] depicts as positively oriented towards the outside world. They offer, by means of publicity, facilities for learning their systems but do not provoke conversions since the important thing is for them to acquire spiritual attitudes rather than to offer specific activities or relationships. The group of life of these movements is often reduced to an absolute minimum, their gnosis being impersonal. Anyone may accept it and use it for his personal ends since its efficacy is not dependent on any relationship or an any mystical process. When the members of these movements come together, the chief function of their assembly seems to be not so much for worship or devotion as to claim prestige and social status for successes achieved using the special teachings of the sect. These movements are often syncretist, even within the Christian tradition. But they use evangelical texts such as those where Christ affirmed that he had many other things to say, but that men could not bear to bear them. Divinity, is understood implicity or explicity, as a source of laws or principles to apply in one's daily life. The idea of a personal saviour is reduced here to a minimum and one notices the absence of any emotional relationship with God, or a relationship of authority. Provided he can take the trouble, anyone can learn the doctrine, which can be applied universally. These sects take little interest in eschatology. They are interested in results in this world, and the hereafter seems of this type in Christian countries are Christian Scientists, Unians, Psychiana, Scientology and Rosacrucians.

The types I now wish to add to this classification are those found within the Christian tradition, but which also can be found elsewhere.

Thaumaturgical sects are movements which insist that it is possible for men to experience the extraordinary effect of the supernatural on their lives. Within Christianity, their principles representatives are spiritualist groups whose main activity lies in seeking personal messages from the spirits, obtaining cures effecting transformations and performing miracles. These sects define themselves in relation to the wider society by affirming that normal reality and causation can be suspended for the benefit of special and personal dispensation. They resist acceptance of the physical process of ageing and death and come together to affirm a special exception from everyday realities which assures each individual and his loved one of perpetual wellbeing in the next world. For the present, they procure immediate advantages by accomplishing miracles. In several ways these groups differ little from manipulations sects, except that their response to the world is less universalist and more personal. Moreover, they do not claim a special gnosis, but tend rather to call upon spirits and other powers to perform oracles and miracles. The ends they seek can be defined in terms of compensation for personal losses rather than the specific quest for cultural goals. Here religious activity is not far removed from magic. When these groups assemble, they form an audience in which the majority hope for personal benefits or watch others obtain them. If they are Christian, these groups put great weight on the various miraculous happenings in the Scriptures. The Gospel according to St mark especially appeals to them. Their most Characteristic activity is the 'Seance' or public demonstration. The relationships they seek tend to be more with lost relatives than with God or a saviour and their conception of a behaviour is seldom elaborated. We find among these groups the national Spiritualist Church and the progressive Spiritualist Church.

The *reformist* sects seem to constitute a case apart. But the dynamic analytic approach to religious movements demands a category corresponding to those groups, which , though sectarian in more than one respect, have effected transformations in their early response towards the outside world. Originally revolutionary this attitude may have become introverted later. The history of the Quakers is a typical example of this. Revolutionary at the start and becoming introvertionist during the eighteenth century, they have gradually adopted a reformist position. This type of possessing a very strong sense of identity, studies the world in order to involve itself in it by good deeds. It takes upto itself the of social conscience. The sect also accepts a place in the world without being of the world or touched by its impurity. It associated with the world but keeps apart from it. The favourite texts of these sects, even if they do not hold fast to them, are those according to which faith without deeds is in vain and which support the view that the sect is itself the leavening of the lump. Their doctrinal position is mitigated, subsumed by their humanitarian orientation and their reformist tendencies towards the outside world. The Christadelphians may at some time in the future end up by being transformed into this kind of sect, even enough their doctrinal position is much more extensive and could not be easily abandoned. The interest in this category lies in the importance it would seem to have for the study of the transformation of sects when the structure persists although the response to the outside world is modified.

The *Utopian* sect is perhaps the most complex type. Its response to the outside world consists partly in withdrawing from it, and partly in wishing to remake it to a better specification. It is more radical than the reformist sect, potentially less violent than the revolutionary sect and more constructive on a social level that the conversionist sect. It sets out through its activities the construct the world on a communitarian basis. It does not seek only to establish colonies but also proposes a progaramme for the reorganization of the world along community lines. Thus it aims at a sort of social reconstruction but of a kind essentially different from that of such socialgroups as the Quakers. It does in fact propose measures for social reorganization, and not only improvements and reforms within the existing framework of society. In the case of a Christian movement, the favourite biblical texts may be those of he Acts recounting the establishment of the primitive Christian community in Jerusalem. But sects of the sort are unlikely to have a clear conception of divinity. They may be conversionist in some measure but the converts they want are distinctive kind. As a consequence of the demand made of their members, they are likely to be rather suspicious of the candidates for conversion, rather like the monastic orders. Among Christian groups (or more or less Christian) of this type, one might name the Tolstoyans the community of Oneida, the Brüderhof and perhaps also certain sections among the Christian Socialists.

In the case of Utopian sects, it seems necessary to distinguishly between those which consider the founding of 'colonies' as their essential religious mission, as the specific means of attaining grace, and those for whom this represents but one reasonable means. Thus groups such as certain minorites, the Aman society and the shakers, communal in practice have become so in response to particular circumstances, rather than as part of their original vision. Their practice of communal living does not constitute their response to the outside world, but their defense against it. This was in particular the appropriate way in which too adapt to the colonial (American) society into which they had immigrated, and which threatened to disperse them and assimilate them in piecemeal fashion into the irreligion of the 'frontier' situation. The practice of communal life, sometimes assisted by linguistic distinctiveness, became for these groups an important means of protecting their way of life from that of the wider society; and in a society where land was cheap and awaited only clearing, vicinal segregation by means of communal living became an almost natural means of defence. Of course, it could have happened that communal living assumed very great significance for a movement and one should not neglect its importance as a decisive factor in the creation of a specific kind of change in introversionist movements. Gradually, as the original inspiration becomes less active – as was the case with the Shakers and the Amana society, introverted groups which at their inceptions claimed special spiritual gifts communal living may then become an end it itself.

It would seem that, when sects do persist, they always undergo processes of mutation; some of the reasons for this have already been studied. Because sects cannot cut themselves off completely for the world they are influenced by external factors. But the internal causes are perhaps even more significant: the response of the founders towards the outside world becomes difficult to maintain for successive generations. The latter may equally re-evaluate and reinstate the devices of isolation set up by the founders, and what were in the beginning only institutional defence mechanicsms may gradually become intrinstically important and no longer just as a means. Communitarianism, first adopted as protection, or the ideology and practices of the sect is thus be transformed for defence to response. It may in turn become the object of new mechanisms of defence and nationalization, and doctrinal or spiritual legitimation may, consequently, take the place of something which originally was entirely circumstantial. Thus one can observe the internal consequences and even the *systematic ideological consequences* of that was at the beginning simply defensive action., and an institutional adaptation is brought about. Communal living alone is not enough to characterize as Utopian the sects which adhere to it any more than the squabbles between the Doukhobors and government agents of British Colombia would justify inclusion of these secretarians among revolutionary groups. To decide otherwise would introduce a foreign criterion of organization into our classification,[2] and reduce its usefulness in the study of the processes of transformation within sects.

Any typology of sects must point up, and not hide, the fact that sects pass through processes of change. It is not only a question of the process of denominalization, which is the typical change with conversionist sects (see Wilson, 1959). All organizations are prone to suffer an attentuation in commitment in their original values and this is especially true among protestant movements. The sect manifests this tendency most particularly in its response to the world. Indeed the structures, duties and official doctrine are much more resistant to change,. But the attitude towards the outside world, which constitutes, the major issue of debate between the sect and the wider society, may itself shift imperceptibly. An extremely clear illustration of this type of change can be found in the case of the revolutionary sect which, while remaining essentially a sect, may gradually change its attitude towards the outside world. An intense revolutionary spirit is difficult to maintain, especially when it depends upon the expection of the supernatural sign, the date of which is of necessity frequently postponed. The revolutionary sect appears to be suspectible of a supernatural sign, the date of which is of necessity frequently postponed. The revolutionary sect appears to the susceptible to two kinds of development. In the firs case, the sect may bind its fate so tightly to the idea of active revolution that it does actually stage a rebellion: in that case it seems impossible to preserve the original religious position in its primitive form, even approximately. Sudanese mahdi-ism the Marching Rule Movement of the Solomon Islands,[3] The Taipaing rebellion (see Wallace, 1956) and perhaps the case of the fifth Monarchy Men (England, seventeenth century) seem to furnish examples of this type of transformation. The change into a military force tends to led to the suppression of the sect by state authorities or to turn it into a secret party, precarious in existence, and henceforward more political than religious. The second possible mutation may be harder to trace. It is difficult to maintain over a long period the hope of a divine appearance or a cataclysm, and it may perhaps be easier to keep it up by recruiting new adherents, enthusiastic for what to them is a new perspective, than to recruit a second generation or successive generations of members from among the children of members. But if the sect is well protected and has a good chance of maintaining its internal recruitment, then its response to the world will probably take on new aspects in spite of the persistence of doctrinal declarations, interpretations of the Scriptures or ritual. It seems that the revolutionary sect which persists in these circumstances, becomes more passive, more withdrawn and that it then grows nearer in fact to the position of the introvertionist sects. The change wrought among the Quakers would seem to be of this order. It is the same as is being wrought at the present time, up to a certain point, among the Christadelphians. These changes do not always go un-noticed within the sects and after often resisted there. Indeed, these processes themselves produce schisms within revolutionary sects rather in the same way as we have seen the process of denominationlization engender schisms in conversionist sects. Thus, among Christadelphians today, and in spite of the reintegration of certain old schismatic groups, tensions can be observed between those holding an introvertionist conception of the movement and those, especially the young, who would prefer ideas of social reform. Some of the latter have moreover been expelled on these grounds. And alongside this can be seen the persistence of older revolutionary ideas. The Quakers have undergone other mutations – from revolutionary sect they become introversionist and social reformist. This came about not only because the Quakers individually were interested in good deeds but by the fact of the movement's concerted action in its entirety. A significant characteristic of the refromist position must be seen in the fact that it does not use this type of good works as a means of proselytizing. The reforming work becomes the raison d' etre of the sect, the central point of its mission and of the image it has of itself – a changed response to the world.

Of course one can best study the typical changes of sects in terms of internal factors (disappointment of eschatological hopes, recruitment of a second generation). But the influence of the wider society must not be omitted in studying the birth and transformation of sects. It is obvious that sects of the manipulationist and introversionist type can only come about at certain stages of social and cultural development. A manipulationsit sect can come into being only when metaphysical thought has extended into the religious and philosophical traditions of a society. Sects of this type tend to succeed among semi-intellectuals who have some knowledge of scientific or philosophical reasoning and imitate it up to a point. Manipulations it sects are universalist and this also is a cultural variable found only at relatively advanced stages of cultural development. These sects comprise more 'educated' people; they are unlikely to originate from the working classes. They tend to offer visions of prestige and power as well as the short cuts for achieving them. they attract groups who have some ambition in this direction. The special means offered by the sects to attain these goals are defined in terms of verbal techniques and metaphysical theories. They use a language which attracts confidence and creates assurance, and their pre-occupation with the explanation of their teories, tends to exclude all other activity, well-being in the world, perceived in terms of health, wealth, comfort and social status, constitutes the practical sanction for these sect's teaching. The achievement–oriented society offers its rewards through extremely competitive processes. In response, these sects offer new methods which allow an escape from tensions and the achievement of cultural goals, especially for those who are sensitive to social status, and struggle to attain it. Sects of this type were particularly significant during the nineteenth and twentieth centuries in industrial societies (see Gris wold, 1954; England, 1954; Wilson, 1961).

For quite different reasons, the introverted attitude also tends to be manifest only in certain kinds of social circumstances. The retreat from the wider society and the rejection of its dominant religious teachings and practices are only possible when the social institutions have reached a certain degree of autonomy from each other, and in circumstance where religious expression and practices have ceased to constitute a necessary public performance. The idea of private life must be established before an introversionist religion can originate, especially in its non-communitarian forms. In monasticism the retreat from the world was practised under the auspices of the dominant social ideology and led to a style of life separated from the world outside, but one could also say that it was undertaken in the name of that world. In the case of the introversionist sect, the retreat constitutes a more radical contracting out', even though it does not renounce all social conflicts, but essentially only the customary and dominant religious and moral consensus. It can thus only originate in a society already partly secularized, or in a society where military conquest, for example,. has put in doubt the traditional religion and made possible some differentiation. Participation in secular activities can continue, but if this leads to difficulties in the field of religious practice then communitarian tendencies and segregation might, in favourable circumstances, occur. But introversionist sects have not always been able or wished to become communitarian; their method of retreat seeks to establish a personal religious privacy, not vicinal segregation. They do not consider that this isolation is necessarily endangered by secular activities if these are deemed "necessary". Thus certain holiness movements and strict Darbyists admit that their members need to expose themselves to the affairs of the world, while keeping their privates lives pure of the contamination of that world. While conversionist and revolutionist sects insist on a doctrine of witness and its public expression, the introversionist sects deny the value of such activity and reject its theoretical implications. Introversionism seems to have constittued an attitude which was tenable in seventeenth-century Europe, but it is clear that the social climate is today less favourable to this kind of religious attitude. Compulsory education, sanitary and social regulations, increased economic control of individual activity on the part of the State, the extension of taxes, obligatory military service to the use of certain procedures approved by nations to secure exemption from it – all these factors bring the sectarian into closer involvement with the wider society. The development of mass communications and the reliance which governments have upon them, the extension of the division of labour, the development of large scale man-power recruitment, the disapperance of the small business – all this makes effective isolation more and more difficult. The diffuse dependence of the individual on society makes his withdrawal harder all the time and individuals' widening social experience, his access to a great variety of cultural, social and leisure activities probably reduce the relative attractions of a life of retreat. Organic solidarity does not necessarily lead to increased allegiance to society and its goals, but it does make complete independence more difficult to attain or even to contemplate. These circumstances may, at least for some tine, produce among the sects responses which facilitate the persistence of those already 'established', but at the same time make less likely the growth of new sects, at least of the introversionist type, and perhaps also of the revolutionist type.[4]

If we now leave the Christian world for what one might call the mission territories, we can quickly see that manipulationist sects and introversionist sects are not likely to develop there.[5] Indigenous sects, which abound in these societies, are either revolutionist or thaumaturgical. These two kinds of responses are primitive and simple. Thaumaturgical practice characterizes primitive religion and magic, and when societies reach the degree of complexity where religious deviation becomes possible, thamaturgy becomes an almost inevitable part of it. Nevertheless, healing sects often owe much to the thaumaturgical tradition of Christianity itself. Sects of this kind are born in primitive societies in reply to social change and to deterioration in the traditional culture. One of the aspects of this phenomenon is the introduction of new ideologies which become in turn a source of religious ideas and practices accessible to purely native religious movements. The 'Zionist' sects of South Africa (see Sundkler, 1948; Dougall, 1956; Hunter, 1936) illustrate this syncretiziation of pagan and Christian thaumaturigical practices, as do the so-called Pocomania sects of Jamaica (Simpson, 1956). But it is quite unlikely that manipulationist or introversionist sects will come into being among he indigenous populations of these two territories , of which one is more or less destrabilized and the other is an under-developed non-tribal society.

We frequently find the revolutionist type of religious movements in these territories, and it has been called, itself 'Ethiopian' (Cook, 1933; Westermann, 1937; Roux, 1945; Sundlker, 1948; Shepperson, 1952; Schösser, 1949; Thwaite, 1936). The Ras Tafari movements of Jamaica are movements similar in their salient features. They insist in the typical manner, but in varying degrees, on the adventist or chiliastic expectation, in the coming reversal of roles between the adherents and their enemies, and all share the same awaiting of the millennium Simpson, 1955). In certain contexts these movements have been identified with a type of incipient nationalism, or, when the term 'nationalism' is anachronistic, they are at least taken for semi-political movements. One may well consider some of them in these terms but in other cases to call them such is to go beyond the evidence. Many of them are nearer to those revolutionist sects which are not completely institutionalized. They do not necessarily lead to revolutionary activity but look forward to revolutionary transformation of their society, or at least of their own circumstances. In general, they believe that a super-natural intervention in their favour will bring about the revolution.

Researchers accept the consideration that revolutionist secterianism is a response to a situation of cultural strain. There seems some reason to suppose that this is a spontaneous response of oppressed or colonized peoples who make their wishworld into their response to the real world. But we cannot always be sure that this type of movement constitutes a spontaneous response, and if we wish to draw a clear picture of the circumstances and cultural conditions to which revolutionary sects respond, we need to be able to dissociate the effects of cultural contact from those of cultural diffusion. Even very slight cultural contact seems capable of producing recognizable effects at the level of religious intrpretation.[6] But the responses of revolutionary sects as such may be provoked and stimulated by missionary activity, even by that of a more or less orthodox kind.[7] We must also consider another factor: the fact that the Christian Scriptures carry a very clear revolutionist element, which forms the doctrinal core of European and American revolutionist sects. These have often actively proselytized in under-developed countries and have disseminated their teaching far and wide. Paradoxically they are not alone in having communicated ideas of the return of Christ and the millenium, since these teachings are also after all part of the message of the many fundamentalist groups we can call conversionist. Nevertheless, in the context of mission territories, it could be that doctrines relatively less significant in the European or American situation may be just those most easily accepted by native peoples.

Thus several pentecostal sects, some of which call themselves holiness movements, and other fundamentalist groups, among them the darbyists, have been working in Jamaica since 1919 the seventh Say Baptists (in Nyasaland), the Brethren Church (in Nigeria), the So-called Open Bible standard Church Group (French West Africa) in many other groups were at work in Africa around 1955. The Seventh Day Adventists were reported to have about two thousand missionaries in the missionary lands at this time, and the American Assemblies of God had about seven hundred and fifty. These two groups have made a considerable number of converts in different parts of Africa and in other territories (see Thiessey, 1955, pp.411 ff.; Pierce Beaver, 1954; Price and Mayer, 1956; Price, 1957). Already in the period around 1930, the penetration of the Seventh Day Adventists into the mission fields of more orthodox groups provoked complaints (Burton, 1936; Keesing, 1941, pp. 225 ff.). The Mormons and Jehovah's Witnesses maintain a substantial but secret number of lay missionaries in these countries, and the latter try to transform all their converts into as many 'publishers' of their particular form of adventism.

The native sects manifesting the direct influence of the Christian missions are legion. In a certain number of cases their leaders are indigenous people irritated by the limited opportunities for prestige and power offered by the missions in which they were educated. Such was the case of Kimbangou (see Lerrigo, 1922; Schlösser, 1949; Comhaire, 1953, 1955; Balandier, 1955); and that of Simon-Pierre Mpadi Chilembwe, whose career owed much to the radical and volatile Joseph Booth, a fundamentalist missionary of changing views, who are prototypes of the mission—influenced leaders of a native revolutionist movement (Shepperson, 1954). The Kitawala, a Rhodesian version of the Jehovah's Witnesses movement, furnished further evidence of the direct influence of indigenous peoples (Quick, 1940; Schlösser, 1949; Cunnison, 1951).[8] And examples in this direction are not lacking for Melanesia, Polynesia and China.[9]

It remains for us to establish in which of their aspects the native revolutionist movements constitute simply a response to cultural contacts without borrowing the eschatological and messianic ideas of Christianity. The nativist movement, the promise of the return of ancestors and their customs, seems to constitute a response of this type.[10] The cargo cults seem also to arise without ideological borrowing. These two movements are of the revolutionist type, but perhaps we have less proof in the case of the returning Messiah as an indigenous myth giving birth to religious activity, although this has been suggested regarding the case of the Manseren cult of Biak in New Guinea.[11] If some revolutionist sects originate outside all Christian influence we have evidence of the wider usefulness of our categories, which are no longer culture-bound. In order to study this question, and some other connected problems, we must analyse the indigeneous sects and make sure of distinguishing between their different elements. We could then link the latter to the condition of cultural contact and to levels of social development. Köbben (1960) has begun an analysis of this type. It seems probable that in less advanced societies the possibilities of response to the outside world are limited, and that only two of them (revolutionist on side world are limited, and that only two of them (revolutionist on thaumaturgical) constitutes possibilities of original response in pre-literate societies. These two responses, it will be noted, permit considerable elements of fantasy. Both clearly existed in the history of Christianity; although the thaumaturgical response has given rise to fewer sectarian organizations as such, it has existed with the Christian tradition in cult movements of some kind another, or as residual paganism. As a primitive position and as a transformation of the revolutionist position the interversionist sect seems only to manifest itself in certain condition of social development. For manipulationist sects, conditions favouring their appearance seem to be those in which the religious, intellectual and educational monopoly of traditional religious functionaries has been broken and in circumstances which make status insecurity common and social mobility possible at least for a certain number.

The conditions for the appearance of the other three types pf response to the world seem even more strictly limited. It seem that conversionist sects are linked with the development of individualism and this perhaps constitutes the condition *sine quanon* of their appearance. The refromist response appears to be essentially derivative. One can consider it partly as a process in the secularization of sects, at any rate as an accommodation in the concerns of the outside world. If Utopian conceptions can be formed to some degree in revolutioanry sects, the idea of undertaking social action with a view to establishing a new society arises only at a stage of social development of a certain realistic relativism. Thus it seems that the birth of this type of sect is also itself limited to certain general circumstances of social development. Few of our types, it seems, can be observed among the religious deviations one finds in pre-literate societies. This fact should not deter us in the attempt to discover the relevance of these types for the analysis of religious movements with the major world religions, as well as in the Protestant development of Christianity from which our types are primarily deprived.

References

Anon (1951), 'A visit to the Apostles and town of Aiyetoro'. *Nigeria*, vol. 36.

Allen, C.H. (1951), 'Marching rule: a nativistic cult of the British Solomon Islands', *South Pacific*, vol.5.

Balandier, G. (1955), *Sociologie actuelle de L'Afrique noire*, Presses Universitaires.

Bhrger, P.L. (1954), 'Sociological study of secterianism,' *Soc. Res.*, vol.21, pp. 467-85.

Bhrdt, R.M. (1952), 'A Cargo movement in the Eastern Central Highlands of New Guinea,' *Oceania*, vol.23, pp. 40-65 and 137-58.

Berndt, R.M. (1954), 'Reaction to contact in the Eastern Highlands of New Guinea,' *Oceania*, vol. 24, pp. 190-228.

Bardman, E.P. (1951), 'Christian influence on the ideology of the Taiping rebellion', *Far Eastern Quart.*, Vol. 10, pp. 115-24.

Bodrogi, T. (1951), 'Colonization and religious movements in Melanesia', *Acta Ethnograph, Acad. Scient. Hungar*, vol. 2, pp. 259-90.

Brewster, A.B. (1922), *The Hill Tribes of Fiji*, Lippincott.

Burton, J.W. (1936), *Missionary survey of the Pacific Islands*, World Dominion Press.

Cato, A.C. (1947), 'A new religious cult in Fiji', *Oceania*, vol.18, pp.146-56.

Chinnery, E.W.P., and Haddon, A.C. (1917), 'Five new religious cults in British New Guinea', *Hibbert J.*, vol. 15, pp.448-63.

Clark, E.T. (1937), *The Small Sects in America*, Abingdon.

Comhaire, J.L. (1953), 'Religious trends in African and Afro-American Urban societies', *Anthrop, Quart.*, vol. 26, pp. 95-108.

Comhaire, J.L. (1955),'Societies secretes et mouvements prophetiques au Congo belge', *Africa.*, vol. 25, pp. 54-8.

Cook, L.A. (1933), 'Revolt in Africa', *J. Negro, Hist.*, vol. 18, pp. 396-413.

Cunnison, I. (1951), 'A Watchower assembly in Central Africa', *int. Rev. Miss.*, vol. 40, pp.456-69.

Bruynm J.V. (1951), 'The manseren cult of Biak', *South Pacific*, vol. 5, pp. 1-11.

Dougall, J.W.C. (1956), 'African separatist churches,' *Int. Rev. Miss.*, vol. 25, pp. 257-66.

England, R.W. (1954), 'Some aspects of Christian Science', *Amer, J. Social.*, vol. 59.

Firth, R. 91935), 'The theory of "cargo" cults: A note on Tikopia'. *Man.* Vol. 55, pp. 130-32.

Fletcher, A.C. (1891), 'The Indian Messiah', *J. Amer. Folk-Lore*, vol. 4, pp. 57-60.

Griswold, A. W. 91954), 'New Thought: a cult of success', Amer, J. sociol., vol. 59.

Hunter, M. (1936), *Reaction to Conquest*, Oxford University Press.

Keesing, F.M. (1941), *The South seas in the Modern World*. Allen and Unwin.

Köbben, A.J.F. (1960), 'Prophetic movements as an expression of social protest', *Int. Arch. Ethnograph.*, vol. 49, pp. 117-64.

Koskinen, A. (1953), 'Missionary influence as a political factor in the Pacific Island's *suomalaisen Tiedeakatemian Tolmituksia, Annales Academiae scientiarum* Fennicae, Sarja Ser. B, Vol, 78 (Helsinki).

Krader, L. (1956), 'A nativistic movements in western Siberia', *Amer. Anthrop.*, vol. 58, pp. 282-92.

Lane, G.H. (1927), *Fox Pitt Rivers, The Clash of Cultures and the Contact of Races*, Routledge.

Lerrigo, P. H.J. (1992), 'The prophet movement in the Congo', *Int. Rev. Miss.*, vol. II, pp. 270-77.

Martin, D.A. (1962), 'The denomination', *Brit. J. Sociol.*, vol. 13. pp. 1-14.

Marty, M.E. (1960), 'Sects and cults', *Ann. Amer. Acad. Polit.*

Soc. Scien., vol. 332, pp. 125-34.

Pierce beaver, R. (1954), 'Expansion of America Foreign Missionary activity since 1945', *Miss. Res. Lib. Occas. Bull.*, vol.5, no.7.

Pos, H. (1950), 'The revolt of "Manseren", *Amer, Anthrop.*, vol.52.

Price, .W., and mayer, K.E. (1956), 'A study of American Protestant Missions in 1956', *Miss. Res. Lib. Occas. Bull.*, vol.7, no.9.

Quick, G. (1940), 'Someaspects of the African Watch Tower Movements in Northern Rhodesia', int. *Rev. Miss.*, vol.29, pp. 216-26.

Roux, E. (1945), *Time Longer than Rope*, Gollancz.

Schlösser, K. (1949), *Propheten in Afrika*, Limbach, Brunswick.

Shepperson, G. (1952), 'Ethiopanism and African nationalism', *Phylon*, vol. 14, pp. 9-18.

Shepperson, G. (1954), 'The politics of African Separatist Movements in British Central Africa, 1892-1916', *Africa*, vol. 24, pp.233-46.

Simpson, G.M. (1955), 'Political cultism in West Kingston, Jamaica,' *Soc. Econ, stud.* Vol., 4. Pp. 133-49.

Simpson, G.M. (1956) 'Jamaican revivalists cults', *soc. Econ. Stud.*, vol.5. pp.321-42.

Sundkler, B.G.T. (1948), *bantu Prophets in South Africa*, Butterworth.

Thessey, J.C. (1955), A *Survey of World Missions*, Inter-Varsity Press.

Thompson, B. (1908). *The Fijians: A Study of the Decay of Custom* Heinmann.

Thwaite, D. (1936), *The seething African* Pot, Constable.

Trodeltsch, R. (1931), *The Social Teaching of the Christian Churches*, Macmillan.

Tallace, A.F.C. (1956), 'Revitalization movements', *Amer Anthropol.*, vol. 58, pp.264-81.

Westermann, D. (1937), *Africa and Christianity*, Oxford University Press.

Williams, F.E. (1934), 'The Vailala madness in retrospect', in E.E. Evans-Pritchard *et al.*, *Essays Presented to C.G.* Seligman. Kegan Paul, pp.36-79.

Wilson, B.R. (1958), 'The appearance and survival of sects in an revolutionary social milier', An analysis of sec development', Amer, soc. Rev., vol. 24, pp.3-15.

Wilson, BR. (1961), *Sects and society*, Heinemann, and California University Press.

Winks, R.W. (1953), 'The doctrine Han-Hanism', *J. Polynes. Soc.*, vol. 62, pp. 199-236.

Worsley, P. (1957), *The Trumpet Shall Sound*, McGibbon & keh.

Winger, J.M. (1946), *Religion in the Struggle for Power*, Duke University Press.

Winger, J.M. (1957), *Religion, Society and the Individual*, Macmillan.

NOTES

1. See Marty (1960). This author suggests that 'cults' collapse in the absence of a charismatic leader. But this type of leader is far from being a instant factor in the movements Marty embraces under this name. They often proper in a completely impersonal context – such in the case in the various branches of New Thought and Rosacrucianism.

2. Clark (1937) presents a classification in which the communitarian sects are regarded as a distinct species.

3. One might hesitate to classify this movement as a sect. Worseley's (1957, pp.170 ff.) account suggests that in spite of its millenarian aspects this movement had distinct political aims since its birth. Allen (1951) seems to suggest that the movement had a much less well-developed political consciousness at its birth.

4. For an examination of the social circumstances favouring the survival of sects, see Wilson (1958).

5. The only example of a sect in an under - developed country (excluding nativistic attitudes) which I have found possible to classify as introversionist, in so far as I have the facts, is the 'Apostles of Aiyetoro' on the Nigerian Seaboard. The evidence reported by periodical is too meagre to make a decisive case. See Anon (1951), pp.387 ff.

6. Berndt and Firth both consider that autochthonous movements arise independently of all foreign influence after very slight contact, or even in reaction to rumours from places where there has been slight cultural contact: see Berndt (1952, 1954) and Firsth (1935).

7. Evidence from for the beginnings of missionary activity in Polynesia is presented in Koskinen (1953). See also Lane (1927).

8. Shepperson (1952) suggests that these movements have become some what different from the Jehovah's Witnesses of Europe and America.

9. The 'Manseren' revolt in Papua led by Stephanus during the Second World War manifested distinct signs of Christian influence, according to Pos (1950), pp. 561 ff. (On Manseren see fn 11.) Williams (1934) suggests that misunderstood missionary teaching played some part in the movement.

   As for Polynesia, see Winks (1953), Thompson (1908), Brewster (1922), pp.141 ff. And 236 ff., and Cato (1947).

   As for Asia, see Boardman (1951) and Krader (1956).

10. Nativistic movements of this sor have been called 'revitalization movemetns by Wallace (1956). They did perhaps appear spontaneously as autochthonous movements in response to cultural contact. The American Ghost dance should be classed among them and perhaps also the Taro in British New Guinea.

11. See de Bruyn (1951), Bodrogi 91951), and Chinnery and Haddon (1917). There seems to be agreement in thinking that the belief in the return of the manseren Kover as a saviour precedes Christian missionary activity. It is perhaps a response to a previous conquest. Later the 'cult' borrowed Christian elements. Fletcher (1891) considered that the Indian had their own messianic myths of a returning cultural hero.

Chapter-8

AFRICAN RELIGIOUS MOVEMENTS

J. W. FERNANDEZ

Chapter-8

Our object here is threefold. We shall first attempt to establish an elementary typology,[1] as simple as is clearly possible, of religious movements in Africa. We shall next examine one type more fully the so-called 'syncretist' movements of equatorial Africa in the interest of exposing their particular configuration and dynamic changes. We shall finally try to asses the present and future place of these religious movements in the sequential process leading to nationalism, Africanism and Panm-Africanism the process in other words, leading form the communal to the modern, the state less to the state societies in Africa. In the way we can perhaps say something useful about the relation of religion to politics in so far as this relationship is evident in African religious movements.

I

Two points must be made to simplify the discussion of types. First only those movements will be discussed which may be defined against a back-ground of Christian evangelization. Religious movements formed under the impetus of Islamic evangelization, such as prophet movements in the Mahdist tradition, will be ignored, through they are of importance, particularly in Sudanic Africa.[2] It was Christian evangelists in their travels throughout the bush who were, from the earliest moments of colonization, generally the most effective agents in making Africans fully aware, first, of the attitude of depreceation taken by the dominant colonial society towards their culture, and second, of the political domination that lay behind the missionaries, ready to support their right to evangelization on those occasions when Africans domination to repel them[3] This emphasises the relevance of the background of Christian

---

Except from J.W. Fernandez, 'African religious movements – types and dynamics, '*Journal of modern African Studies*, vol. 2. (1964), pp.531-49.

evangelization to our discussion. The colonial administrations, concerned always to establish their district and regional administrative centres, were less given to travelling and thus made more super official contact in the bush. The Christian missionaries, in most cases then, were the first agents of domination and deprecation, in reaction to which most religious movements arose.[4] The throughgoing identification of the evangelical with the colonial and imperial enterprise in the minds of Africans has been often remarked. Historically, however, Christian evangelization was frequently the first term of this identification, colonial administration the second.

We cannot presume, however, in discussing the types of religious movements which arose under Christian domination to find their origins solely in this unique situation. It is clear, given the turmoil, extensive migrations and Kaleidoscope of succeeding domination and sub-ordinations in African history and Pre-history, that revitalization movemetns of a religious character were a fairly frequent traditional pattern. Herskovits (1962, p.418) argues that 'many of the separatist movements are to be thought of as reinterpretation of the prophet movements widely prevalent in Africa long before European control. While noting this continuity we shall consider the movements only in response to the colonial, predominantly Christian presence.[5]

If we compile a list of types of African religious movements we recognize at once that we are confronted with too broad and redundant a typology. A partial compilation would include prophetism, faith healing, Bible Church, Ethiopian, Zionist, Messianic, millenarian, separatist, contra acculturative independent, syncretist and nativist, to go no further. It is a considerable challenge to reduce this plethora to the four basic types we propose – reformative, separatist, nativist and messianic – because the various regions of Africa have become attached to the typologies that have grown out of original local research. Thus Sundkler's (1961, pp. 38-43) typology, Ethiopian-Zionist, has currency in Southern Africa, yet, as Parrinder (1953, p.108) points out, it is not really satisfactory elsewhere. For one thing, other areas do not have the same racial problems as South Africa. These have been a dynamic factor in separatism there and are expressed in the term Ethiopianism. For another thing all, areas have not had the same close contact with New World revivalism and millenarianism: this contact was primarily with American Negro separatist churches such as the African Methodist Episcopal Church in the United State or the various Negro Baptist Churches. Penrecostal revivalists such as the Christian Catholic Apostolic Church of Zion Illinois, the Adventists and especially the Jehovah's Witnesses, whose watch tower doctrines have had such an impact on Central Africa, were also important. No one can deny, within the framework of South African history that Sundkler's two terms are appropriate in typing the religious movements that occurred there. We must seek for terms, however, that are less bound to a specific area and a specific history.

The classic typology for movement of the kind we are considering here remains that of Ralph Linton (1943). By such movements he mean's any conscious organized attempt on the pat of a society's members to revive or perpetuate selected aspects of its culture'. Linton discusses two sets of criteria whether the movements are perpetuative or revivalist, and whether they are magical or rational. He combines these sets into the four theoretical types – revivalistic - magical, revivalistic - rational, perpetuative – magical and perpetuative rational. A percent and particularly cogent criticism of Linton by Worsley (1957, pp.267-76) points out however, that practically all religious movements are ready to adopt new elements, invent new ritual or reinterpret the old and hence the categories perpetuative and revivalistic suggest a state of affairs so delimited as to be uninformative. Worseley also criticizes the term rational, pointing out that it risks evoking an old argument as to logical and pre-logical mentality. What looks magical to us may be perfectly rational in another less sophisticated frame of reference with other premises. Reason should not be after all a function of range of awareness.

Nevertheless movements do differ as to the degree to which they perpetuate the old or incorporate the new. The clue to a more appropriate set of characteristics to which to refer a apology is found in Linton's statement that 'what really happens in all nativistic movements is that certain current or remembered elements of culture are selected for emphasis and given symbolic value (London, 1943, p.231). If this is true, the question arises, When does the particular movement obtain its symbols? From its own cultural tradition, or from the culture of the society or societies with which it is in contact? We find ourselves thus on a continuous, or a continuous series of gradual and movements which are largely committed by acculturation to the symbols of the contact culture. The continuum thus lies between the two poles of a traditional or an acculturated symbolism.

But the larger question remains as to how these symbols are used: whether instrumentally or expressively. This suggests a second dimension, which may be defined as follows. An instrumental type of religious movement chooses the elements for symbolic use in a realistic and goal-minded fashion and with a view to perpetuating them under existing conditions. We find fairly pragmatic attempts to compensate for the deprivations and other frustration involved in the situation of subordination without endangering the continuity and survival of the religious group, since it is seen as the only institution that can achieve its goals. In an expressive type of religion the emphasis is upon escape by symbolic displacement from the situation which is causing frustration. This is done by means of symbolic forms in ritual and ceremony, song, drama and dance. Intense involvement of the participants in these activities draws their attention away from the frustration and deprivations of their everyday situation. In such movements the group as an entity is not all-important. It and its activity are but means to this symbolic displacement.

In an expressive movement there is no calculated attempt to deal with a difficult situation directly. Rather the frustration involved often spontaneously produce supernatural and visionary experiences in persons of charismatic qualities.[0] These movements rely on intense evocation of the supernatural and are given over to enthusiastic religious behaviour. Their emotional tone is high and they count heavily on ritualization. Their leaders are preoccupied with internal concerns and not with representing the group to the larger situation of which it is a part. Moribund elements of culture may be revived, not in anticipations of practical advantages, but as part of a magical formula which will miraculously change a frustrating environment and returns an unrealistic reliance on their ability to create and constitute their own universe through expressive symbolism.

In summary, then, movements whose emphasis is primarily instrumental keep enough cognisance of the total situation to which they are reacting to remain adapted to it and thus guarantee their survival. They are exocentric well aware of their place in a larger field. Movements whose emphasis is expressive institute kinds of behaviour which compensate the individuals for the deprivations they feel at the moment; but they remain preoccupied with these compensations, their symbolic gratification, without reference to the outside world of time and place, of which they are a part. They are not so much concerned with their group survival as they are with directly reducing the frustrations and anxieties with which they are living.[7]

We have some examples of what we mean in the Gabon religious cults studied by the writer (Fernandez, 1964). These cults, ordinarily typed syncretist, are in two different places along the expressive instrumental continuum. Those concerned with expressive satisfactions insist on ritual procedure regardless of administrative disapproval of certain practices such as use of the purpose or ritual flagellation. Other cults, more instrumental in orientation, attempt to modify their practices to some extent to accord with the directives of the government and local administration. It is the latter who have had, quite naturally, greater survival value but they have not provided the range of symbolic satisfactions available in the former. For example the expressive groups have always freely taken the alkaloid stimulant, *eboga* (tabernenthes eboga), an important guarantee of a satisfying ritual experience. The instrumental-type cults have been, because of their awareness of administrative disapproval, more sparing in the use of this drug, denying thereby some ritual satisfactions to their members for the sake of the survival of the group. The price of survival has been the pain of accommodation.

We may now locate the four types of religious movements proposed earlier in relation to our two-bipolar continua. Nativist movements are those oriented towards a *traditional* symbolism which they manipulate *expressively*. Messianic movements generally employ an *acculturated* symbolism, which despite their acceptance of historic time they manipulate *expressively*, conjuring up millennial satisfactions. Separatist movements employ an *acculturated* symbolism, which they tend to manipulate *instrumentally*. Reformative movements find their base in a *traditional* orientation with which, because of their *instrumental* orientation they deliberately and creatively combine an acculturated symbolism. This theoretical placing of the four types may be indicated in a diagram using two co-ordinating axes.[8]

We now turn to individual cases. Every concrete movement may be located in a particular position on the co-ordinate system of the diagram, though there are difficulties cause by overlap and interpenetration.

Separatism. Most of the movements within this category have the organizational characteristics of a church. They place, in fact, heavy emphasis upon the social organization and coordination of the membership. They are concerned with the group's status in the larger society and think usually, though not necessarily, of improving that status.[9] Usually they separated from European-dominated parent organizations for non-religious reasons. In respect to Christian symbols, religious belief and ceremony, they continue to adhere very closely to the practices of the parent organization and they remain therefore fairly orthodoxy in liturgy and theology. The separation from the parent body was designed to make possible greater status in church organization, which was achieved. Members of the best examples of movements of this kind, the African Congregational Church and the Bantu Methodist Church in South Africa, are very conscious of their social status within the larger community, and are anxious that their religious behaviour should be instrumental in promoting or maintaining it. Many of the African churches which are classed as Ethiopian by Sundkler would fall fully into this category, as would all of the native churches reorganized by the South African Government. If, for reasons of continuing frustrations or weak leadership and organization, fission occurs in a separatist church, and Sundkler testifies to the extent of this, it is likely that the newly formed groups will forget their concern with orthodoxy and tend more and more to a syncretism and perhaps eventually to nativism. Also, continuing

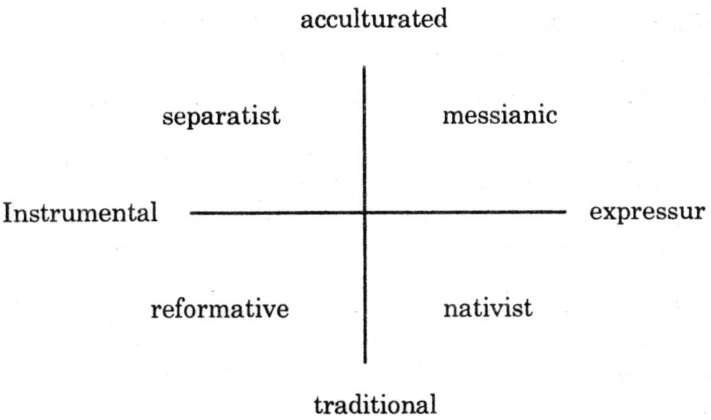

Figure 1

frustrations may lend importance to visionary experiences and give the movement substantial qualities of messianism, the dynamism of these movements has been amply portrayed by Sundkler, in whom the problem of orthodoxy is a main concern.

Other examples of this type of movement may be mentioned. One is the Church of the Lord Aladura, which had its beginnings among the Yoruba in Lagos in the twenties, and has since spread to the other three regions of Nigeria, and to Ghana, Sierra Leone and Liberia as well (Turner, 1962). Here again we are dealing with founders who were all *bona fide* members of the Church Missionary Society affiliates in West Africa, but who claimed to have become dissatisfied with the immorality of European Christianity as evidenced by the foolishness of the First World War and compounded by succeeding metropolitan barbarities. Nevertheless the leaders of this movement have been resistant to the symbolism of traditional African religion, and greatly desire to be accepted by the Christian community. Evidence of their concern with Christian orthodoxy has been their habit of enrolling their leaders in a two-year course at the Missionary Bible Institute in Great Britain.[10] The African Methodist Episcopal Church of South Africa and Rhodesia, the Watchtower Society of Jehovah's Wittnesses (as opposed to any of the kitawala or Watchman offshoots) and John Chilembwe's Providence Industrial Mission, all fall within the separatist division, though at rather different positions (see Taylor and Lehmann, 1961. Ch, and pp. 227-38; Cunnison, 1951; Shepperson and Price, 1958.

A final example of the separatist type is the African Greek Orthodox Church in Uganda, founded by Reuben spartas in the twenties in dissidence and protest against the paternalism of missionary Anglicanism. At first linked with the marcus Garvey movement and the African Orthodox Church in the United States, the remarkable thing is that by a long series of skilful negotiations Spartas finally gained in 1946 corporate acceptance by the Greek Orthodox Church. Thus, as Welbourn (1961, ch. 5, esp. pp. 80-81) points out, both Romans and Anglicans in Uganda are faced not with a purely local schism but with a recognized branch of a world church in their midst. What is demonstrated in this course of events for our purposes in the goal-minded, instrumental and acculturated orientation of the movement, which eventually resulted in a full return to orthodoxy.

Nativist movements contrast in every way with separatist movements. In so far as they begin in the context of Christian colonization, they express a fundamental disaffection with Christian Symbolism and with the way Christianity confronts the supernatural. These movements turn to tradition for effective and more penetrating belief. They are, like messianic movements, often preoccupied with directly healing or ceasing the multitude of physical and spiritual ills that afflict Africans, they do this by ecstatic techniques and highly emotionalized in a purely nativist movement the sources of these techniques and rituals should be exclusively traditional. But, as Worseley has indicated, this is rare in the situation of culture contact which gives rise to religious movements. We almost always have a syncretism. Thus the churches which Sundkler calls 'Zionist' in South Africa would seem to fall into this category, although a good many traditional curing practices have been prohibited.

Moreover, in the type-movement of South African 'Zionism', the *amra Nazaretha* or Nazarene Church of Isaiah Shembe, there is a patent search for a new messiah, partially made out in tembe himself. Though the nativist orientation is strong here, he also is the messianic tendency. An indication of the strong traditional orientation is seen in Shembe's construction of an old-type Zulu village, Ekuhakameni, in order that his followers might worship and be cured in appropriate surroundings. the minds of conditions created by European cities and farms could only further sicken his people (Sundkler, 1961, pp. 93-9). Another example of a nativist movement with overtones of messianism was Mau Mau in Kenya and, before it, Maji Maji in southern Tanganyika. The various modern anti-witchcraft movements which have been so abundant in Africa in recent years, and the Congo 'Holy Water' movements discussed by Kopytuff also fall in this category (see Richards, 1935; Marwick, 1950; Field , 1960; Kopytoff, 1962).

Reformative movements are those which have preserved a strong sense of the viability of the traditional African religious attitude with its associated symbolism.[11] However, these movements have been inescapably aware of Christianity and the attractiveness of some of its symbolism, and have therefore made calculated attempts to integrate Christian elements into their beliefs and ritual. A Prime example of this type of movement is Bwiti in Gabon (Balandier, 1955, 1957; Fernandez, 1964); its marginal example is *Blalouisme* or the Abadice Cult in the southern Ivory Coast (Paulme, 1962). The air of calculated recreation in all these movements is reflected in the name Abadice – coined from ABC – as well as their susceptibility to the obvious advantages of Western civilization. In the case Bwiti we find, over time, the gradual reinterpretation and creative eleboration of an ancestor cult, Bieri, in the presence of Christianity. The orientation remains traditional, with the purposeful accretion of Christian elements. We may mention, as a movement marginally reformative in the direction of separatism, the National Church of Nigeria and the Cameroons, which was organized by *Azikiwe* N.C.N.C. as its religious wing – mainly, to be sure for instrumental political purposes, but also with the purpose of preserving a denigrated African tradition.

A better example of reformatism from Nigeria would be the Reformed Ogboni Society among the Yoruba. This traditionally had important social and political functions as a secret society. Which have been much reduced, while its religious dimension have been much reduced, while its religious dimensions have been carefully syncretized with Christian elements (Parinder,

1953, pp. 175-81). The Reformed Ogboni Society indicates in its very name the important feature of these movements, their sense of continuity with African tradition and, at the same time, their readiness to reform themselves by appeal to acculturation.

Messianic movements are commonly seen as those that arise out of intense xenophobia – in most cases the hated object is European and colonial domination. The prophet or black messiah, responding to visionary experiences, which confirm his election and provide him with charismatic personality, works upon this emotion in expressive ways. A *Weltanschaung* is created irrespective of the actuality in which the movement exists, and the prophet guarantees for his followers either a return to the golden age of African culture or the coming of a future millennium The unrealistic promises and expressive practices of these movements reduce the frustrations of social domination and cultural appreciation by elaborating a compensatory universe. It is of interest, and may be due to African pragmatism, that a pure example of this type of movement is rare though many African religious movements have moved through a messianic stage. It is of further interest that messianic movements characteristically reject a good portion of their own traditional religious This is true of *Kimbanguisme*, which in its early form was messianic movement largely influenced by missionary protestantism (Anderson, 1958, p.49). Other movements which through their expressive character and acculturation fall into this quarter of the diagram would be the Society of the One Almighty God in Uganda, with its adamant reaction to medicine of all kinds (Welbourn, 1961, pp.31-53), and the Elliot Kamwana and Bamulonda movements in Rhodesia and Nyasaland (Taylor and Lehmann, 1961, pp.238-47; Shepperson, 1962, pp. 149-52). As marginally messianic we would include Alice Lenshina's Lampa Church (Taylor and Lehmann, 1961, pp. 248-68; Rotberg, 1961) and the Musama Disco Christo Church of Ghana (Baeta, 1962, pp.28-67). It is clear that the expressive orientation and messianic qualities of the Lenshina movement encouraged the fanaticism to which it succumbed in its recent confrontation with the Government. Because of the heightened emotion characteristic of these movements, the unrealistic expectation they create in their followers, and their neglect of the larger situation of which they are a part and to which they have reacted but remain unattended, they are usually short lived. Their organizational thrust is customarily expended in ritual and cosmological elaborations, and not in more viable social and political forms.

II

It will be useful now to examine more closely a type which appears with frequency in the literature – the so called syncretist cults of western equatorial Africa. Since syncretism – that is, the coalescence of differing religious forms appears in all the movements so far indicated, it is not an apt term for a typological scheme.

Our discussion up to this point intimates that movements frequently do not stay placed in one quarter of the diagram, but pass through typological phases. The importance of dynamic shifts can be best seen in *Kimbanguisme.* This movement was as we have said, in origin strongly messianic. The appearance of Kimbangu as a visionary was accompanied by a rush of expressive behaviour and adherence to the apocalyptic promise implicit in his visions the purification of the earth and the banishment of the Whites. The Belgian adminsitration, however, dealt swifting wit Kinmbangu and prevented him from stabilizing the movement personally. Balandier (1955, p.431) makes it clear that '*nourveaur organisteurs*' came forward to establish the '*missions des noirs*' in Kimbangu's name. These successors were much more organizational and nationalistic in intention even though they kept alive the millenarian vision. The Eglise Jesus Christ Sur Terre Simon Kimbangu (E.J. C.S.K.) and Ngunzism, the surviving forms of the Kimbanguist movement, display likewise a much more instrumental and hence spearatist character, since the orientation towards acculturated symbolism has been maintained. The shift towards instrumentalism is no doubt responsible for the movement's growth and political significance in the Congo (Leopoldville).[12]

Three more examples of these kinds of shifts are Matswaism and Mpadism in the Lower Congo, and Bwiti in Gabon. The original intentions and the programme of André Matswa and his followers were instrumental and almost wholly secular in nature.

He was very clearly assessing the nature of the colonial situation and seeking to deal with the existing abuses and deprivations as realistically as possible. Neither Matswa's movement nor that of Mpadi – whose Ngunza, a Khaki cult, was a reworking of latter day Kimbanguist enthusiasms (Anderson, 1958, pp. 139-40), began with a visionary experience and apocalyptic promise. Matswa's original intention, in the Paris founding of *Association Amicale des originaires del' AEF*, was that of creating an economic union to improve the situation of Africans. Though he acquired early a religious symbolism, it was mainly acculturated; for he constantly endeavoured to obtain, and at first succeeded in obtaining, administrative approval for his activities. But what began as a totally instrumental movement in Paris, rapidly acquired messianic overtones, when carried forth in the Congo. Salvation from white oppression and rapid restoration of dignity were in the minds of many who responded to Matswa's call. Even features of nativism became apparent, and the Association became known as *amicale Balali*, after a subgroup of the Bakongo. The messianic-cum-nativistic characteristics became so marked that the movement was soon suppressed and Matswa himself, at first deported, was later imprisoned.

From very early days it appears that Matswa and his followers permitted, if they did not actually encourage, syncreticisms and interpretations of Chrisitanity, and the traditional ancestor worship (Andersson, 1958, pp. 124-5); though very probably the intended the movement to maintain an instrumental orientation moving from separatist to reformative. But his followers, particularly after his death, identified Matswa with Christ and shifted the movement into a messianic configuration, bringing both passive and active detachment from the colonial situation and considerable unrest (Balandier, 1955, p. 398). One surviving form of Matswaism, Nzambiya Minda (God of the Candle) plays down the messianic element and is more reformative, combining Christian elements with traditional forms of ancestor worship. the history of Matswaism, in sum shows us the subversion of an intended shift from separatist to reformative subverted by an exaggerated swing to messianism which was suppressed. Due to the exigencies of the Second World War, the colonial authorities also imprisoned Simon Mpadi. But his movement did not make the broad shifts of Matswaism. His original Salvation Army-oriented movement has simply shifted to a later and rather inactive reformative stance (Andersson, 1958, p.146).

It may be pointed out, incidentally, that the shift made by Matswaism from a modern instrumental orientation towards the expressive pole is also seen in the Chilembwe movement in Nyasaland in 1915, and in Harry Thuku's Young Kikuyu Association and its immediate successors in Kenya in the 1920s. Both of these latter movements began with pragmatic attempts to deal with the colonial situation. A series of frustrations led Chilembwe to the obortive revolt in 1915 and Thuku's successors through a series of transformations to Mau Mau in the 1950s.

Bwiti, in Gabon and Rio Muni, is the oldest movement in western equatorial Africa, extending its roots back into the century. But, like practically all the African religious movements it was given great impetus by the European moral débacle of the First World War. Bwiti was, from the first, a reformative type cult of nativistic inclinations. It represented in the early years of the century the attempt by a minority of Fang to rework their own ancestral cult, Bieri, by adding elements from the more elaborate rituals and cosmologies of neighbouring Bantu peoples with whom the Fang had been brought into contact by their conquest of northern Gabon. The ancestral cult that most impressed the Fang was that of the Mitsogo Massango peoples called Boeti. The shift towards Christian symbolism occurred much later. For a surprising length of time Bwiti resisted them authority of Christian evangelization. After the Second World War, however, an increasing number of Christian elements found their way into most branches of the cult, so that at the present time there is a Christian dimension to most cult symbolism.

As we have already noted, fission has produced a diversity of forms in Bwiti, and the various subcults differ in their acculturation and their instrumental orientation. Under the impetus of Christianity and colonial development in the late forties and we even find, for the first time, the Charismatic authority of leaders expressing itself in messianic fashion. In general we may say of the dynamism of Bwiti that it has shifted from antivism-reformative through reformative to the present tendency become separatist. One branch of Bwiti, however, rapidly showed through a separatist stage into messianism. Those that did this shift were dissident Catholic catechists or seminarians.

We may illustrate the dynamics of the movements we have just discussed in another simple diagram, based on the first (see pp.398.)

III

Having offered a simple set of characteristics by which African religious movements may be typed, and their dynamics assessed, we return to a larger perspective. The questions which most frequently arise in relation to these movements are of a social and political nature. This, in fact, has been such a preoccupation that C.G. Baeta feels obliged to emphasize the religious thrust in the movements he studied, taking to task Schlösser's (1949, p. 401) emphasis on economic and political motivations. He points out:

If the prophets whose preponderant interest was religious appear to have been few it must be remembered that those who have assembled the data at present available have been for the most part persons primarily interested in and on the look-out for any happening which might have political import (Baeta, 1962, p.5).

Banton, in a more recent article, has also voiced caution against in social economic political bias in assessing these cults. Though they may 'serve political functions these are not so immediate as some writers have implied'. Banton (1963) also points out, as we have above, that the distinction between politics and religion is by no means as relevant to Africans as to post-reformation westerners.

These cautions are no doubt well taken; but the scheme we have presented is not encumbered by this bias (though the classification we have tentatively made may very well be, by reason of the data on which we are forced to rely). Since it cannot over look expressive elements, it is sensitive to the most characteristic features of religion. In its awareness of instrumental actions it recognizes the political intentions of these cults.

Reference to it is thus an aid in all the major questions asked of these movements, whether of a religious or political nature.

For example, it is frequently argued that African religious movements offer to their members a sense of competence and creativity in face of the colonial denigration of these qualities. Indeed, it is more than a sense or feeling of these qualities. The church organization that was required of the South Africa separatists, for example, or the need for a more comprehensive and more African elaboration of dogma and ritual that resulted in the aesthetic creativity of the Shembe movement or Bwiti, actually produced these qualities. But this argument cannot be adequately pursued without assessing the instrumental or expressive nature of the groups involved. In the colonial period, when Africans were largely excluded from wielding the substantial tools of progress, life within movements of an instrumental kind offered them possibilities of developing competence in the ways of a more complex world, thereby acting to secularize the membership. For movements of expressive type, a transitory substitution of autonomy for dependence was achieved.

Again, anyone who has experienced present-day village life in Africa, and the comparative deprivation that progress has brought upon it, cannot ignore the entertainment value in the social and ritual life of the movements. They almost all act to

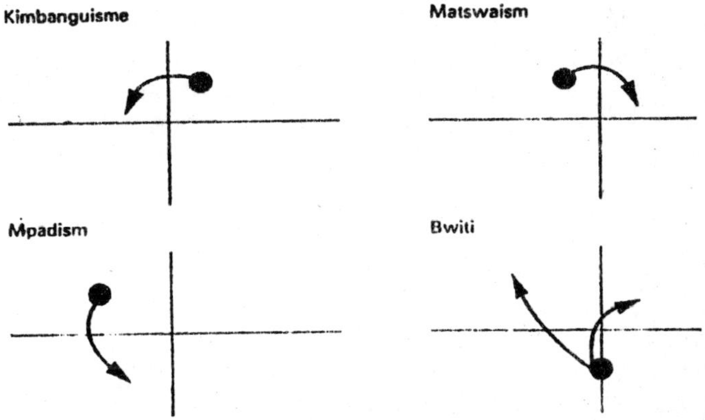

Figure 2

replace the village boredom and deprivation with the satisfaction of sociability and religious adventure: a social invitation to an enthusiastic in-group: a ritual invitation to a spiritual universe, apprehend sed but not fully grasped, full of possible surprises, but always exhilarating. The more expressive the orientation of the cult, of course, the more satisfying and the more involving is this ritually created spiritual universe the more instrumental the more are the satisfactions of a purely social and political nature.

The major question remains as to the present and future place of these movements in an independent Africa. Where autonomy was not politically possible it is understandable that Africans should have sought for it in other realms. But now it may be asked, as Welbourn (1961, p.161) ask concerning the Kikuyu, whether 'the desire for independence is likely to express itself in manifestly religious symbols'. For it is now possible to achieve autonomy by manipulating political symbols. While this question ignores the host of other satisfactions, from aesthetic to psychomatic, achieved by these movements, as well as the extent to which Africans have identified political with religious symbols, and may continue to do so, it remains of foremost importance (cf. Evans-Pritchard and Fortes, 1940, pp. 16-23).

To put it in another way, the viability of these movements is said to hinge on the organizational retionality that is produced in African societies in the processes of modernization. Greater rationality, it is supposed will militate against them. But it may be argued that some of these movements, despite their minority status, might be rationally employed as religious vehicles of national integration. This would be particularly likely with those that have attained pan-tribal distribution, such as Bwiti in Gabon, Aladura in West Africa and Kitawala in Central Africa. In the late 1950s there seemed to be this possibility with the Lumpa church. Otherwise whatever organizational rationality is achieved, if colonial domination in Africa is replaced by a sense of ethnic domination, the situation of sub-ordination and deprivation will persist and continue to produce religious movements of a compensatory character.

As for the movements themselves, it remains true that their

survival depends upon their powers of organization, in terms of long-term goals and a correlated senstivity to the larger situations of which they are a part.[13] If we return to our scheme we recognize that those movements which have persisted longest are those which have stayed within or passed into the instrumental hemisphere. Similarly Voget (1956, p.259), in his study of American Indian movements, notes 'a progression towards more secular, pragmatic and accommodative adjustment'.

The survival capacity of religious movements is thus roughly predictable by reference to the rapidity of their shift away from expressive and totally traditional orientation. Prolonged inertia as a messianic or nativist movement seriously diminishes its viability.

What seems to be implied in a broader frame of reference by our scheme is a movement from religion to politics. This is surely the tendency though not an inevitable one, and we cannot exclude, for reasons which we have exposed, the possibility of moves from politics to religion.[14] Nor should this tendency be taken to imply that politics is in every way a functional alternative to religion, or that religion is inert as an instrument of politics. In fact, the scheme we employ suggests, without specific reference to politics or religion, that there are varying proportions of instrumental and expressive tendencies in all acts and institutions. In fact, every viable institution must strike an appropriate balance for its circumstances between the instrumental and the expressive. There must therefore be numbers of African religious movements which combine a 'right' proportion of the expressive and the instrumental for the times, both adapting the group to the larger situation while at the same time providing adjustment for the individuals involved by expressive techniques.

What this optimum proportion may be in the changing Africans situation remains to be ascertained. That it will be primarily instrumental seems clear. That it will be exclusively instrumental seems doubtful. These movements, in short, embody many cultural imperatives, primarily expressive techniques which can and will facilitate African adjustments to modernization, just as they provided adjustment to the colonial situation. In other words, African politics, should its instrumentalism lead to abolish African religious movements as irrational and intractable enclaves, must still provide some the of the gratifications previously referred in these movements.

References

Andersson, E. (1958), *Messianic Movements in the Lower Congo*, Almquist och Wiksell.

Baeta, C.G. (1962), *Prophetism in Ghana*, S.C.M. Press.

Balandier, G. (1955), *Sociologie actuelle d'Afrique noire*, Presses Universitaires.

Balandier, G. (1957), *Afrique Ambigue, Plon.*

Blanton, M. (1963), *'African prophets', Race*, vol. 5.

Cunison, I. (1951), 'A Watchtower assembly in Central Africa'. *Int. Rev. Miss.*, vol.40.

Evans-Pritchard, E.E. and Fortes, M. (1940), *African Political Systems,* Oxford University Press.

Fernandez, J.W. (1964), 'The idea and symbol of the saviour in a Gabon syncretist cult,' *int, Rev. Miss.*, vol.53, pp.281-91.

Field, M.J. (1960), *search for security*, Faber.

Fisher, H.J. (1963), Ahmadiyyah – *A Study in Contemporary Islam on the West African Coast*, Oxford University Press.

Herskovits, M.J. (1962). *The Human Factor in Changing Africa*, Knopf.

Hamil, A.N. (1963), 'The Salifiiya movement in Morocco the religious bases of the Morocan National Movement, *Mid. East. Affairs*, no.3, pp.90-105.

Kopytoff, I. (1963), African religious movements: indigenous versus acculturative factors, unpublished manuscript.

Linton, R. (1943), 'Nativistic movements', *Amer. Anthrop.*, vol.65, pp.230-40.

Marwick, M. (1950), 'Another modern anti-witchcraft movement in East Central Africa', *Africa* vol. 20, pp. 100-12.

Mitchell, R.L. (1963), The Aladura movement among the Yoruba in Nigeria, unpublished manuscript.

Parrinder, G. (1953), *Religion in an African City*, Oxford University Press.

Parsons, T. 91951), *The Social System*, Free Press of Glencoe.

Paulme, G. (1962), 'Une religion syncrétique en Cate d'Ivoire', *Cahiers d'études Africaines*, vol. 3, pp. 5-90.

Richards, A.I. (1935), 'A Modern movement in Witch-finders', *Africa*, vol. 8, pp.448-61.

Rotberg, R. (1961), 'The Lenshina movement of Northern Rhodesia', *The Rhodes – Livingstone* Inst. J., vol. 29, pp. 63-70.

Schlösser, K. (1949), *Propheten in Afrika*, Braunschweig.

Shepperson, G. (1962), 'Nyasaland and the millennium', in S.L. Thrupp, ed., *Millennial Dreams in Action*, Mouton.

Shepperson, G., and Price, T. (1958), *Independent African John Chilembwe and Nyasaland Native Rising of 1915*, Mouton.

Spiro, H.J. (1962), 'Comparative politics – a comprehensive approach *Amer. polit., Scien., Rev.*, vol. 41, pp. 577-95.

Sundkler, B. (1961), *Bantu Prophets in South Africa*, Butterworth.

Taylor, J.V., and Lehmann, D. (1961), *Christians of the Copperbelt*, S.C.M. Press.

Turner, H.W. (1962), 'The Church of the Lord', *J. Afr. Hist.*, vol. 3. pp. 91-110.

Voget, F.W. (1956), 'The American Indian in transition reformation and accommodation' *Amer, Anthrop.*, vol. 58. pp.249-63.

Welbourn, F.B. (1961), *East African Rebels a study of some Independent Churches*, S.C.M. Press.

Worseley, P. (1957). *The Trumpet Shall Sound*, McGibbon & Kee.

Zessner, W. (1961), 'Co-operation and competition in geometric vectorial symbolism,; in M. Mead, ed., *Co-operation competition among Primitive Peoples*. McGraw Hill.

NOTES

1. The types we propose are simple not complex ideal types. They and not mutually exclusive. The features defining the type are fewer than those possessed by any member within the type. The discussion is from the observer's rather than the participant's point of view.

2. See Jamil (1963) and fisher (1963). It is clear that Islam in

the Maghreb and west Africa can almost be regarded as one long succession of religious movements.

3. What is remarkable in the evangelization of Africa is the general tolerance with which it was at first received. This testifies to African religious electicism and to the identification of Christianity with the material benefits of European civilization. The failure of evangelical Christianity to produce these goods was one of the frustrations which gave arise to religious movements which have sought these by other means. Most clearly evident in the Cargo Cults of Melanesia, this is present as well in Africa. George Shepperson notes and similarity between the Cargo Cults and Nyasaland religious movements, and refers to Livingstone's view that 'Africans identified the coming of the missionary with the arrival of cornucopia of material goods' (Shepperson, 1962, pp.19 and 146).

4. We ignore here the impact of traders, which in most cases was transitory, and their contacts limited to the trading situation.

5. Kopytoff (1963) identifies the Holy Water movement in the south western Congo as just one in a long series of re-examination of religious and magical technology with the object of replacing the outmonded and fatigued with more vigorous forms. Because of a very few items like the Holy Water itself we tend, he points out, to see this as a specific response to the colonial situation. But the colonial situation was not the first disaster and frustration faced by the Suku.

6. The expressive-instrumental continuum is basic in the work of Talcott Parsons (1951, p.348). He says of the expressive orientation: "The essential point is the primacy of "acting out" the need disposition itself rather than subordinating gratification to a goal outside the immediate situation.'

7. It should be repeated that this is an analytic distinction; no religious movement is exclusively instrumental or expressive, nor could it be. We are concerned with the relative primacy of one mode or another of action. Know-

ledge of the relative primacy is of value in assessing the order of minorities in a movement's economy and is useful in predicting its capacity to survive.

8. Herbert J. Spiro (1962) makes highly illuminating use such a scheme in his article. Walter Zessner (1961) makes a similar presentation called by him geometric vectorial symbolism. Such diagrams have, he maintains, inherent advantages over descriptive language. Both schemes are more comprehensive than the one presented here. They attempt to assess the cycle of activities within a system, they embody more dimensions and they imply what is equilbrium and disequilbrium, symmetry and asymmetry, in a given system. I am elsewhere elaborating the scheme presented here.

9. Such separatist movements as the *Apostolowa Fe Dedefia Habobo* the Apostolic Revealation Society) in Ghana, as described by Baeta (1962), pp.77-93, have many of the instrumental characteristics of improvement associations. On the other hand south African separatist churches, though sensitive to their relationship to the larger society, strongly support apartheid and the social *status quo*. Sundkler (1961), pp. 310-11, however, makes clear that this support is strongest from those movements of a zionist, that is, messianic disposition.

10. Recent research by Mitchell (1963) shows a preoccupation with alleviating the physical and spiritual sufferings of members by expressive techniques. His insistence that the Aladura movement must be studied from 'the perspective of the Protestant religious system' confirms in our view, however, its separatist character.

11. The term reformative is taken from Voget (1956, p.250) who defines as 'conscious creative attempt on the part of a subordinate group to obtain a personal and social reintegration through a selective rejection modification and synthesis of both traditional and alien cultural comunenements'. He suggests that these movements are the most stable and induring – most successfully providing for dignified accomodation with universalistic pan-ethnic

implications. In fact Pan-Africanism may well most solidly on an instrumental approach consciously combining old and new. This kind of posture is, of course, difficult to maintin.

12. Balandier points to reformative tendencies; see (1955, pp.434-5).

13. This is not to deny the importance of the attitude taken by the main forces in the superordinate, that is, outside situation. An expressive, tradition-oriented movement can survive for a very long time if the administration takes a permissive view, and of the world-view implied by the cult's symbolism does not too strongly imply their elimination. However, the administration, whether colonial or independent, is invariably goal minded and instrumental, and therefore in fundamental tension with the more expressive and traditional movements. Thus with Bwiti in Gabon, despite its modest instrumentalism, it is nevertheless the constant complaint of the present administration that 'dancing all night and eating *eboka* does not much contribute to the building of modern Gabon'. 'Think how much energy is going into that which could be going into road, building', said one administrator.

14. Worsley in his New Guinea study is led to distinguish between activist and passivist movements. All the former movements ultimately result in the emergence of secular political organization, or failing him are eventually themselves led, much in the manner of the South African separatists, to a state of passive resignation. See Worseley (1957), p.236.

Chapter-9

Gods, Magicians and Priests

M. WEBER

Chapter-9

Just as the forms of the gods vary, depending on natural and social conditions, so too there are variations in the potential of a God to achieve primacy in the pantheon, or to monopolized divinity. Only Judaism and Islam are strictly monotheistic in their essence. The Hindu and Christian forms of the sole or supreme deity are theological concealments of the fact that an important and unique religious interest, namely in salvation through the incarnation of divinity, stands in the way of strict monothesim. The path to monothesim has been traversed with varying degrees of consistency but nowhere was the existence of spirits and demons permanently eliminated. Even in the Reformation spirits and demons were simply subordinated unconditionally to the one God, at least in theory.

The decisive consideration was and remains: who is deemed to exert the stronger influence on the individual in his everyday life, the theoretically supreme God or the lower spirits and demons? If the spirits, then the religion of everyday life is decisively determined by them, regardless of the official God-concept of the ostensibly rationalized religion. Where a political God of a locality developed, it was natural enough that he frequently achieved primacy. Whenever a plurality of settled communities with established local gods expanded the area of their political association through conquest the usual result was that various local gods of a religious totality. Within this amalgamated totality, the empirical and functional specializations of the gods, whether original or subsequently determined by new experiences concerning the special spheres of the gods influences, would reappear in a division of labor, with varying degrees of clarity.

M.Weber, *The Sociology of Religion* Beacon Press, 1963. chapter 2. (First Published 1920).

The local deities of the most important political and religious centers (and hence of the rulers and priests in these centers), e.g Marduk of Babel or Amon of Thebes, advanced to the rank of the highest gods, only to disappear again with the eventual destruction or removal of the residence, as happened in the case of Assur after the fall of the Assyrian empire. Once a political association as such has come to be regarded as a society under the tutelage of a particular deity, it would seem to be unprotected until the gods of the individual members were also incorporated, amalgamated and even adopted locally in a sort of synoecism. This practice, common in antiquity, was re-enacted when the great sacred reilcs of the provincial cathedrals were transferred to the capital of d unified Russian empire.

The possible combinations of the various principles involved in the construction of a pantheon or in the achievement of a position of primacy by one or another god are almost infinite in number. Indeed, the jurisdictions of the divine figures are as fluid as those of the officials of patrimonial regimes. Moreover, the differentiation between jurisdictions of the various gods is inter sected by thc practice of religious attachment or courtesy to particular god who is especially cultivated or directly invoked and who is treated as functionally universal. Thus all possible functions are attributed to the universal god, even functions which ha' been assigned previously to other deities. This is the 'henotheism, which Max Muller erroneously assumed to constitute a special stage of evolution. In the attainment of primacy by a particular god, purely rational factors have often played an important concommitant role. Wherever a considerable measure of constancy in regard to certain prescriptions became clearly evident—most often in the case of stereotyped and fixed religious rites—and where this was recognized by rationalized religious thought, then the deities that evinced the greatest regularity in their behavior namely the gods of heaven and the stars had a chance to achieve primacy.

Yet in the routinized religion of everyday life *(Alltagsreligiositat),* only a comparatively minor role was played by those gods who, because they exerted a major influence upon universal natural phenomena, were interpreted by metaphysical speculation as very important and occasionally even as world creators. The reason for this is that these natural phenomena vary but little in their course, and hence it is not necessary to resort in everyday religious practice to the devices of sorcerers and priests in order to influence them. A particular god might be of decisive importance for the entire religion of a people (e.g. Osiris in Egypt) if he met a pressing religious need, in this case a soteriological one; it even so, he might not achieve primacy in the pantheon. The process of rationalization *(ratio)* favored the primacy of universal gods; and every consistent crystallization of a pantheon followed systematic rational principles to some degree, since it was always influenced by professional sacerdotal rationalism or by the national striving for order on the part of secular individuals. Above all, it is the aforementioned relationship of the rational regularity of the stars in their heavenly courses, as regulated by line order, to the inviolable sacred social order in terrestrial affairs, that makes the universal gods the responsible guardians of both these phenomena. Upon these gods depend both rational economic practice and the secure, regulated hegemony of sacred norms in the social community. The priests are the primary protagonists and representatives of these sacred norms. Hence be competition of the stellar deities Varuna and Mithra, the guardians of the sacred order, with the storm god Indra, a formidable warrior and the slayer of the dragon, was a reflection the conflict between the priesthood, striving for a firm regulation and control of life, and the powerful warlike nobility. Among his warrior class, the appropriate reaction to supernatural powers was to believe in a heroic god avid for martial exploits as well as in the disorderly irrationality of fate and adventure someness. We shall find this same contrast significant in many other contexts.

The ascension of celestial or astral gods in the pantheon is advanced by a priesthood's propagation of systematized sacred ordinances, as in India, Iran or Babylonia, and is assisted by a rationalized system of regulated subordination of subjects to their overlords, such as we find in the bureaucratic states of China and Babylonia. In Babylonia, religion plainly evolved toward a belief in the dominion of the stars, particularly the planets, over all things, from the days of the week to the fate of the individual the afterworld. Development in this direction culminates in astrological fatalism. But this development is actually a product of later sacerdotal lore, and it is still unknown to the national religion of the politically independent state. A god may dominate a pantheon without being an international or universal deity, a transnational god of the entire world. But his dominance of a pantheon usually suggests that he is on his way to becoming that.

As reflection concerning the gods deepened, it was increasingly felt that the existence and nature of the deity must be established unequivocally and that the god should be 'universal' in this sense of unequivocal. Among the Greeks, philosophers interpreted whatever gods were found elsewhere as equivalent to and so identical with the deities of the moderately organized Greek pantheon. This tendency toward universalization grew with the increasing predominance of the primary god of the pantheon, that is, as he assumed more of a 'monotheistic' character. The growth of a world empire in China, the extension of the power of the Brahman caste throughout all the varied political formations in India, and the development of the Persian and Roman empire: favored the rise of both universalism and monotheism, though not always in the same measure and with quite different degree of success.

The growth of empire (or other comparable social processes that tend in the same direction) has by no means been the sole or indispensable lever for the accomplishment of this development. In the Yahweh cult, a case of fundamental importance in the history of religion, there evolved at least an approach to universalistic monotheism, namely monolatry, as a result of concrete historic event the formation of a confederacy. In this case, universalism was a product of international politics, which the pragmatic interpreters were the prophetic protagonist of the cult of Yahweh and the ethics enjoined by him. As consequence of their preaching, the deeds of other nations that were profoundly affecting Israel's vital interests also came to be regarded as wrought by Yahweh. At this point one can see clearly the distinctively and eminently *historical* character of the theorizing of the Hebrew prophets, which stands in sharp contrast in the speculations concerning nature characteristic of the priesthoods of India and Babylonia. Equally striking is the ineluctable obligation resulting from Yahweh's promises: the necessity of interpreting the entire history of the Hebrew nation as consisting the deeds of Yahweh and hence as constituting a pattern of history. In view of the many dire threats to the people's rival, its history appeared contradictory to the divine promises, as well as inextricably interwined with the destinies of other nations. Thus, the ancient warrior god of the confederacy, who become the local god of the city of Jerusalem, took on the prophetic and universalistic traits of transcendently sacred omnipotence and inscrutability.

In Egypt, the monotheistic, and hence necessarily universalistic, transition of Amenhotep IV (lkhnaton) to the solar cult resulted on an entirely different situation. One factor was again the extensive rationalism of the priesthood, and in all likelihood of laity as well, which was of a purely naturalistic character, in marked contrast to Israelite prophecy. Another factor was the practical need of a monarch at the head of a bureaucratic totalitarian state to break the power of the priests by eliminating the multiplicity of sacerdotal gods, and to restore the ancient power the deified Pharaoh by elevating the monarch to the position supreme solar priest. On the other hand, the universalistic monotheism of Christianity and Islam must be regarded as derivative of Judaism, while the relative monotheism of Zoroastrianism was in all likelihood determined at least in part by near Eastern other than intra-Iranian influences. All of these monotheisms were critically influenced by the distinctive character of 'ethical' prophecy, rather than by the 'exemplary' type[1]. All other relatively monotheistic and universalistic developments are the products of the philosophical speculations of priests and laymen. They achieved practical religious importance only when they became associated with the quest for salvation.

Almost everywhere a beginning was made toward some form of consistent monotheism, but practical impediments thwarted its development in the workaday mass religion *(Alltagsreligion)*, with the exceptions of Judaism, Islam and Protestant Christianity, here are different reasons for the failure of a consistent monotheism to develop in different cultures, but the main reason was 'generally the pressure of the powerful material and ideological interests vested in the priests, who resided in the cultic centers and regulated the cults of the particular gods. Still another impediment to the development of monotheism was the religious need the laity for an accessible and tangible familiar religious object which could be brought into relationship with concrete situations or with definite groups of people to the exclusion of outsiders, an object which would above all be accessible magical influences. The security provided by a tested magic manipulation is more reassuring than the experience of shipping a god who—precisely because he is omnipotent—is not subject to magical influence. The crystallization of develop conceptions of supernatural forces as gods, even as a single transcendent god, by no means automatically eliminated ancient magical notions, not even in Christianity. It did produce however, the possibility of a dual relationship between men and the supernatural. This must now be discussed.

A power conceived by analogy to living persons may be coerced into the service of man, just as the naturalistic power a spirit could be coerced. Whoever possesses the requisite charisma for employing the proper means is stronger even then the god, whom he can compel to do his will. In these case religious behavior is not worship of the god but rather of the god, and invocation is not prayer but rather the exercise of magical formula Such is one ineradicable basis of popular religion, particularly in India. Indeed, such coercive religion universally diffused, and even the Catholic priest continues practice something of this magical power in executing the miracle of the mass and in exercising the power of the keys. By and large this is the original, though not exclusive, origin of the original and mimetic components of the religious cult - especially of song dance, drama and the typical fixed formulae of prayer.

The process of anthropomorphization may take the form of attributing to the gods the human behavior patterns appropriate to a mighty terrestrial potentate, whose freely disposed favor be obtained by entreaty, gifts, service, tributes, cajolery and bribes. On the other hand, his favor may be earned as a consequence of the devotee's own faithfulness and good conduct in conformity with the divine will. In these ways, the gods are conceived by analogy to earthly rulers: mighty beings whose power differs only in degree, at least at first. As gods of this type evolve, worship 'divinity comes to be regarded as a necessity.

The two characteristic elements of 'divine worship', prayer sacrifice, have their origin in magic. In prayer, the boundary been magical formula and supplication remains fluid. The technically rationalized enterprise of prayer (in the form of prayer 'wheels and similar devices, or of prayer strips hung in the wind attached to icons of gods or saints, or of carefully measured wreaths of roses—virtually all of which are products of the methodical compulsion of the gods by the Hindus) everywhere stands closer to magic than to entreaty, individual prayer as real supplication is found in religions that are otherwise undifferentiated, It in most cases such prayer has a purely business-like, rationalized form that sets forth the achievem- ents of the supplicant on behalf of the god and then claims adequate recompense therefore.

Sacrifice, at its first appearance, is a magical instrumentality that in part stands at the immediate service of the coercion of the gods. For the gods also need the soma juice of the sorcerer-priests, substance which engenders their ecstasy and enables them to reform their deeds. This is the ancient notion of the Aryans as why it is possible to coerce the gods by sacrifice. it may even held that a pact can be concluded with the gods which imposes obligations on both parties; this was the fateful conception of the Israelitis in particular. Still another view of sacrifice holds that a it is means of deflecting, through magical media, the wrath of god upon another object, a scapegoat or above all a human sacrifice.

But another motive for sacrifice may be of greater importance, and it is probably older too: the sacrifice, especially of animals, intended as a *communio*, a ceremony of eating together which serves to produce a fraternal community between the sacrificers and the god. This represents a transformation in the significance of 'the even older notion that to rend and consume a strong (and or a sacred) animal enables the eaters to absorb its potencies. Some such older magical meaning—and there are various other possibilities—may still provide the act of sacrifice with its essential, even after genuine cultic views have come to exert considerable influence. Indeed, such a magical significance may even regain dominance over the cultic meaning. The sacrificial rituals of the Brahmins, and even of the Atharva Veda, were aim purely sorcery, in contrast to the cultic sacrifices of the ancient Nordics. On the other hand, there are many departures for magic, as when sacrifices are interpreted as tribute. First it may be sacrificed in order that the god may not deprive man of enjoyment of the remaining fruits; and sacrifice is often interpreted as a self-imposed punishment or sacrificial sin-offering that averts the wrath of the gods before it fails upon the sacrificer. To be sure, this does not yet involve any awareness of sin, and, initially takes place in a mood of cool and calculated trading, as for example in India.

An increasing predominance of non-magical motives is later brought about by the growing recognition of the power of a god and of his character as a personal overlord. The god becomes great lord who may fail on occasion, and whom one cannot approach with devices of magical compulsion, but only with entreaties and gifts. But if these motives add anything new to mere wizardry, it is initially something as sober and rational motivation of magic itself. The pervasive and central theme *do ut des*. This aspect clings to the routine and the mass religion behavior of all peoples at all times and in all religions. The normal situation is that the burden of all prayers, even in the most other-worldly religions, is the aversion of the external evils of this world and the inducement of the external advantages of the world.

Every aspect of religious phenomena that points beyond evil and advantages in this world is the work of a special evolutionary process, one characterized by distinctively dual' aspects. On the other hand, there is an ever-broadening rational systematization of the god concept and of the thinking concerning the possible relationships of man to the divine. On the other hand, there ensues a characteristic recession of the original, practical and calculating rationalism. As such primitive rationalism precedes, the significance of distinctively religious behavior is sought less and less in the purely external advantages of everyday economic success. Thus the goal of religious behavior is successively ' irrationalized' until finally otherworldly non-economic goals come to represent what is distinctive in religious behavior. But the extra-economic resolution just described requires as one of its prerequisites he existence of specific personal carriers of the otherworldly goals.

The relationships of men to supernatural forces which take he forms of' prayer, sacrifice and worship nay be termed 'cult religion', as distinguished from 'sorcery', which is magical coercion. Correspondingly, those beings that are worshipped and treated religiously may be termed 'gods', in contrast to 'demons', which are magically coerced and charmed. There may no instance in which it is possible to apply this differentiation 'absolutely, since the cults we have **just** called 'religious' practically everywhere contain numerous magical components. The historical development of the aforementioned differentiation frequently came about in a very simple fashion when a secular or priestly power suppressed a cult in favor of a new religion, with older gods continuing to live on as demons.

The sociological aspect of this differentiation is the rise of the priesthood ' as something distinct from ' practitioners of magic'. Applied to reality, this contrast is fluid, as are all sociological phenomena. Even the theoretical differentiae of these types are not unequivocally determinable. Following the distinction between 'cult' and 'sorcery', one may contrast those professional functionaries who influence the gods by means of worship with those magicians who coerce demons by magical means; but in any great religions, including Christianity, the concept of the priest includes such a magical qualification.

Or the term 'priest' may be applied to the functionaries of a regularly organized and permanent enterprise concerned with influencing the gods, in contrast with the individual and occasional efforts of magiciàns. Even this contrast is bridged over by a sliding scale of transitions, but as a pure type the priesthood is 'unequivocal and can be said to be characterized by the presence of certain fixed cultic centers associated with some actual cultic apparatus.

Or it may be thought that what is decisive for the concept of priesthood is that the functionaries, regardless of whether their office is hereditary or personal, be actively associated with some of social organization, of which they are employees or organs pertaining in the interests of the organization's members, in contrast with magicians, who are self-employed. Yet even this distinction, which is clear enough conceptually, is fluid in activity. The sorcerer is not infrequently a member of an organized guild, and is occasionally the member of a hereditary caste which may hold a monopoly of magic within the particular Community. Even the Catholic priest is not always the occupant of official post. In Rome he is occasionally a poor mendicant who lives a hand-to-mouth existence from the proceeds of single masses, the acquisition of which he solicits.

'Yet another distinguishing quality of the priest, it is asserted is his professional equipment of special knowledge, fixed doctrine and vocational qualifications, which brings him into contrast with sorcerers, prophets and other types of religious functionaries who exert their influence by virtue of personal gifts (charisma made manifest in miracle and revelation. But this again is simple and absolute distinction, since the sorcerer may sometime be very learned, while deep learning need not always character working priests. Rather, the distinction between priest and magician must be established qualitatively with reference to it different nature of the learning in the two cases. As a matter of fact we must later, in our exposition of the forms of domination distinguish the rational training and discipline of priests from the different preparation of charismatic magicians. The latter preparation proceeds in part as an 'awakening education' using irrational means and aiming at rebirth, and proceeds in part as training in purely empirical lore. But in this case also, the two contrasted types flow into one another.

'Doctrine' has already been advanced as one of the fundamental traits of the priesthood. We may assume that the on standing marks of doctrine are the development of a rational system of religious concepts and (what is of the utmost importance for us here) the development of a systematic and distinctively religious ethic based upon a consistent and stable doctrine which purports to be a 'revelation'. An example is found in Islam which contrasted its scriptural religion with simple paganism. But this description of priesthood and this assumption about the nature of doctrine would exclude from the concept of priesthood the

Japanese Shinto priests and such functionaries as the mighty hierocrats of the Phoenicians. The adoption of such an assumption would have the effect of making the decisive characteristic of the priesthood a function which, while admittedly important, not universal.

It is more correct for our purpose, in order to do justice to the diverse and mixed manifestations of this phenomenon, to set up the crucial feature of the priesthood the specialization of a particular group of persons in the continuous operation of a cultic enterprise, permanently associated with particular norms, places and times, and related to special social groups. There can be 'no priesthood without a cult, although there may well be a cult without a specialized priesthood. The latter was the ease in China, here state officials and the heads of households exclusively conducted the services of the official gods and the ancestral spirits. On the other hand, both novitiate and doctrine are to be found among typical, pure magicians, as in the brotherhood of the Hametze among the Indians, and elsewhere in the world. These magicians may wield considerable power, and their essentially magical celebrations may play a central role in the life of their people. Yet they lack a continuously operative cult, and so the term 'priests' cannot be applied to them.

A rationalization of metaphysical views and a specifically religious ethic are usually missing in the ease of a cult without priests, in the case of a magician without a cult. The full development both a metaphysical rationalization and a religious ethic requires an independent and professionally trained priesthood, permanently occupied with the cult and with the practical problems involved in the cure of souls. Consequently, ethics developed into something quite different from a metaphysically rationalized religion in classic Chinese thought, which lacked an independent priesthood and this also happened with the ethics of ancient Buddhism, which lacked both cult and priesthood.

Moreover, the rationalization of religious life was fragmentary entirely missing wherever the priesthood failed to achieve dependent class status, as in classical antiquity. Wherever a class of primitive magicians and sacred musicians did rationalize magic, but failed to develop a genuinely sacerdotal occupational pattern (as was the case with the Brahmans in India), the priesthood developed in a rather strange way. Not every genuine priesthood developed the distinguishing features of a rational metaphysic and a religious ethic. Such developments generally (though there were exceptions) presupposed the operation of one or both of two forces outside the preisthood: prophets, the bearers of metaphysical or religious ethical revelation, and the laity, the non-priestly devotees of the cult.

NOTES

1. For Weber's account of these types see above, p.39, -Ed.

Chapter-10
Diviners in Dinkaland

G. LIENHARDT

Chapter-10

All Dinka assert that divinity is one, *nhialic ee tok*. The implications of this affirmation are that their for is the same divinity as that which different peoples know under different names, the divinity the Nuer call '*Knwoth*', the Muslims 'Allah', the Christians 'God' and so on. Yet *nhialic* is also a comprehensive term for a number of conceptions which differ considerable from each others. Powers of which the most important religiously are those I have called free divinities and clan divinities, are distinct from each other, though of most of the, the Dinka may say simply ee *nhialic*, 'It is Divinity'. This unity and multiplicity of Divinity causes no difficulty in the context of Dinka language and life, but it is impossible entirely to avoid the logical and semantic problems which arise when Dinka statements bearing upon it are translated , together into English.

The most important and active of the free divinities known in western Dinkaland are Deng, Garang, Macardit and Abuk. Deng, Garang and Macar are common personal names for men and Abuk is probably the commonest name for women, so here the names of the free divinities appear in italic letters to distinguish them from human personal names. Among the Agar and Cic Dinka, another free divinity called *Loi* is also important, but knowledge of this divinity had not spread farther westwards during my visits to Dinkaland, ending in 1950.[1] Elsewhere in Dinkaland there are others, which are unkwnon in the west, or have been forgotten in all but name because they are thought no longer to be active there.[2]

None of the free divinites, with the possible exception of *Macardit*, also sometimes called *Colwic*, is thought to exist independently of the particular name by which the Dinka know it. That is, unlike Divinity, who is thought to be universal and

---

Excerpts from chapter 2 of G. Lienhardt. *Divinity and Experience*, Clarendon Press, 1961, pp.56-7, 64-74.

known by various names to different peoples, the free divinities are active only where their specific names are known and where effects in human life can be attributed to them.

Free divinities make their presence known by causing illness, by possessing human beings and announcng through their mouths their names and demands, and sometimes by speaking in dreams. They do not, strictly speaking, *appear*, for in themselves they are held to be formless, though each has a set of colour and other associations. [...]

There are several categories of 'religious' specialist (I here use the term widely) in Dinka society and the boundaries between some of them are not very clearly defined. The permanent hereditary preisthood of master of the fishing-spear is described elsewhere.[3] Here we consider those seers, diviners and prophets whose powers, unlike those of the priests, are not necessarily hereditary.

I first consider and then dismiss as marginal a number of magical practitioners whose powers reside in their possession of fetish bundles, which they may have bought or inherited. A man who possesses such fetishes is called *ran (lo) wal,*' a person with medicine'. *Wal* is the term for grass and vegetable life generally, and hence for medicine, in the dual sense of herbal remedies and magical medicines. Among the western Dinka the most famous of such magical medicines is one called *Mathiang gok*, though the varieties of wal may by as numerous as the private superstitions of which individuals are capable. *Mathiang gok*, however, is the very type of potent medicine possessed by medicine men , and a brief account of it will be enough to suggest the nature of all; as I have said, they are not to be regarded as of great religious importance, and the Dinka themselves are quick to point out the difference between the characters and abilities of such earthly medicines and their owners, and those of priests and prophets. In their roles as such.[4] I say 'in their roles', because anyone may possess and use such medicines; they serve individual human ends and, as individual human beings, priests and prophets may acquire them like anyone else. I think, however, that they are less likely to do so, as although they fear them they pretend to despise them.

Mathiang gok, like other medicines of a magical nature, is in the general category of powers, *jok*. It resides in the physical fetish bundle and can be bought with it; but its action is of a spiritual nature, and is attributed to a power informing the fetish bundle but which also moves outside it, to effect the consciences and fortunes of men against whom it is directed. *Mathiang gok* is called a 'black power' (*joing col*), or sometimes an 'earth power' (*jong piny*), to distinguish it and other medicines of its kind form the higher powers, the divinities.

I do not know what the physical constituents of a *mathiang gok* bundle are; the one I saw consisted of bits of unidenifiable wood and withered roots, and I think that roots of some kind are always included. The connexion of the medicine with the earth is thus perhaps reinforced, for I do not think that among the various material things associated with the higher powers, the divinities, there are any which come from under the ground. The name, *Mathiang gok*, is not given any consistent etymology by the Dinka. *Mathiang* indisputably means 'dark brown', but it might also be a man's name, as is supposed by Captain Fergusson.[5] *Gok* similarly may been told by a Dinka that the name means 'brown dove', since, he said, the name of the medicine *may really be mathiang guk, and guk is a dove. Yet I cannot think that this is more than a piece of ad hoc etymology, since in Dinka the adjective follows the noun and 'brown dove' would correctly be guk mathiang.*

The circumstances in which *Mathiang gok* is thought to operate and its mode of operation, are consistently described by all Dinka. Its main function is to obtain for its possessor and influences over those whom he thinks to have wronged him, particularly to enforce the payment of cattle debts. Its mode of operation is said to be as follows. A man has enemies, or he has a grudge against others for keeping for him what is rightfully his own. He does not feel strong enough to obtain his rights without the assistance of a power which will work for him individually. Perhaps invocation of divinity has been of no avail. He therefore buys *mathiang gok*, a purchase which will normally involve a trip to another part of the country, or into the land of the non-Dinka peoples to the south. People may suspect what this trip is for; they will not be quite sure, as a Dinka does not usually piblicly admit to the possession *mathiang gok* and it is not lightly spoken about. This may be partly because the Government has imposed heavy penalties on those who are found with it, though I doubt of it is these alone which surround the transaction with secrecy. The Dinka themselves tolerate, but do not really approve, dealing which involve the manipulation of amoral medicines for purely individual ends. Members of any particualr group of Dinka are convnced that *mathiang gok* is a foreging importation, some say for the Agar Dinka, who say it comes from the non-Dinka ('Jur Beli and Sofi) to the south and some even say it comes from the Nuer, who also know it, but trace it to the Dinka.

The man returns and hides the bundle of roots somewhere in his cattle byre. For time to time he speaks to it and tells it his desires, and will also make it small offerings. It, in its turn, will demand sacrifices, which may be covertly carried out, or which may be secretly included by the man in the intention of other sacrifices made to powers which are not in the same way publicly disapproved. In return for these attentions, *mathiang gok* will go out after a man who owes its owner it owner cattle. The Dinka say that it will come to such a man when he is walking alone, and will speak to him and threaten to injure him or his family unless the debt is paid. It may go further, and actually kill an enemy of its owner by causing swellings, most commonly in the throat and head or in the belly. A man intimidated by *mathiang gok* will often pay his debts, though a man who feels himself to have wrongly injured violence of he is sure of the source of his suffering.

I have found that Dinka are never prepared to admit that they are quite sure that a man possesses or is using *mathiang gok* until a further stage is reaches, that is until a man, having by recourse *mathiang gok* obtained what he desires, is many years later taken seriously ill himself. He may then either announce himself that he has in the past bought *mathiang gok* to which he has for long failed to pay appropriate attentions, or a diviner will distribute his sickness or death openly to this cause. Then the possession of *mathiang gok* by the man is openly admitted, and sacrifice is made to the power to try to divert its wrath from the neglectful owner. By this time, of course, the original disputes and enmities for which the *mathiang gok* was obtained are probably no longer live issues, though the Dinka are less sympathetic towards its owner and victim than they are to those who suffer through the unsought intervention of a higher power, which they have themselves attempted to harness to their own individual advantage.

Anyone may be a *ran (lo) wal*, one who possesses medicines. More specifically, however, a *ran wal*, 'medicine-man', is one who is suspected of trafficking in medicines, and though he may not himself admit to possessing them knows their qualities and knows where to get them. a medicine-man is the lowest form of specialist in control and knowledge of powers, just as medicine bundles are informed with the lowest, if yet dangerous and fearful, powers. A *ran wal* is usually, I think, in any part of Dinkaland, a visitor, perhaps an itinerant Nuer or Dinka. Such people may purvey roots and charms as no permanent member of a Dinka village could, for by selling medicines or admitting to their possession within his own community a man would also be suspected of causing the sickenss of his neighbours. The line between *ran wal* and *apeth*, the possessor of the evil eye, is often not very clearly drawn; both injure others for their own advantage, whatever their justification may be thought to be.

Though 'medicines' like *mathiang gok* are thought to inhere sufficiently in particular bundless of roots to make it possible to transfer them with roots, and to regard them as residing in the roots, they are yet not toally bound to their material homes. Their influence or virtue their power emanates for them and its action is upon the mind and hearts of men as well as upon their physical health. So even these lower powers transcend any material form with which they are associated. There is no question for example, of sample contagious magic in the use of fetish bundles. They 'speak' to men or we might say to men's consciences, for we cannot fail to notice how like the workings of our 'conscience' is the action attributed to them and when they speak to men, they are not necessarily visually imaged. I have heard it said that *mathiang gok* may speak, when conjured by a diviner, from the walls of a cattle byre, and that it has no occassions appeared to people in the form of a small brown dog. When functioning as a power it does not seem to appear to others in the from of a bundle of roots, though this is known by all to be its physical basis and vehicle, as far as transmission from hand to hand is concerned. The active principle even of this lowly power capable of being detached, in thought, from any specific material form in which it may be supposed at times to inhere, and this is true of the relation between any power and its emblem. It is never, among the Dinka, simply material things in themselves which are of central religious importance, but something formless, immaterial, invisible, associated with them.

Much higher in esteem than men who possess only such fetish bundles are people called *tyet (pl tilt)*, a class of specialists that comprises individuals of widely differing reputations for occult knowledge and powers. I begin with a brief description of one of the least of them, one of those who may also be called *Acoor, Acoor* is related to the world car, meaning to divine, and is also I think connected with the word *coor*, blind, blind people may often be thought to have special insight. It could be unlikely that any *tyet* with a high reputation would be spoken of as *acoor*, though an *acoor* would also be referred to as *tyet* by those who thought highly of him. Diviniers of lower and higher reputation stand in a relationship similar to that between minor fortune tellers and will-known clairvoyants in own society.

When we were all a long way from home, my companions who were worried about what might be happening to their families announced that they wished to consult an itinerant *tyet*, diviner, who had arrived in the village. The man had some schooling. He was asking 10 piastres (about 2s.) to tell fortunes. His mode of procedure was first to set a ring – the gift, he said of missionary in the dust in front of him. We sat around him, and after a few moment's of apparently deep concentration he began to trace tracks in the dust between himself and the ring. As though reading these tracks as a hunter follows spoor, he would pause and consider for a while now and then, and then put forward tentative statements about matters which he could easily have pickes up in the course of a few hours of ordinary village gossip. For his clients, he referred to their kinsmen's minor illnesses that would pass, cattle that would eventually be settled, and other generalities such as he might rightly suppose any Dinka away from his home to be troubled about. It was clear that he was following up leads given to him the conspicious heightening of interest shown by audience where he was on the right lines, and he would hazard guesses, again in generalized and tentative from, until the manner of his audience convinced him that he should continue in a particular direction. when he divined for me, I deliberately misled him by showing interest in suggestions which could not possibly be true – such is for example, that my father has four wives, and that I was worried about half-sisters, who did not exist, and he reassured me about these matters. The Dinka, who then knew what was happening, lost faith in his statements about them, saying that after all there were many fraudulent *tiit*, diviners, or people who are real *tiit*'; but of course the experience of one false diviner, far from calling into doubt the abilities of all, reminded them of many others who really had the insight which this man claimed.

The following text from the Twij Dinka illustrates something of the thought of the Dinka in this matter, and the ambivalent attitudes they may adopt towards diviners:

> A young man was very ill, and his father called in a diviner who lied and said that Divinity (*nhialic*) wanted a very big fat ox. And the father of the man said 'Good;, and fetched an ox from the herd and killed it. But the young man was still on the point of death.
>
> And a lion used to come to the homestead and watch the man from a hiding-place near by, so that some day when he found him alone he could eat him. And the father of the sick man had walked and walked until he was tired out [because he was searching for more breasts to sacrifice from the herds of his relatives and friends]. And everything was finished [in sacrifices]. And that lion knew what was injuring the man.
>
> One day a man went into the woods to get honey. He lit a fire under tree (to smoke out the bees) and climbed the tree to cut more wood. The lion heard the axe and made for

the foot of the tree. The man heard him coming and put out his fire and sat in the tree.

Two lions met at the foor of the tree, and greeted each other and asked about each other's affairs. The lion called mangar Dit said I ate two men one was thin but the other was fat.' And the other lion said. 'They have sent for your home, for your father and mother say 'If you see Mangar Dit, and he has eaten a man, tell him that his sister has menstruated, and will heaplease bring the man's puddings[6] for her to eat."

Mangar Dit said: 'Good. I have found a sick man in the village here, but I can't get hold of him because his people sleep by him day and night. And I will tell you that the Power which injuries him is not a big power at all, it is merely a little one.' And the other lion asked 'What sort of a Power is it?' And the first said 'It is a tiny Power which is in the pool in the village. If they bring a small *mangok ox* and kill it in the pool the man will get better at once.' Then the lions picked up their spears and went off to the cattle-camp. And that man in the tree heard all they said.

So the man went off to the home of the sick young man, and said 'You people of the sick man, give me a little *mangok ox* and I will see what I can do.' The father of the sick man brought a little ox, and the ox was taken along to the pool with the sick man. And the ox was prayed over; and the sick man was possessed. Then they killed the ox.

And the sick man arose at once and ate the meat of the sacrificed ox. The next morning he went to the cattle-camp, and people were astonished by his recovery.

And that man who had climbed the tree had no power in this body (was not a diviner); they wanted to reward him with a cow in calf, but the man refused and said, 'Just reward me with a single goat.'

Minor practitioners of divination may use mussel-shells, like the Nuer, or scatter grain and interpret its fall, or, more commonly, draw in the sand as a *mise-en scene* for their display of insight. Their reputation naturally varies according to their sick in hitting upon something which their clients are prepared to recognize as true and perceptive; but their standing is never nambiguously respectable for, as in the above story, they can be thought to defraud while still being called *tiit*,[7] diviners.

A higher type of diviner is one who is thought to have an important power, a free divinity, in his body. This may come without in several ways. He may have become sick and been told by another diviner that he has been possessed by a power of such a name. This power then becomes his divinity it becomes related to him, that is, and he sacrifices to it. When he recovers from the illness he may come to regard himself as inspired by this divinity and gain a reputation for diagnosis of other people's illness and misfortunes by displaying an insight which he attributed to his divinity. Many people whose illnesses are attributes to his divinities are content merely to offer sacrifice to them and return to their normal way of living; but a few (and, from those I have seen, I should say a few who are nervously very highly organized) become practising diviners. They continue to hoe and tend their cattle like other Dinka, but are called in to diagnose illnesses and causes of misfortunes. The divinity may pass from a diviner to any, or none, of his children. Once the divinity has seized a man, he may learn more of the technique of divining from an established diviner.

The least regarded of these are also consulted about suspected witchcraft, and they may extract from the patient's body bits of wood or sand which have been shot into the body by witches, apeth. Such people again may also be suspected of being also prone to bewitch people/ More highly regarded are those whom the Dinka sometimes assimilate to the yet higher category of inspired person, later described, by calling them also *ran nhialic*, a person of Divinity', or *aciek*, prophet or 'creator;. The Categories shade into each other, but a famous 'person of Divinity and prophet would be demeaned by being called only *ryet*, a mere diviner.

All Dinka give consistent accounts of the way in which established diviners operate. The diviner is invited to the home of a sick man, whose kinsmen sit around him. They place on the ground spears and money as an initial payment, and an earnest of their intention to give a larger present, perhaps even a calf, if the séance is successful. The people of the sick man will then ask the diviner the name of the divinity through whom he divines, and he will tell them. the free divinities earlier mentioned *Garang, Deng, Macardit* or *Colwic* are the commonest and most widely reorganized in Rek country. In Western Twij country there are also several others *Atem, Aiwel, Yath* and *Biar yath*. It is interesting to note that possession by divinities is thought both by Wester Twij and Rek Dinka to be more common among the Twij than among the Rek, and that some divinities known in Rek-land are said to have entered from the land of the Twij to the north and east, in the direction of kordofan. This was a point of contact in the nineteenth century with the great Arab prophet, the Mahdi a matter the significance of which we later discuss.

When the diviner has announced the name of the divinity through which he divines, the people ask him if he wants them to sing to it. It is considered usual for the diviner to ask that they should, and they then sing hymns, in some of which his particular divinity may be mentioned. After a period of singing the diviner beigns to shake himself and to appear to feel pains in his neck and his back. He then begins to quiver and tremble and make curious squeaking noises (these I have heard from possessed people) and to breathe heavily. It is then thought that the divinity has begun (as the Dinka say) to 'rise', or to 'wake up' (*pac*) in his body, or to 'warm' his body. He is then progressively 'seized' by the divinity, which speaks in an unknown tongue through his mouth. He translates the sounds, usually twittering and groaning sounds, into partly intelligible Dinka He thus announces, guided by his divinity, the grounds of the trouble which he has been asked to treat. The commonest and expected diagnoses are that the sick man or his father or mother of grandfather committed some hidden sin, or disposed lightly of a cow dedicated to a divinity. In one case I heard of, but did not see treated, a diviner called in to cure the paralysis of a girl marriageable age attributed the illness to an act of her grandfather who had cut off the arm of an enemy to take his ivory and had thereby offended the ghost (*atiep*) of the dead man. In this case the ghost required satisfaction in the from of an expiatory sacrifice. I had seen the girl before the sacrifice, and supposed that she was suffering from sleeping-sickness. She could not stand and appeared to be permanently dazed. A few weeks after the sacrifice this girl who had appeared to be incurable was walking about cheerfully with the help of a stick. I mention this to suggest that cures are sometimes conspicuously effected, though the Dinka are prepared to find that their sacrifice may be ineffective. They then simply resign themselves to the refusal of divinity to help in a particular case, or suppose that the grounds of the trouble have not been diagnosed by the diviner.

The diviner's usual suggestion for treatment is that a sacrifice, or dedication of a beast for later sacrifice, should be made. He may kill the beast himself, or he may leave it to the senior man of the homestead or someone asked by him to officiate. A master of the fishing spear may be asked to carry out a diviner's instruction on behalf of the sufferer, adding his own prayers, to divinity and the clan divinity of his clan, to those of the diviner and the people. They pray to divinity and to the clan divinities of those descent-groups most concerned in the case, and to such free divinities or other powers as are indicated by the diviner,. These divinities are left for fuller description and illustration later.

As I have said, diviners vary very much in reputation. There are minor personalities, of no great importance, whom many may suspect of practising fraud, or witchcraft, or even sorcery. In the middle ranks are respectable and reputable men whom the Dinka always compare to Arab or European doctors, sometimes those who know a little Arabic try to distinguish between the lower class of diviners, who shade into practitioners with magic roots, by referring to the latter as *Kujur*, a general Sudani, and I think, originally Nuba term, which might be translated roughly as 'magician', and to the former as *Zara*[8], diviners or soothsayers, At the higher level of reputation the *tyet* shades into a figure ideally of a quite different type, the *ran nhialic*, man of divinity, or *aciek*, 'creator', which we here call the 'prophet'.

Prophets of outstanding reputation are not, and nave not

been, numerous in Dinkaland. In the area I knew best there had been only two whose names were widely known. One, Cyer Dit may be still alive at the time of writing. The other Arianhdit, died in about 1948 after a long period of exile, following a patrol carried out against him by the Government in 1922. I failed to reach Arianhdit before he died and Cyer Dit showed no disposition to receive me, so I thought it better not to force my company upon him. Both men, however, represent an ideal type of religious leader, a type in which the Dinka include also the prophets of other peoples, in particular the outstanding Nuer prophet Ngundeng (Deng Kur) and also, where they have heard of him the inspired Arab who, as the Mahdi, led his people against the British.

It is said of the great Dinka 'men of divinity' that they unite two 'things' two principles in their bodies. They are overtly inspired, more than others of their clans, by their clan divinities. And it is said that the really great prophets are always also hereditary masters of the fishing spear, or members of the spear master clans, whose clan divinities are in any case thought to be more powerful than those of other clans. the special strength of their clan divinities in them is one of the the principles of their effectiveness. The other is that they are in addition vehicles and representatives on earth, of divinity. Unlike ordinary diviners, therefore, they necessarily have a place in the priestly organization of Dinkaland, but by special inspiration they are able to show powers which denied to ordinary masters of the fishing-spear. These genius is thought to show itself less in the states of possession which the ordinary diviner induces in himself than in the direct insight they have into the truth of situation ,and their ability to help or injure others by a mere word or gesture. They are universally acknowledged by the Dink as true prophets, while many diviners may be thought, by some who have consulted them, to be capable of falsehood or former. Further, the Dinka think of them as being essentially men of peace, who, nevertheless, may be forced by external circumstances into uniting their numerous followers against a common enemy.

Reference

Fergusson, V.H. (1923), "Mattiang Goh" witchcraft', *S.N. and R.*, vol. 6.

Shaw, Archdeacon (1915), 'Dinka Songs', *man*, vol. 15.

NOTES

1. As will appear, it is characteristic of these free divinities that they should extend the range of their activities, and it would not be surprising if *Loi* were now more widespread.

2. Such are *Adim*, a free divinity laid to have originated in Agar country and connected with hyaena and the protection of stock against hyaena; *Ayak*, the mother perhaps of *Abuk*, known among the Bor Dinka; and *Dayim*, also known among the Bor Dinka and the subject of a hymn translated by Archdeacon Shaw (1915), p.20.

3. Leinhardt discusses the masters of the fishing-spear at a later point in the book from which this excerpt is taken. – *Ed.*

4. Fetishes are thought by the Dinka to be particularly characteristic of the Sudanic-speaking peoples to the south of their country.

5. V.H. Fergusson (1923, p.112) calculates that there in about 1902 an Agar Dinka called Mattiang went to settle near the Gell river. There he found the root, which a Jut' (non –Dinka) of Tonj told him to call 'Mattiang Goh', Since Goh was his father's name. Fergusson says that the root protects its owner against theft.

6. In Dinka *abyar*, an euphemism for the anus, frequently a topic of jocular impropriety.

7. The world *tyet* is sometimes confused by non-Dinka with the word *atet*, which means simply 'someone who has a special skill of facility'. It is supplied to bonesetters and masseurs, and more widely to anyone clever with his hands. Some diviners also have these skills many who are not diviners also have them.

8. This probably to the Arabic *zar*, spirits which possess people.

9. Following Professor Evans-Pritchard's usage in his writings on the Nuer.

Chapter-11

Authority and Power in the American Baptist Convention

P. M. HARRISON

Chapter-11

Emerging as they did from the neo-Calvinist Free Church movement of the seventeenth century, the Bpatists have always regarded the problem of authority and power as a fundamental concern. The attitude of the left-wing Protestant churches was expressed by John Cotton when he cautioned all the world to 'learn to give mortal man no greater power than they are contents they shall use, for use it they will—It is necessary—that all power that is on earth be limited, church-power or other, (Cf, Hudson, 1953, p.53).

While it is true that the radical ideals of the Puritan left-wing were stimulated with an environment of religious persecution they were 'derived in the first instance from the two theological doctrines of the sovereignty of God and of human bondage to 'sin' (Hudson, 1953, p.49). Because concentrations of power lead to rebellion against God, the churches must be independent of government, voluntary in membership, and limited in authority. No official could be trusted to wield the administrative instruments of both church and civil government. Thus the Baptists insisted upon the separation of church and state, and for the same reason they were of the opinion that church officials should not exercise authority over more than a single congregation. No church leader could legitimately claim special access to the divine power, and since God is the only obsolute sovereign it follows that all religious authority must be penultimate and limited. The church 'executive must always be subject to correction by the will of Christ, for which a partial criterion was at hand in the Scriptures' (Nichols, 1951. p. 268).

But difficulties arose when these doctrinal ideas were expressed through the polity of the churches. The baptists

---

Excerpt from chapter 4 of P. M. Harrison, *Authority and Power in the Free Church Tradition*, Princeton University Press, pp.53-64.

believed it was sufficient to point to the Scriptures, the personal experience of the Holy Spirit, or to the gathered Congregation of believers as the principal mediators of divine authority. But emphasis upon the autonomy of the local churches ignored the sinful potentialities within these religious groups. The divine presence among the people was sometimes interpreted to signify the possession of God by the community, so that the will of the congregation was adequated with the will of God. When God is possessed by the local church, external direction from ecclesiastical officials is obviously superfluous.[2]

One of the primary problems in every religious community is the discovery of a method for historical expression of the divine sovereignty. In any case, the sovereignty of God must be historically mediated, whether it be through 'spontaneous inspiration' of special individuals or by means of an official preistly class which preserves and transmits the oral or written tradition. However, every form of polity lies in the conception of the limitation and balance of power; but his form of church government tends to break down when an effort is made to eliminate the effective authority of those leaders who have been given acclesiastical responsibilities.

The Authority of the American Baptist Convention

The crux of the problem of authority was recognized by many of the leaders who participated in the formation of the Convention. Some believed the Convention itself would provide the answer:

> So far as organization, these problems center in the task of getting efficiency without dependence upon external authority.
>
> We are our own spiritual masters. Of course there is difficulty in having so many masters, and the process of getting cooperative efficiency with us been one of long development. We have taken step after step, and at last we have evolved the Convention (Mathews, 1916, p. 22).

The need for some form of social mediation of God's sovereignty led the Baptists to locate ultimate historical authority in the Holy Scriptures. But even the authority of the Bible must gain social expression in the religious community. The Bible may be the normative referent to which the various personal authorities turn, but in every casc its meaning must e interpreted and the problem remains: who are the interpreters and what is their authority? The Baptist answer is ambiguous.[3]

On the one hand, the authority of Scripture 'was to be exercised under the guidance of the Spirit of Christ operative in the Christian community' (Harrelson, 1954, pp.3-4). Therefore under the gospel, the local church was the ultimate authority. But the Baptist effort to scatter authority throughout the land does not cease with the positing of authoritty in the local communion. On the foundation of the doctrine of the priesthood of all believers, the same people who affirm the authority of the community hold that 'one saved, any person has free and direct access to the Father through the one and only High Priest, Jesus (Pruden, 1951, p.2). In Baptist thought there often seems to be more involved than an effort to sustain a tradition of prophetic criticism of the community by means of an inspired individual McNutt (1935, p.9) affirms that the true church 'will be a fellowship of the religiously competent, with every man a priest, spiritual democracy, with every man in God a king'. With such royal opportunities offered every individual in the Baptist denomination it is not difficult to discover one of the primary sources of a constantly threatening disorder.

However, there are many spokesman who deplore the individualism inherent within the Baptist doctrine of the church. Individualistic voluntarism has no place in the New Testament,' says one Baptist who was writing a report for a committee of the convention. 'The fellowship,' he continues, 'is the mother which gives birth to each new child' (Skoglund, 1954, p.18). In the contemporary situation some of the basic issues have been discerned. For example, the contradiction of positing two ultimate authorities. The individual and the community to which he belongs has been recognized. Nonetheless, the tension still exists between the Kings 'each man on his throne' holding absolute sway over has own realm' (McNutt, 1935, p.24) and those who believe that 'private interpretation of the Bible must always be subjected to the testing of the Spirit, and this testing takes place in the regenerate Christian community...(Harrelson 1954, p.19).

It is clear that the Baptists are faced with a more critical problem than the autonomy of the local church.[4] The intramural tensions inherent in this principle may be superseded by the monarchic potentialities of a radical individualism. The problem of authority of the regional or associational group in relation to the local church would be considerably simplified if the focus of authority at the congregational level were a settled issue.

But Baptists have a genius for obscuring the problem of authority by means of a labyrinth of theological doctrines. There is no effective way of predicting what a given document will pronounce on this vital issue. According to open source there may be no possibility of a mediated authority beyond the New Testament: Christ as the only Head over, and Law-giver, to His churches. Consequently, the churches cannot make laws, but only execute those which He has given. Nor can any man, or body of men, legislate for the churches. The New Testament alone is their statute book, by which, without change, the body of Christ is to govern itself' (Hiscox, 1890, p.14).

Or, the local church may be the primary locus of authority.

We Baptists are recognized democrats of the Protestant world. The local church is our depository of ecclesiastical authority. The Association has no authority over the local church; and the Northern Baptist Convention has no authority over the State Convention. All these are voluntary cooperative associations created for the sake of greater effectiveness in the business of the kingdom (Montgomery, 1922. P.38).

A third possibility is that the individual under God may be the supreme authority. A fourth variation, of more recent origin may be expressed in many ways. This final perspective represented a more realistic effort to account for the existing power of the association groups and to discover a biblical rationale for the support of this power.

In 1954 a committee of the American Baptist Theological Conference observed that authority extends beyond the limits of congregational membership. If missionary work is an 'integral' part of the responsibility and authority given to the church by its Lord,' then Baptists must agree that in working through national society or its board, the local church' (Pruden, 1951, p.19). But this unanticipated shift of power and confirming of authority is not to be treated lightly by the national leadership. They receive a warning form the same committee which indicates that final ecclesiastical authority remains with the local Church. The authority given to the national executives is provisional and the position they enjoy is precarious, depending as it does upon proper rendition of the Baptist tune composed by he local churches:

> At the same time it must be clear that such delegation of authority can remained justified only in so far as the board retains the confidence of the church and can be regarded as a fit repository for the authority involved. Unless the church has the right to terminate the delegation of authority when the necessary confidence has been shattered, then it could have had no right to delegate the authority in the first place. Under the Baptist system the Boards and their officials are necessarily the servants of the churches, not their masters. To give up authority since for all would be, not a justifiable limitation, but a violation of the autonomy of the church (Pruden, 1951, p.20).

This quotation seems to indicate that God may work through the national boards only if the local churches permit him to do so since. He had nothing to do with the creation of these boards, except in an indirect way, he can guide them only though the medium of the local churches. If for some reason communication between the local churches and the national boards is seriously impaired the according to the Baptist theology of the church, these boards inevitably would become secularized because God's only means of communication with them has been destroyed. On the other hand, if the local churches become corrupted the national boards posses no legitimate authority to criticize or correct them. According to Baptist polity, in such a situation the national boards would be servants of God but only by means of the diseased churches.

It is beyond argument that the boards should serve the local churches and in some sense should be responsible to them. In a historical sense they were brought into being by the churches, but from a theological perspective a distinction must be made between the desires of the churches—which may be corrupted—and the needs of the churches. Since it is possible that God conceived the national boards as a corrective for the sins of the churches, it is dangerous on principle to preclude the possibility of conferring official authority upon the ecclesiastical officer of the board. This authority need not be unlimited, and according to Baptist principles it should not be. But it seems no less a violation of the freedom of God and of the original intention of the Baptist fathers to deposit ultimate authority under God with any historical individual, whether it be the local church, the state association, the national boards, the General Secretary of the Convention or a prophetic layman in the local congregation. The recognized democrats of the Protestant world' seem to have forgotten the first principles of democracy as developed by the independents: the separation of powers and the freedom of God to speak through the most unlikely of historical individuals.

This is not surprising, since with regard to the authority of leadership Baptists have been preoccupied with control and restriction rather than with the element of freedom which is no less necessary for leaders that for the constituency. Baptists attended to the limitation of the leader's authority and power, but they have largely ignored the problem of the fulfilment of his duties. From the Baptist point of view the chief responsibility of a leader is to avoid seeking enough power to meet his responsibilities. But without authority and freedom the ecclesiastical leader cannot be held accountable for failing to achieve goals to which he has been assigned. Baptist voluntarism has resulted in an effort to pulverize ecclesiastical authority and power. Realizing that concentrations of power contain great demonic potentialities, the Baptists have placed a higher value on the minimization of power than on establishing effective means to attain other goals. If the Baptists haa enjoyed substantial success in achieving the primary goal of their polity there would be considerably less ground for criticism. But the Baptist denomination had been no more successful in establishing a 'democratic polity' than many other Protestant denominations which do not place primary emphasis upon this goal.

According to Pruden's (1951, p.20) committee on church government, 'our system is based upon the assumption that churches of regenerate believers will be sensitive to the promptings of the spirit and will do their proper share coluntarily'. This places an unbearable pressure upon the motivations of the regenerate soul and reveals a faith in the power and goodness of the individual which is unsupported by traditional Christian doctrine. 'Moral and spiritual suasion,' the committee reports ' are the means at our disposal. If they fail us it is because we have failed' (Pruden, 1951, p.21.)

The Problem of Authority in the Present Situation

Notwithstanding the ambiguities and restriction on their authority, the executive officials of the American Baptist Convention have managed to gain enough power to meet their responsibilities with reasonable effectiveness. Since hey have no official ecclesiastical authority they seek to secure their position by other means, and they have been remarkably successful in their efforts. It has often been observed that the American Baptist Convention 'has no authority, but has very great influence.[5] In order to analyse the character of this influence as well the problems and which surround the executives of the Convention, it is best to draw a clear distinction between power and authority. Power signifies the ability to carry out one's own will despite the *criteria* or resistance of others (Weber, 1947, p.152; it is the reality to influence or control the actions of others even though there is no institutional sanction for this control. However, power may be, and generally is, used to acquire legitimized status and symbols of recognition; (Parsons, 1949, p.172). Therefore, power is a more comprehensive term than authority; in fact, authority is a speacialized function of power.[6]

Authority is defined as formalized or institutionally recognized power. 'Authority is thus the expected and legitimate possession of power'.[7] Since authority is the more specialized concept it will be used whenever the intent is to indicate that and of power which is officially legitimated and voluntarily concepted by the group. This does not signify that those who held authority always satisfy every member of the constituency, that despite particular dissatisfactions the constituency recognizes the right of the leader to lead. However, when a leader exercises power, which, within this analytical framework should be called 'illegitimate authority', he is controlling the of others despite their wishes, or he is controlling them without their knowledge. The latter often occurs in the Baptist situation because the Baptist are unwilling to confer authority upon their leaders and are equally unwilling to recognize that they have attained power apart from authority. Thus they do not posses adequate analytical instruments to discern the existence of 'illegitimate authority.'

Those Baptists who do recognize the existence of power either ignore the situation because they enjoy its fruits and recognize as a functional necessity of every social system, or they deplore it because they enjoy no benefits and engage in an effort to eliminate it as an 'un-Baptist' phenomenon. But power is required for achievement in any field whatsoever (Heiman, 1947 p.119). Even though it contains the seeds of corruption,[8] power in itself is not an evil thing. It is necessary for life, which is capable of both good and evil.

Those leaders in a social group who are given responsibilities and goals to achieve will strive for legitimate authority for their constituency in order to gain the necessary support for the achievement of the group's goals. Those who hold power who seek to legitimate it; that is, they will seek authority (Lasswell and Kaplan, 1950, p.137). If, as in the case of the Baptists , the ideology of the group does nor permit the granting of legitimate authority to the leaders, any struggle for power will probably be increasingly complicated. Each group will strive to establish itself as the legitimate authority.

The Baptist denominational executives are given responsibility and limited power, but no legitimate authority. In order to overcome the lack of officials status, they seek more power and when they are successful in this enterprise they seek authority. Relatively speaking, it has not been difficult for them to acquire the power necessary for the achievement of their assigned tasks. This has been accomplished by means of an unanticipated formation of an informal system of inter personal and inter - group relations which bypasses the formal rules of order. The distinction between the formal, and informal systems of action is a category of interpretation which enables the observer to answer crucial questions concerning the Convention. Why do the national leaders posses considerable power when the Convention itself does not have any legislative power or legal authority? What is the actual distinguished from the official – locus of authority in the convention is the informal power of the executives gradually becoming legitimated on a formal basis? Or, to reformulate the last question; are there any signs that the Baptist interpretation of the nature of the church is changing in order to adjust to changes in the environment?

According to sociological theory, authority is generally associated with the formal system of action, i.e. the officially sanctioned relations of the group. Power is associated with the informal system.[9] Even before the Convention came into being the national executives of the missionary societies discovered that their duties extended far beyond the specific functions of the organization. Whether they wanted it or not[10] their positions enabled them to exercise tremendous influence in the life of the denomination. They made decisions about the content of the denomination's educational and plamphering enterprises, the fund-raising activities, the development of semainaties and colleges, in addition to determining the policies of the missionary boards (Hudson, 1958, pp.14 ff.)

Hudson notes that fifty years before the Convention was formed a large number of important posts were held by a small group of influential men. Francis Wayland, President of Brown University, was active in the affairs of the Triennial Convention from its conception until the middle of the century. During those years he held the following posts: recording secretary of the Triennial Convention, secretary of the Baptist Convention of Massachusetts, secretary the Boston Baptist Foreign Missionary Society, member of the board if Trustees of Newton seminary, board member of the Baptist Missionary society of Massachusetts, board member of Society of Massachusetts, board member of the Evangelical Tract Society member of the Boston Standing Committee for the Triennial Convention and editor of the *American Baptist Magazine*. 'Wayland was not unique figure in this respect. Actually, all the offices of the various societies and board in Massachusetts were held by a dozen men. In New York and elsewhere the situation was the same (Hudson, 1958, p. 20).

The by-laws and resolution of the convention prevent single individual from holding so many posts today, but the situation has changed only in degree. This circumstance, however should not necessarily be interpreted as an undesirable appropriation of power by men of evil intent, but rather as an inevitable emergence of leadership which occurs in any social system.

References

Buber, M. (1946), *Moses*, East and West Library.

Daviers, R.E. (1946), *The problem of Authority in the Continental Reformers*, Epworth Press.

Harrelson, W.J. (1954), 'The biblical basis of the Gospel', *Basic Papers Prepared for the American Baptist Theological Conference* (Mimeogrpahed).

Heiman, E. (1947), *Freedom and Order*, Scribner.

Hiscox, E.T. (1890), *The Standard Manual for Baptist Churches*, The American Baptist Publication Society.

Hudson, W.S. (1953), *The great Tradition of the American Churches*, Harper.

Hudson, W.S. (1958), 'Stumbling into disorder', *Foundations*, vol. 1.

Lasswell, H.D., and Kaplan, A. (1950), *Power ad Society*, Yale University Press.

Levy, M.J. (1952), *The Structure of Society*, Princeton University Press.

McNutt, W.R. (1935), *Policy and Practice in Baptist Churches*, Judson Press.

Mathews' S. (1916), 'President's Address to the Convention', *Annual*.

Montgomery, W.A. (1922), 'President;s Address to the Convnention Annual.

NewBigin, L. (1954), *The Household of God*, Friendship Press.

Nichols, J.H. (1951), *Democracy and the Churches*, Westminister Press.

Parsons, T. (1949), *Essays in Sociological Theory Pure and Applied*, Free Press.

Pruden, E.H. (1951), *Interpreters Needed*, Judson Press.

Skoglund, J.E. (1954), 'The nature of the Church', *Basic Papers Prepared for the American Baptist Theological Conference* (mimeographed).
Weber, M. (1947), *The Theory of Social and Economic Organization*, Oxford University Press.

NOTES

1. Some modern Baptists insist that the minister has no special authority even in his congregation. 'The pastor of a Baptist church is simply the preaching member of that church. In a congregational meeting he has one vote... and the vote of the most in significant member of the church counts for just as much as the vote of the pastor' (Pruden, 1951, p. 56).
2. This phenomenon is neither new nor is it confined to the left-wing Protestant tradition. Martin Buber shows that primitive religious societies undermined the authority of the chief priests by establishing within the tribe but external to the official tribal life, a secret society in which the actual the true, the "holy" communal life is lived, free from the bonds of the "law" but in holy action.' The problem always arises, that if the authority of the priests is disputed and extended to all, then the actual dominion is taken away from God; for without law, that is, without any clear-cut and transmissible line of demarcation between that which is blessing to God and that which is displeasing to Him, there can be no historical continuity of divine rule upon earth' (Buber, 1946, pp.186 ff).
3. The Baptists are not alone with the possible exception of the fundamentalists, the enire Protestant view of authroity is ambigious . (Cf. Davies, 1946, pp. 10, 154.)
4. Lesslie Newbigin simplifies the problem of congregationally ordered churches when he asserts that there is no 'intelligible reason why we should be asked to acknowledge the spiritual authority of the local fellowship over the individual but to deny the spiritual authority of

the regional or ethnical fellowship over the local'. It is evident that many Baptists do not acknowledge the spiritual authority of the local churches over the individual except in a very limited way. See Newbigin (1954), p. 120.

5. 'Baptists', *Encyclopaedia Britannica*, vol.3, 1953 edn.

6. Marion Levy defines power as 'the ability to exercise authority and control over the actions of others'. More accurately, it should be 'authority and or control'. Power can exist apart from institutional sanction. See Levy (1952), p. 333.

7. Lasswell and kaplan (1950), p.133. This definition is in agreement with Parsons, who describes authority as the 'institutionally recognized right to influence the actions of others, regardless of their immediate personal attitudes to the direction of influence'. It is also in agreement with Weber's definition of authority or imperative control which 'is the probability that certain specific commands (or all commands) from a given source will be obeyed by a given group of persons'.

8. Never 'absolute corruption'. Action's dictum is in error because absolute corruption presupposes absolute power, which is historical impossibility. Power and authority are both relational concepts. Even in the limiting case of slavery the leaders must exercise caution because of the constant threat of a revolutionary uprising (Weber, 1947, pp.62 f., 276 ff.)

9. Recall that Lasswell and Kaplan defined authority as formal power. Conversely, power could be called informal authority (1950, p.133).

10. Indications are that most executives desired all the power they could acquire. Hudson notes that a power struggle was in progress among the denominational leaders shortly after the creation of the Triennial Convention (predecessor of the Foreign Mission Society) in 1814. At one of the annual meetings a movement to create a General Convention was set aside. Apparently, Luther Rice had feared that some maneuver to seize control of the

Convention was afoot because he pointed out that the ... arrangement could easily be abused by an "active and intriguing man" (Hudson, 1958, pp. 5 ff).

Chapter-12

The Social Status of the Anglican Minister

R. TOWLER

Chapter-12

One of the most significant differences between the denominations of the Christian Church has always been the variation in forms of full-time leadership. The ministry of each denomination is unique, and ministers occupy quite different statuses both with respect to the wider members of thier own denomination and also with respect to the wider society. This is a situation with which all are familiar. At the present time, however, less familiar situation has arisen, where the ministry of each denomination terms to be changing from its established fromtrs, and moving towards something new. An attempt will be made here to clarify, Sociological terms the changes which appear to be taking place in the ordained Ministry of the Anglican Church. Such changes are not limited to the Church of England, but are felt like in the Roman catholic and free Churches in varying degrees, it seems best to limit the discussion to the Anglican situation for the sake of simplicity, but it should be possible to how the same points apply to other religious organizations without spelling out the details.

It can be maintained that the problems of the ministry, in common with all problems of organized religion, are due to the manchronistic relationship of religion to a secular society and culture. Dr. Bryan Wilson 91966) has referred to the. 'alienation of the clergy', and the resemblance of sections of the clergy to the charcoal burners or alchemists in an age when the processes in which they were engaged had been rendered obsolete, technically or intellectually'. This may be so, but secularization has been much written about recently, and it seems best to try to find the roots of the problem within a more limited context, if that is possible.

Towler, 'The changing status of the ministry? '*Crucible*, May (1968). 73-8 [With slight alterations by the author.]

A Threefold Problem

Crisis is an over-worked expression, but the Ministry does face something of a crisis at the moment. This is not to suggest that the dilemma is insoluble, but there are a number of problems which require some radical changes from what has been a traditional pattern, in order to reach a new pattern of Ministry which will prove viable under our changed social circumstances. There are those who maintain that the established pattern with modifications in personel deployment such as are suggested in the report *Partners in Ministry*, is still perfectly satisfactory However the problems go deeper than that, and they come under three broad headings. It is hoped that the sociological statement of the problems, if accurate, may go little way towards finding a solution.

The first general problem to be faced in the shrinkage of the Ministry. This shrinkage itself has four separate aspects. The absolute numerical strength of the Ministry has declined by some 20 per cent since the turn of the century. The decline is even greater when compared with a 40 per cent rise in the total population. A third aspect of the shrinkage is seen in the age profile of the clergy as a whole, which has become progressively more biased towards older men. This accounted for by an increasing proportion of older men entering the Ministry, as well as by the drop in recruitment. This shift in the age profile results in an effective reduction in the number of years of work available from personnel, even when numbers are held constant. Yet fourth aspect is to be found in the number of clergy leaving the parochial Ministry, and this loss is made the more serious by the high proportion of younger men involved, thus biasing the age profile even more.

The second problem is the loss in social status which the Ministry has suffered. Of course it is possible to dismiss this, and claim it as an advantage rather than an hindrance in the discharge of their office by men who have been classically defined as *servi servorum Dei*. But it remains a radical break from tradition, even if readily accepted, and as such demands a readjustment on the part of the clergy, which they have yet to make. Although the factual basis of this contemporary problem is rarely questioned. It is nonetheless difficult to substantiate empirically. Perhaps the nearest we can come to a demonstration of this loss of social prestige is the relative drop in clerical incomes. Although the phenomenon of the 'poor clergyman, has been with us for a long time, it is a trend of this century that clergy incomes have come to be on a level with, and often below, those of manual workers. But the relationships of prestige to remuneration is neither simple nor direct. The results of most investigations shows that clergy are held in great respect. Thus in one study (Richards, 1962) Clergy were ranked as the fourth most prestigious occupation, after suregeons, G.P.s and solicitors; and a recent study conducted by Gallup Poll (1965, para. 285) found that clergy were thought to be 'influential in the community, devoted to public service, useful in the parish, sincere, overworked and underpaid...'Dr Wilson (1966, p. 82) suggests, perceptively, that the reason for these findings might be that there are 'spiritual affinites of the occupation which induce respondents to give relatively high ratings to clerics, since people with any religious dispositions at all cannot but pay some attention to the traditional claim of all religious professionals to have the highest calling of all'. Perhaps an effective measure of the social status of the clergy has yet to be devised but for the moment a real loss in prestige must be granted, of a sort well described by a recent speaker (Furlong, 1966):

> The clergyman has suffered throughout this century (and it still continues) a decline in status. This is indicated, as well as accentuated, by the fact that his income is less than that of the majority of his parishoners. In some cases he earns about the same as an unskilled worker and this is perhaps how an un-churched society is coming think of him —as someone who is not qualified as the twentieth century understands qualification. In an age which is not particularly interested in faith it is difficult for people to understand what the clergyman is up to, and so they are apt to suggest that he isn't upto anything in particular. He is thrust on one side where serious issues are being discussed he isn't social workers, he isn't a psychiatrist, he isn't a doctor, he isn't a probation officer, or a teacher or a welfare worker. He is granted a little elbow room in hospitals or prisons—after all

> ıt is well known that when people are unhappy, ill or dying they like a bit of religion, and the clergyman can at least talk about God without getting uncomfortable. But I believe there is a growing feeling in the community as a whole that the church is played out and the clergy with it, and this is perhaps as obvious in the exaggerated respect—an almost superstitious awe—which is sometimes shown to the clergy and which indicates how little religion is a part of people's ordinary, everyday lives ....

The third problem may be termed the 'role uncertainty' of the clergy, mentioned in the preceding quotation. By this meant the uncertainty on the part of the clergy themselves as to preciseiy, what they are there to do. The full impact of this problem is yet to be felt, but it is perhaps the biggest single problem. In the established pattern of the ordained Ministry, a parochial clergy man has had a number of different roles which he has exercised. He has been the teacher of the Christian faith, the organizer of his Church activities, the preacher of the word of God, the administrator of Church affairs, the pastor of his flock and the priest of the parish in his sacramental duties.[1] In the present trends of church affairs, almost all of these roles are affected. As Dr Trevor Ling (1967) has pointed out, the drop in the proportion of clergyman who have had a university education in theology has been accompanied by an increase in the number of lay people, especially in the teaching profession, who have got theological degrees. In the next few years an increasing proportion of parishes will have among the laity persons admirably trained to teach the Christian faith; better trained in fact than their clergy, who have has less theological education and no training whatever in teaching methods. The clergy have been trying to persuade members of their congregations to assume more responsibiliy in the spheres of organization and administration for some time now, and in many places the clergy have already been relieved of msot of this work. Where this is not yet so, it may be expected to become so in the foreseeable future. Lady readers have for many years assisted in the Ministry of the word, and there is no reason on why the number of readers should not increase, to ease the work of the declining number of clergy and utilize the theological knowledge which is becoming more current among the laity. Action arising from the 'People Next Door' campaign and trends in Church organization are increasing a most dramatic way the share of pastoral responsibility taken by the non-ordained members of the local church.

In short the professional activities of the clergy, other than their duties in the administration of the sacraments, are coming to be shared more and more by the laity. As this change becomes more widespread it is increasingly difficult to define the extra surgical role of the parochial clergyman as anything other than full-time Christian. This trend, when seen in conjunction with lowering prestige of the Ministry as an occupation, and its rapid shrinkage, leads to a conclusion, stated in its boldest terms by Dr Ling 91967, pp. 142-3), that;

There are no clear or compelling reasons for supposing, that this process of decline will be other than temporarily halted; and it is possible that what we are witnessing, therefore, is the gradual disappearance of a once familiar figure, the full-time parochial clergy man —,Whether the complete disappearance of a paid (or more accurately half-paid) professional caste of clergyman is a tragedy for the Churches or not is still something of a matter of controversy.

The Ministry as a Profession

Dr king's use of the term 'caste' when speaking of the parochial clergy has something more than a derogatory implication. It raises the question of the nature of the social group we call the ordained Ministry. It is assumed almost universally that the clergy constitute and occupation—albeit a rather special occupation - which takes its rightful place among the other professional occupational groups. Thus Professor Gordon Dunstan (1967), considering the relationship of the Ministry to groups such as doctors, social workers and psychiatrists, says it is the duty of the clergy, 'as a condition of proper co-operation with men and women of *other professionals*, to search out the ground, meaning, opportunity, disciplines, of *our own*' (author's italics).

Space does not permit a discussion of Professor Dunstan's argument, but it is not in any case central to this paper. What is open to serious question is the assumption, not that the Ministry is a profession, but that it is an occupation at all. Any definition of an occupation, and especially a sociological definition, is based on an understanding of what activities and goals characterize it. The prerequisite of an occupation is that it should be possible to make a definite statement of what its members *do* in their work.

We have seen three major problem areas which emphasize the dilemma of the Ministry in contemporary society, and it should be noted that none of the problems arises as a result of a change in the Ministry itself. In each case the problem arises as a result of changes in Western industrial society. Hence the [original] title of this article – 'The changing status of the ministry?' – with an emphasis on the query. The sociological nature of the Ministry has not changed to a significant extent since the Middle Ages and the period of 'Christian imperialism' But society has changed fundamentally.

Seen in an historical perspective (see Carr-Saunders and Wilson, 1933), the 'learned professions' grew of the social group of the clergy. This was perfectly natural, since the first, second and third Estates were in broad terms the social groups in which were located respectively leadership, learning and labour. So it is not surprising that the professions bear many marked similarities to the Ministry in terms of their organization and behaviour. But the clergy, as such, have never constituted on occupation, let alone a profession. Even the post-Reformation parson's position in society was more akin to that of the squire than that of the physician; parson and baron alike were social positions highly relevant to the structure of medieval society, and each is now alike in having not but honorific consequences in contemporary social structure.

Of the many ways in which our society has changed, the way most relevant here is its shift from a structure in which social status was based on ascription, to one in which social status is based on achievement. In technical terms, we live in an achievement—oriented society. But clergymen are made, not qualified clerical status is ascribed, not achieved. Membership of occupational groups (and pre-eminently of the professions) is achieved. To be a barrister or a sheet-metal worker is to occupy a position in society which is defined by what the member of the occupation *does*. Skill, competence and legitimation in these characterizing activities is achieved and it is achievement of occupational status which forms the fundamental basis of contemporary social structure. The clergyman is an odd-man-out in any sociological analysis of his position. He has a social position, but it is ascribed; it is comparable to that of a Knight of the Bath, or earl or Doctor of Letters, each of which was relevant to the structure of an ascription oriented society , but fundamentally irrelevant to contemporary social structure.

For these reasons, which cannot be expanded here, the Ministry cannot be considered as an occupation, as we currently understand that concept. I am arguing that this change in the character of the ordained Ministry relative to Western society as it has evolved is at the root of the three major problem areas which a present face the Churh Ministry.

Possible Innovation

The particular problems which face the Ministry will demand some form of solution before the end of this century. Solutions are not to be found in relatively minor modifications in deployment and payment of clergy. Nor will any structure of Ministry prove viable for future generations if the Church continues to ignore the basic fact that the Ministry, as we have it, is not an occupation.

There seem to be roughly three lines of development which could lead to a stable and viable form for the Ministry. Each seems equally feasible sociologically, though recent trends in theological writing seem to suggest that all would not prove theologically acceptable. It goes without saying that any change in the structure of the Ministry would imply a prior change in church organization as a whole.

1. One line of development would be for clergy increasingly to become efficient, full-time religious organizers, co-ordinating and administrating Church affairs. This change would presuppose a change in local churches in developing more clearly and exclusively as social units, and their becoming gradually more sect-like. In a de-Christianized, or secular society this would make

sociological sense. In the U.S.A. this is the trend, as it is also in some of the best-attended Anglican churches in English suburbs.[2]

2. Another possible development which is really no development at all, would be acceptance of shrinkage and loss of prestige, and conscious acceptance by the clergy of their anomalous social status. They would have to accept that they have not only a social role different to other members of the 'helping professions', but a quite unique position in society. While this is a possibility it is improbable, in sociological terms, that any substantial number of men and their families would find this impecunious and economic mode of existence commending itself to them. It is rather more likely that the first line of development would spontaneously set in.

3. The other possible development would be the gradual decline of service of the full-time clergy, and their replacement by lay leadership in the church. Liturgical functions would be exercised by members of the church in lay occupations, who had been ordained. As Dr Ling points out, in the article quoted above there could still be full-time religious functionaries such as members of the religious orders and teams of evangelists.

Before the end of this century there will be sociological changes in the nature of the Church and its group of fulltime employees. Of that there can be no doubt. What direction the changes take depends on a large number of factors, most of which have yet to be discussed. Prediction and the possibility of control must rest, however, on an accurate analysis of the present position. This paper is simply an attempt to clarify some of the facts about the social position in which the Church finds itself at present.

References

Carr-Saunders, A.M., and *Wilson*, P.A. (1933), 'The professionals before the industrial revolution', *The Professions*, Clarendon Press.

Daniel, M. (1967), *unpublished M. Phil. Thesis, University of London*.

Dunstan, G.R. (1967), 'The sacred ministry as a learned profession'

Theology, vol. 10, pp.142-51.
Furlong, M. (1966), *Address to a conference of Clergy in the Diocese of Wakefield.*
Gallup Poll (1965), *The Television Audience and Religion*, Social Surveys ltd.
Ling, T.A. (1967), 'Religion, Society and the teacher', *The Modern Churchman*, Vol. 10, pp.142-51.
Richards, N.D. (1962), *unpublished M.A. thesis, University of Nottingham.*
Wilson, B.R. (1966), *Religion in secular Society*, Watts.

NOTES

1. Work on the clergy role components has been done notably by Professor Samuel Blizzard.
2. Recent research on clergy in the London area (Daniel, 1967), shows, interestingly, that the degree to which the crisis in the Ministry is felt by clergy is in inverse proportion to the size o their congregations.

Chapter-13

RELIGION IN TRIBAL SOCIETIES

Chapter-13

It is common to draw a dividing line between the 'world religions' and 'primitive religion' or the religion of 'primitive' societies, folk religion, 'primary' religion, and so on. It is often a misleading division since included in the world religions one usually finds Confucianism, Taoisim, Hinduism, Jainism, and Sikhism all of which are confined to particular communities or parts of the world. One might argue that the only truly world religions are Buddhism, Christianity and Islam, while Judaism is in an ambiguous position.

If the distinction is expressed in terms of 'higher' versus 'primitive' or 'primary' religion, however, it does make some sense. The higher religions may be characterised as having a transcendental emphasis which primary religions lack. The transcendental religions are concerned with wider questions of the meaning of human existence while in the primary religions such concerns are largely absent. In them, the dominant concern is with immediate events in this world—pragmatic and concrete purposes—whereas the higher religions are oriented towards salvation.

It would be a mistake, however, to characterise the higher religions as *exclusively* concerned with the transcendental. They, too, share with primary religions *a* concern with the avoidance of pain and the promotion of wellbeing and prosperity. It is simply that this is often subordinated in them to the more transcendental aims. It would be a mistake, also, to think that all primary or primitive religions are exclusively concerned with the concrete and the practical, with this worldly concerns. The Hopi belief that they existed as a people in order to perform religious rituals which ensured the daily rising of the sun and thereby the continuity of the world must surely be interpreted as a moving attempt to give their life in this world significance.

A second major difference between the transcendental and primary religions is that, in the former, systems of morality are always central whereas in the latter moral questions, at least in the universalistic sense, are absent. Primitive religions may involve ideas concerning the fulfilment of specific obligations to kin and so on but do not embody wider and more general moral conceptions.

If the distinction between higher or transcendental and primitive or primary religions is useful, it is still rather crude. There have been a number of attempts to classify religious systems in a more elaborate way. These schemes frequently assume an evolutionary aspect.

Types of Religious System

A. F. C. Wallace proposes a fourfold classification of religious systems (1966). The four types are termed *shamanic, communal, olympian* and *monotheistic.*

Shamanic religion is the type found among such peoples as the Indians of North America, the Siberian tribes, the Eskimo, Andaman Islanders and many hunter-gatherer societies. Rituals are performed by non-specialists or part-time specialists. Divining the causes of misfortune and propitious times to undertake activities are prominent, as are curing and healing rituals. Mortuary and transition rituals are usually found and taboos and ritual avoidance beliefs are common.

In *communal,* systems, found widely in Melanesia, Polynesia and Africa, the shaman is supplemented by belief in a pantheon of deities associated with aspects of nature, the seasons and events in the individual life cycle. These deities can be approached through rituals and there may be a greater degree of specialisation among those who mediate between men and the gods than in the shamanic type.

The *olympian* type is characterised by a pantheon of high gods who are worshipped and propitiated in temples through the mediation of full-time priests. Examples are the Inca, Aztec, Ashanti, and Dahomey.

Finally, *monotheism* covers the world and higher religions. It is characterised by a belief in a supreme deity or principle which controls all other supernatural beings or forces.

A second attempt to reduce the great variety of religious

systems to an ordered classification is that of R. N. Bellah (1964). Bellah's classification contains five types which he terms *primitive, archaic, historic, early modern* and *modern*. While Bellah thinks of these as stages in the development of religion and thus adopts a clearly evolutionary approach he warns against any interpretation of his scheme as an actual, historically accurate description of the development of religion. The scheme is an admitted oversimplification.

Bellah discussed each of his five types in terms of three general aspects of religion, namely its symbol system which covers beliefs, the type of religious actions which predominate, that is the form of ritual, and finally the type of organisation.

In the *primitive* stage of development, best exemplified by societies like that of the Australian aborigines, we find a set of beliefs in a mythical world which is seen as being closely bound up with the natural environment and prominent features of it. Ritual is basically participatory involving all members of the group without specialists.

There is no distinct religious organisation. Bellah sees this type of religion as largely to do with the promotion of social integration and solidarity.

The *archaic* stage is characterised by the development of distinct deities with whom human beings interact. The religion takes the form of a cult involving worship of the deities and frequently involving sacrifice to them. The beginnings of a priesthood can be seen hut which is not yet clearly differentiated from or subordinate to the political realm.

In the *historic* stage religion becomes increasingly transcendental. The gods and the sacred realm are now seen as separate and distant from the everyday world. World rejection and a concern with salvation become dominant themes. The priesthood acquires a degree of autonomy since the political and religious spheres are now distinct. Priests and religious functionaries become a distinct and separate elite. This allows religion to come into conflict with the political regime and it may provide, by this stage, ideological backing for reform movements and protests. Religion may now play a more dominant role in social change rather than merely legitimating the social order.

With *early modern* religion there is a swing away from world-rejection. Salvation remains the primary concern but is now seen as something to be attained not through withdrawal from the affairs of this life and world but through activity in the midst of it. Early modern religion begins with the Reformation and Protestantism. There is a greater emphasis upon personal conviction and the hierarchical character of the priesthood is weakened or abandoned. Early modern religion tends to promote social change through its emphasis on worldly activity.

By the *modern* period this de-emphasis of the transcendental, world-rejecting aspect of earlier traditions develops to the point where the notion of a superior sacred realm disappears. Social action and community work become the ideal and the organisation becomes fluid and impermanent, often taking the form of special purpose groups. The emphasis is upon individual responsibility for working out personal solutions which may take the form of 'secular' types of activity. Modern religion is ambivalent in its social impact, either tending to undermine social stability or, on the other hand, opening up opportunities for creative innovation.

Bellah sums up the development as one of increasing freedom of personality and society through religious ideas.

The range of terms used by Wallace and Bellah to classify types of religion, especially the religions of the less complex societies, suggests, then, that it is not useful merely to contrast primitive with transcendental religion. Also, many of the transcendental religions retain 'primitive' elements. Christianity could be argued to have its magical side; ancestor worship was as important in Confucian China as in West Africa. Nevertheless, it will be convenient to treat the pre-transcendental religions together since there are a number of common themes and similarities between them. The religions of primitive societies, described and analysed by anthropologists, also offer an opportunity to examine in detail the primary aspect of religion, shared by the 'higher' religions but difficult to examine clearly in that context because of its subordination to the transcendental dimension. Work on this aspect of the transcendental religions is, also, so much less abundant than that on primitive societies. Where possible, however, attention will be drawn to the similarities between primitive religions and the transcendental religions or at least to the primary aspects of belief in those societies in which the latter predominate. The lessons that anthropological studies have for the study of the transcendental religions are considerable.

The diversity of pre-transcendental religion is so great that it would be a foolish endeavour to attempt to summarise and discuss here the whole of the very extensive body of material written about it. Discussion, therefore, will be limited to three major themes or aspects, namely ancestor worship, witchcraft and spirit possession. These themes are particularly revealing of the relationship between social structure and religious beliefs and practices which is a central purpose of this book to demonstrate.

Ancestors and Ghosts

The notion of a spiritual essence or aspect of the human being which 'survives' death as a soul, ghost, ancestor and so on, is a universal one. It is found in societies from the most simple to the most complex although with considerable variations of detail. The soul might, as in ancient Sumeria for example, enjoy nothing more than a shadowy subterranean existence, or it might in other cultures enjoy the delights of an everlasting paradise. Very often more than one non-material aspect of the human being is distinguished, each separating at death to go its way. The ancestor spirit may be distinguished from the personality and this from the breath, and so on. In ancestor worship it is only the first aspect that is the concern of ancestor cults. It is with these that we shall largely he concerned here.

As we have seen in Chapter 1 some early theorists in the sociology of religion believed that the origins of religion lay in the belief in the continued survival and importance of ancestral spirits for the living. Herbert Spencer in his *Principles of Sociology* traced the origins of beliefs in gods and spirits to a primal belief in a soul which survived the death of the individual. The existence of this non-material dimension of the human being was suggested to early man, he speculated, by their experience of dreams in which the dead might appear. The earliest forms of religious ritual took the form of propitiation of the dead. The notion of gods derived from prominent and heroic ancestral figures, founders of clans and lineages, and so on.

The study of ancestor worship, then, is not without a degree of general theoretical significance. Ancestor worship is (or was) prominent in China, Polynesia and West Africa. Most studies of it have been carried out in Africa where it is closely connected with the explanation of and reaction to *misfortune*. Among the most detailed studies are those of Meyer Fortes, carried out mainly among the Tallensi of Ghana (Fortes, 1959, 1965) who attribute nearly all events in a person's life, both good and bad, to the actions of ancestral spirits or to something similar, namely a Personal Destiny spirit, also associated with ancestral spirits.

Ancestor worship, Fortes claims (1965), is always rooted in domestic, kinship and descent-group relations and institutions. It is certainly not simply a cult of the dead. Not just anyone becomes an ancestor but only a person with living descendants of the right category. To become an ancestor establishes and expresses, therefore, the continued relevance of the dead person for his or her community and society. Ancestors are those who stood in a specific politico-rural relationship to their descendants and thus have nothing to do with attachments and affections which develop between one generation and the next nor even with the aspect of nurturance, protection and care between parents and children but rather with authority relationships. What becomes an ancestor is solely the aspect of authority that the deceased had over the descendant. Thus in matrilineal societies the father, who has the responsibility of bringing up and caring for his children and who often has a close, affectionate and easy relationship with them does not become an ancestor of any significance. Rather it is the mother's brother, a figure of authority who has legal responsibility for his sister's son, who becomes an ancestor and must be worshipped.

Ancestor worship, then, Fortes argues, is a representation or extension of the authority component in the jural relations of successive generations and not simply the expression in supernatural form of the total complex of affective, educative, and supportive relationships. It is not the whole person but only the jural status as someone vested with authority and responsibility that is transmitted into ancesterhood. This explains why beliefs about the mode of existence of ancestor spirits are usually very vague (see also Newell, 1976, pp. 223). Those who venerate ancestors are generally unable to say very much about what form they take, where they are or what kind of existence they lead. They are unconcerned, what is more, about such things since they are irrelevant from the point of view of the significance of ancestor worship in their lives.

Neither does veneration of ancestors depend at all upon what actual relations between the deceased and the descendant(s) were like when the former was alive. It has nothing at all to do with individual feelings. The relationship may have been characterised by tension and even dislike and hostility. The deceased may have been a paragon of virtue or the worst reprobate in life, but whatever the case becomes an ancestor and the object of veneration and cult worship. A senior descendant, an eldest son for example, whether virtuous or competent, wicked or inept, will have the responsibility of conducting the rituals of the cult.

In most cases, and particularly in West Africa, failure to conduct the appropriate rituals, make the necessary offerings, or to do whatever is required by the cult, will result in dire consequences and punishments being visited upon the living by their ancestors, once again quite regardless as to the degree of affection in which they were held or had for their descendants or of their character and personality in life. Proper veneration of the ancestors, on the other hand, will bring good fortune and prosperity.

This power of the ancestors and the attribution of misfortunes to their intervention in the lives and fates of the living is well described by Fortes in his study of ancestor worship among the Tallensi (1959). The Tallensi are organised into patrilineal kinship groups in which complete jural and ritual authority is vested in the father and the head of the household. Filial piety is considered to be of the utmost importance and as a result there is usually a high level of tension and suppressed hostility and antagonism as well as affection between father and son. This repressed hostility can be seen in the taboos that first sons have to observe (Fortes, 1987). From the age of six a first son is forbidden to have direct or symbolic contact with his father. He cannot eat with him nor use any of his belongings.

When a father dies he becomes an ancestor and it is largely through the father's ancestral spirit that the son contacts all the various ancestral spirits which are important for him and which are thought to affect his life and fate. Misfortunes are commonly attributed to the action of such ancestors.

Very often, however, misfortune is attributed to a spirit which Fortes calls Prenatal Destiny. This spirit will usually be divined as the cause of a misfortune when the afflicted party is in some way out on a limb with respect to the social structure. Either the person is too young to be implicated in social relationships in a significant way, suffers from an incurable physical or psychological handicap or is in danger of being permanently forgotten because he or she has and is likely to have no offspring. Prenatal Destiny serves as an alibi for such 'failures' and handicaps, relieving kin of the responsibility and potential guilt as well as exonerating the individual concerned in his or her own mind.

Prenatal Destiny is likened by Fortes to Oedipal fate. This is more than simply an analogy used illustratively by Fortes. His whole analysis is heavily influenced by Freudian psychoanalytic theory. Prenatal Destiny symbolises those experiences which are characterised by an inability to become integrated into society and ultimately this amounts to a failure in the primary relationships between parents arid children. Patenthood is the critical. irreducible determinant of the whole social structure. Prenatal Destiny is like the Oedipal idea because it recognises forces in social and personal development that cannot be changed or regulated by the social order. In Tallensi doctrine, Fortes tells us, those with bad or evil Prenatal Destiny are unconsciously rejecting society - the trouble lies in inescapable, inborn wishes.

Evil Prenatal Destiny, however, does not necessarily determine life-fate inexorably. There are ritual procedures for casting out evil Prenatal Destiny. Such rituals, Fortes argues, help to dispose of the emotional and moral tensions generated in structural contradictions and antagonisms and by this means the onus of rejection is shifted onto a supernatural plane. The feelings of helplessness and depression in the face of misfortune are made tolerable. Prenatal Destiny conceptualises that experience in which parental failure leads to the latent hostility towards parents getting the upper hand.

The opposite of Prenatal Destiny is Good Destiny. Every Tallensi man has a Good Destiny shrine associated with a particular configuration of ancestors. In return for submission and service these ancestors bring the owner of the shrine good fortune. The owner must sacrifice at his Good Destiny shrine and if he does so and carries out his kinship obligations to the living he will enjoy prosperity.

The powers of ancestors, Fortes points out, are the powers that a father has over his children but immeasurably magnified and sanctified. They are also removed from the normal controls that operate in everyday relations such as cooperation and reciprocity. Fortes likens the ancestors to Job in the Biblical story. The Tallensi can never be quite sure that they have fully satisfied the ancestors. Ill fortune does not, of course, follow anything but a fairly random pattern. Those who are scrupulous in performing their duties towards ancestors and kin are just as likely to suffer it as those who are lax. The Tallensi rationalise the apparent contradiction by saying that one can never be sure that some small thing has not been overlooked; in other words within the terms of the belief system. The reality, however, is that they experience the actions of ancestors as unpredictable and even capricious.

Good Destiny is the expression in religious symbols and sanctions of the ideal of parental care, success and the correct response by children and their growth into adulthood and maturity. Whereas Prenatal Destiny serves to identify the fact of irremediable failure in the development of the individual to full social capacity, Good Destiny recognises that the hostile component in parental-filial relationships has been overcome. Oedipal predisposition is transformed into Jobian fulfillment.

For Fortes this set of beliefs amounts to something like an official ideology. Ancestor worship, he says, is 'a body of religious beliefs and ritual practices, correlated with rules of conduct, which serves to entrench the principle of jural authority together with its corollary, legitimate right, and its reciprocal, designated accountability, as an indisputable and sacrosanct value-principle of the social system' (Fortes, 1965, p.139).

Such a belief system is a powerful aid to authority since those who exercise it can claim that they are themselves bound by a superior authority which is beyond their control. Jural authority is placed upon a pedestal where it is inviolable and unchallengeable. The key ritual of sacrifice to the ancestors is a means of symbolising such subordination and also of making reparations to predecessors who have, in a sense, been ousted from their positions of authority.

Why should the Talensi express these ideas in terms of ancestor beliefs? Fortes says little about this except that by projecting the whole thing onto a supernatural plane much anxiety inherent in the situation is avoided. Also, he says, the Tallensi cannot see the real nature of their beliefs because they do not have the cultural resources for analysing their religious symbolism in the way that is possible for the anthropologist. In any case, if they could analyse the belief system in this way they would have no need for it.

In this type of society jural authority is vested in persons by virtue of kinship and descent and so it is the deceased kinsmen - ancestors - who represent this authority and the continuity of the social structure. And it is the condition of filial dependence from childhood to adulthood which provides the model of subordination to authority in such societies and therefore the code of symbolism and ritual by means of which reverence for authority can be regularly affirmed and enacted. 'In their ancestor worship', Fortes says, 'Tallensi make clear to themselves the fact that, though parents depart, the authority and jurisdiction they wielded—and which enabled them also to be protective and benevolent—still goes on' (ibid.). The parents are seen to survive in transmuted form but what in fact survives is the web of kinship and descent relationships generated by the parents and the filial experiences standardised in the norms, values and beliefs inculcated by them.

Ancestors, Fortes suggests, are demanding, persecutory and interfering because parents are like this in the eyes of children. It is also an effective' way of representing the sovereignty of authority. The absence of any connection between good fortune and good behaviour in reality serves to make the ancestors appear to be to be somewhat persecutory. Since misfortunes befall everyone to some degree regardless of their behaviour, the authority of the ancestors is always demonstrated, if only infrequently in some cases. The ancestors, nevertheless, however persecutory they may seem, always act justly and good behaviour, while it cannot in reality guarantee good fortune, does bind the ancestors to act justly. If misfortunes occur it can only be the fault of the descendants.

In concentrating heavily on the importance of ancestor worship in the maintenance and legitimation of jural authority, Fortes' work is inevitably focused upon descent group ancestors and their relationship with the living. If descent group ancestors are essentially punitive as a result of their authority role, McKnight (1967) has pointed out, then extra-descent group ancestors, as he calls them, should in theory be largely benevolent or at least not at all punitive. For example, the mother's brother in many patrilineal kinship systems has an easy and affectionate relationship with the sister's son. This ought to be reflected in the ancestor beliefs. Among the Tallensi, upon which Fortes' theory of ancestor worship is largely based, we should expect to find that maternal ancestors are tender and indulgent, as are maternal kin in life, and certainly not the cause of misfortune. Yet we find quite the opposite. Among the Tallensi and in many other patrilineal societies, maternal ancestors are even more punitive than paternal ancestors. Similarly, in matrilineal societies, patrilineal ancestors may well be punitive, contrary to the expectation that Fortes' approach would lead us to hold. Whatever its merits for understanding the cult of descent-group ancestors Fortes' approach seems not to be at all applicable to extra-descent-group ancestors.

The explanation for the punitive character of extra-descent-group ancestors lies, McKnight suggests, in the tensions generated between members of descent groups linked by marriage as must be the case where descent group exogamy is practised. One also fights with those one marries, as McKnight puts it. These conflicts concern such things as bride-wealth payment, of final duties of sons-in-law and treatment of the wife. In a patrilineal society, the tensions and conflicts tend to centre on the mother's brother-sister's son relationship. The sister's son is caught between his own and his mother's descent group which makes him the target for revenge on the part of the latter group as a means of enforcing their rights. Resort to physical force is not possible between affinal groups so supernatural sanctions tend to be used. Hence the attribution of misfortunes to the action of maternal ancestors among the Tallensi and other patrilineal peoples. In matrilineal societies the paternal ancestors, as we have seen, may similarly be seen as the most punitive.

In drawing attention to the tensions and conflicts between affinally related groups and the role of ancestors in their expression and pursuance, McKnight presents Fortes' approach as being somewhat incomplete or partial, applying only to descent-group ancestors. It is tempting to go further than McKnight and reassess Fortes' approach in the light of McKnight's observations. The actions of ancestors in punishing descendants by bringing misfortune upon them might be seen in the more general light of the inevitability of tension in both descent and affinal relationships. Fortes, for example, describes the ambivalence and tension in the relationship between father and son among the Tallensi centred upon the authority role of the father and the desire for independence on the part of the son. He also shows how those responsible for exercising authority are able to legitimate it by appeal to a higher authority - that of the ancestors. Both in this relationship and that between a man and his mother's people there arc close ties characterised nevertheless by conflicts of interest. In both cases ancestor beliefs are utilised in these relationships to control others. Seen in this way ancestor beliefs are less an ideological legitimation of authority structures, or not simply or primarily so, but also a means of managing conflict or even of pursuing it- a means of manipulation, control and the exercise of power as well as authority.

A second major challenge to Fortes analysis has focused upon the differences between ancestors and elders. Kopytoff (1971) has argued that the notion of ancestor cult carries with it extensive ethnocentric connotations which are misapplied in the case African belief and practice. It is not helpful, he contends, to speak of 'worship', 'sacrifice' and 'cult' in connection with the relationships that many African peoples have with their ancestors. In Africa ancestors should be seen as nothing more than deceased elders, the fact that they are not living elders does not mean that they belong to a different category of being. The relationships that the living have with them are the same in every significant respect that people have with living elders as far as the formal as opposed to the personal aspects of the relationship are concerned. Ancestors are not 'worshipped'; they are simply shown the same respect that elders are shown. People do not 'sacrifice' to ancestors they simply give them the gifts or tribute that are due to elders. It is just that people such as the Tallensi do not believe that the formal relationship they have with their elders ceases upon death although the personal and informal relationship does. Western observers of such cultures are inclined to apply, illegitimately, concepts such as worship, sacrifice and expiation where relationships with what are seen to be spirits of the dead are concerned.

This reformulation, Kopytoff argues, helps avoid many misunderstandings and remove puzzles that Fortes' account creates. Sacrifice to ancestors is seen by Fortes as expiation for the living having ousted the ancestor and a means of assuaging the guilt that is felt. But there is no evidence of guilt or of its relief in many African societies where belief in ancestors is prominent. Such notions are not necessary once we realise that ancestors have not been ousted at all but simply that the relationship that existed with them when alive continues to exist after their death. Similarly, the problem of explaining why some societies structured rather like the Tallensi along lines of unilineal descent do not, nevertheless, have strong beliefs in the importance of ancestors, is solved. In societies such as the Tiv and Nuer, although unilineal descent groups are important, elders are not. Ancestors have little importance for the living because when alive as elders they had little importance.

Ancestors are not significant among the Songye even though elders have considerable authority because the Songye believe they are reincarnated in their grandchildren.

Thus ""ancestorship" is but an aspect of the broader phenomenon of "eldership"'. Understanding it is riot so much a question of un-covering deeply rooted psychological processes as of finding an adequate means of expressing African cultural categories in terms of Western concepts.

Kopytoff's challenging arguments have stimulated, lively debate, to no small extent because they raise some fundamental questions relating to the understanding of unfamiliar belief systems and the dangers of ethnocentricity in utilising concepts derived from Western traditions of belief. Brain (1973) and Calhoun (1980) question Kopytoff's equation of ancestors with elders. Brain points out that unlike elders ancestors know the thoughts of the living. The cult of the ancestors is also, in his view, far more than simply reverence for dead elders. Similarly, Calhoun considers that elders and ancestors are distinct categories. Ancestors, because they are dead, can be idealised and can represent collective as opposed to personal interests for more than elders can and as a result play a distinct role in the legitimation and maintenance of the social and moral order.

Clearly, there are similarities and differences between ancestors and elders in African societies. It is tempting to try to decide which are more important, the similarities or the differences. Janelli and Janelli (1982) come down in favour of the similarities in their study of ancestor worship in Korea. Mendonsa (1976), however, points out that this may well be a pointless exercise. Whether the similarities or the differences are crucial depends upon context. In the case of the Sisala of Northern Ghana the similarities are greater, for example, between office-holding jural elders and ancestors than between ancestors and elders who have no jural authority. Fortes' point that ancestor beliefs are a projection of the jural element onto a socio-religious plane is thus well made according to Mendonsa. On the other hand, it could be argued in defence of Kopytoff's position that in this particular society it is only certain elders with whom a significant relationship will continue after their death, those with jural authority.

A question one might ask at this point is why it is that only the formal and jural authority relationships with elders continues beyond death if Kopytoff is correct in his analysis. Why does the personal relationship not continue? Elders are also fathers, brothers and so on. Why do other relationships not continue beyond the grave? This observation tends to lead us to favour Fortes' as does the fact that ancestors often have shrines devoted to them with all the trappings of ritual and ritual objects associated with them. Ancestors are indeed dead elders but it is difficult not to acknowledge that death transforms them in some sense and makes them no longer purely, or at least much less, mundane.

So far we have considered only African material. Studies of ancestor worship in China and Japan have added new perspectives to the anthropological work on Africa. One issue that immediately arises when one compares African and Asian studies is that of the degree of punitiveness of ancestors in Asia. If ancestor worship is a means of exercising' authority then we should expect to find that ancestors behave in a similar way in China and Japan where, as in Africa, unilineal descent groups have also been a central feature of traditional social organisation. It has often been claimed, however, that ancestors in China and Japan are primarily benevolent and rarely (Freedman, 1967; Jordan, 1972), or even never (Hsu, 1949, 1963) punitive. So dependent is the welfare of each generation upon its predecessors in this type of society, Hsu argues, that hostility between them is virtually unthinkable. This has been disputed by many who have carried out fieldwork in these countries (Ahern, 1973; Wolf, 1974a; Kerner, 1976; Smith, 1974; Yonemura, 1976; Janelli and Janelli, 1982) all of whom document cases of often quite punitive action attributed to ancestors.

Wolf suggests that the ideal in many Chinese communities is that ancestors will be benevolent and that there is reluctance to assent to the proposition that they might cause misfortune whereas the reality is that misfortunes may well be attributed to their intervention in specific cases, usually as punishment for neglect.

In their study of ancestor worship in Korea the Janellis explore this point further. There has also been a tendency on the part of researchers who are themselves from East Asia to overemphasise the benign aspects of ancestors, reflecting a general reluctance in the area to admit that ancestors can be punitive in popular belief. The Janellis reformulate Hsu's hypothesis arguing that intergenerational dependence explains why ancestors ought to be entirely benevolent in popular belief and why there is a reluctance to report that they are anything other than such but acknowledging that, at the same time, misfortunes are often attributed to them.

More than this, there is no uniformity of popular opinion or perception on this question, at least as far as Korea is concerned. Women, for example, are more likely to acknowledge the punitive character of ancestors than are men. This reflects, the Janellis argue, tile different experience of men and women in typical social relationships and the varying degree of conflict entailed in them. A woman has two sets of relationships, those with her natal kin and those with her husband's kin whereas a man has only one set, those with his natal kin. The relationships a woman has with her husband's kin are frequently more conflictual than those men have with their natal kin, it is the lower dependence upon and greater strain with the affinal kin that makes women more inclined to see ancestors as punitive. Such differences find institutional reflection. Women's dealing with ancestors is largely in the context of shamanistic rites in which ancestors demand sacrifices, appear to be self-interested and are thought to have caused afflictions. In the ancestor rites-conducted by men they appear much more passive, patient and benevolent.

However, in other parts of East Asia this difference between men and women in their perceptions of the punitive character of ancestors is less marked. This tends to be the case where men more often marry uxorilocally (post-marital residence in the home of the female partner), as in Japan, where the difference between the perception of men and women is slight, and in parts of Taiwan where a high rate of uxorilocal marriage combined with other factors seems to obliterate it altogether.

It does seem, however, that Chinese and Japanese ancestors

are not thought to be as powerful and potentially harmful as many African ancestors are. Fortes himself admits that Chinese and Japanese ancestor beliefs do have a different character to those of Africa (1974, pp. 910). Whereas in Africa ancestor worship is largely concerned with expiating offences and atoning for ritual neglect, in China and Japan it is rather more concerned with keeping the ancestors content and at peace. In Africa it is geared to the protection of the living and in China and Japan to the consolation of the dead. This difference may well be explained by the fact, as Wolf points out (1974b, p. 168), that the African societies in which ancestor worship is prominent are for the most part stateless societies in which all authority is vested in senior kinsmen who dominate all aspects of lineage life and affairs whereas in China kin simply do not control many of the forces and agencies that shape an individual's life and fate. Here the state and local authorities are equally, if not more important. Wolf offers this as an explanation of why in China major disasters are not attributed ancestors. They are, he argues, not seen as being that powerful. Great misfortunes were attributed to the actions of gods modelled on the imperial bureaucracy. His point could easily, however, be extended to account for the generally less punitive nature of ancestors in China and Japan.

Fortes (1961), on the basis of comparative African data, argues that where transfer of authority and property from father to son is relatively smooth and takes place step by step ancestors are seen to be less punitive, echoing the point made earlier by Freedman (1967) who suggests that in societies where corporate kinship groups larger than the family are important, ancestors are not so powerful or punitive. This is the case in China, where there is also a slow and more progressive transfer of authority from father to son.

Wolf (19746) also points out that in China misfortunes may be attributed to a category of dead persons who are not ancestors, namely ghosts. Ghosts include the neglected dead - neglected because they have left no descendants or who have died far away from home and have been forgotten as well as murder victims, suicides and the unjustly executed. They are like homeless wandering bandits outside the accepted social structures and are wholly malevolent. Between ancestors proper and ghosts there are also other categories of dead - those who contributed to a persons line but were not members of it and those who were dependants of the line and have no one else to care for them. The ancestor tablets of the latter are placed on the right of the ancestor alter (the tablets of ancestors proper are placed on the left) while the tablets of the former are placed in a corner of the kitchen or in a hallway and they are thought of almost as ghosts. There is, then, a continuum of dead persons extending from full ancestors to malevolent ghosts.

Jordan (1972) also shows how in the South Western region of Taiwan that he studied family misfortunes such as illnesses are attributed to the ghosts of those who have no descendants or who are in some similar way social-structurally anomalous. The misfortune can be alleviated it is believed by altering this anomalous situation. For example, if an unmarried girl dies a spirit marriage may be arranged so that she will not be without descendants. The girl is married after her death to someone whose descendants will count as hers and who will commemorate her as an ancestor. Wolf (1974b) reports similar practises in the Taipei region.

Contrary to this view that kin without descendants can become malevolent ghosts, Weller (1987) argues that it is necessary to distinguish between two categories of ghost in Taiwanese belief, or at least two distinct ways of thinking about ghosts. In relation to ancestors the dead who are without descendants are regarded as pitiful. These, marginal ancestors' are not feared for the misfortunes they might bring; people feel sorry for them. The gifts given to them are not so much to propitiate them as to express sympathy for them. Other categories of dead, such as those who have died in battle or who have no known kinship affiliations, are better seen as 'marginal gods' rather than marginal ancestors. These are propitiated because they are malevolent and feared. The key distinction, then, between ghosts and ancestors rests on the presence or absence of kinship links. As Weller puts it ghosts are strangers, ancestors are relatives. The dangerous ghosts are those who are no one's ancestors.

Despite reference to Jordan's data on ghost marriage as a

means of removing the malevolence from those who are clearly marginal ancestors, Weller denies that marginal ancestors are seen as malevolent. Clearly there are uncertainties relating to the logic of Chinese beliefs pertaining to ancestors and ghosts stemming either from different interpretations of data or reflecting ambivalence and contradictions in the way they are conceptualised by the believers themselves. We have relatively little information about the circumstances in which misfortunes are attributed to ancestors or to ghosts in China and Japan. More information on this question might reveal a great deal relevant to the general understanding and interpretation of ancestor beliefs. There is clearly a great deal of work to be done in this field before theories such as that of Fortes or the modifications to it suggested above can be reliably evaluated and tested.

Witchcraft

There are other reactions to misfortune than attributing it to the actions of ancestor spirits. It might be blamed upon the malevolence of a living fellow human being with mystical ability to cause harm – that is to witchcraft or sorcery. Witchcraft is generally the term used where the power is inherent in the individual and sorcery when it is learned knowledge of techniques using, for example, spells and substances or calling upon supernatural or mystical powers. The distinction, however, is not always as clear cut in practice.

Witchcraft has been extensively studied in primitive societies and there are also a number of studies from a sociological perspective of European forms of it. A common theme in such studies is that witchcraft accusations are related to the moral state of the group or of particular relationships within it. Through an examination of the pattern of accusations and the social relationships, tensions and divisions underlying this pattern, sociologists and anthropologists have shown how through witchcraft accusations individuals are made responsible or held liable for the welfare of their fellows. The association made between witchcraft and misfortune implies that if social relations were harmonious, misfortunes would not occur or would occur less often.

The classic study of witchcraft is Evans-Pritchard's *Witchcraft, Oracle's and Magic Among the Azande*. This work was important for three main reasons. Firstly, it showed how conceptions of causation which go beyond the ordinary, everyday kind of causation that science is concerned with are central and crucial in understanding primitive beliefs, particularly witchcraft. The Azande usually attribute misfortunes such as sickness and death to witchcraft or sorcery not accepting that these things are matters of chance.

Most deaths are attributed by the Azande to witchcraft. In explaining a death as being due to witchcraft the Azande would not disagree about what for the Western observer would count as the 'facts' of the case, For example, if the deceased had been bitten by a poisonous snake and had died as a consequence, the Azande would not dispute this as a cause of the death but they will persist, nevertheless, in their attribution of the death to witchcraft. It is certainly not a question of them being ignorant of the fact that some snakes are poisonous and that' their bite can cause death. They may not understand how the action of the snake toxin in the body brings about death but this is irrelevant to their belief that the death was caused by witchcraft. The questions they pose about the event go beyond a need for a 'normal' causal account to ask why the event should have happened at all. Why was the person bitten by the snake? Why was the snake in just that place at just that time? Why was it the deceased that was bitten and not someone else standing nearby? For the Azande these questions are answered by the attribution of the chain of events to the action of the power of witchcraft. It is because of the malevolent intentions of someone with witchcraft powers that the person stepped on the snake. It is because of witchcraft that the snake was there in the grass just at the time the person put their foot down in that particular place. This cliam of events was brought about by an enemy of the deceased who out of hatred of them wished to cause harm to them.

The Azande do not dismiss the possibility of a purely natural or accidental death, but although all human beings must eventually die the time and manner of their death is explained in nearly every actual and particular case in terms of witchcraft.

Secondly, Evans-Pritchard's study showed how apparently bizarre and incomprehensible beliefs could be seen to have a kind of coherence when placed in their social context and also to have a degree of practical value for dealing with situations. Evans-Pritchard describes how he himself, for a period of time, used the Azande techniques of divination, employed for a variety of purposes such as determining propitious times to undertake journeys or economic ventures as well as for uncovering crimes including witchcraft activity, quite successfully. He also showed how the beliefs formed a closed, self-reinforcing system within which Azande thought was imprisoned so that it was unthinkable, almost literally, to challenge it as a system. There were, consequently, many ways in which beliefs false in our eyes could actually be upheld by experience. In fact, Evans-Pritchard lists 22 reasons that Azande can give to explain apparent contradiction of their beliefs by evidence. If an oracle,[2] for example, were to give contradictory responses to questions this might be attributed to the person consulting it not having observed all the required taboos beforehand or to counter-witchcraft acting against it, and so on.

Thirdly, the study showed how witchcraft beliefs are closely associated with strained personal relations, particularly where no institutional controls or means for resolving conflicts and antagonisms exist—where the relationships concerned are not governed by known and accepted procedures of regulation.

Evans-Pritchard found that among the Azande witchcraft accusations tended to occur in a patterned way between persons who stood in particular relationships to one another. Witchcraft tended to operate primarily among neighbours (the Azande believe, in fact that it is only effective over short distances) who were not kinsmen, superior in rank or of the opposite sex. In short, accusations of witchcraft were only made between persons who lived close to one another but whose relationship was not regulated by the rules and customs of kinship, rank and sex. And, of course, the oracles always produced names of people who were very plausible suspects since the Azande only ever put to the oracles the names of likely candidates, in other words those with whom they had recently quarrelled. To do otherwise would obviously, in their eyes, have been a waste of time.

All this suggested to Evans-Pritchard that witchcraft operated as a means of social control in areas where other institutionalised means were absent. Neighbours frequently came into conflict with one another but their conflicts were not regulated by the kind of conventions which regulate the relationship between kin, between commoners and chiefs or between the sexes. The notion of witchcraft, he argues, could be seen as a means of condemning vicious and hostile feelings generated by conflicts of interest, tensions and rivalries. Those who bore grudges or showed animosity to others would have to control their feelings lest their name be placed before one of the Azande divinatory oracles and ultimately be accused of being a witch. Witch-craft is thus bound up closely with morality and correct behaviour towards others. It is a means of expressing moral values and of condemning anti-social attitudes. The witch among the Azande, as in Europe, is seen as a reversal of everything that a good person should be.

The picture that Evans-Pritchard gives us is clearly a rather functionalist one and this is perhaps the chief weakness of the analysis. It probably overemphasised the positive role of witchcraft beliefs in promoting social order and harmony. Witchcraft beliefs might equally have tended to generate and intensify conflicts in the pre-colonial era when it was acceptable to take revenge upon a witch believed to have caused the death of a kinsman. It may bean effective means of showing someone that they are harbouring resentments which prevent good relations being maintained but it is not necessarily always the best means of preserving good relations to accuse someone of such a wicked and vile thing as using witchcraft, especially when the accused believes himself or herself innocent. In the past witchcraft accusations which were rejected by the accused may well have been followed by retaliation leading to blood feud. Witchcraft, as later studies showed, could be a means of pursuing conflicts as well as a means of resolving them-it can be a useful weapon for the furtherance of interests against others or in other words of exercising power.

Later studies of witchcraft and sorcery in primitive societies have brought out more clearly its role in power struggles and Gluckman, in a review of this work, has also shown that witchcraft is often an expression of deeply rooted conflicts and contradictions inherent in particular social structures (Gluckman, 1972). It is often an important factor in the breakup of communities and groups rather than a major force for social control and cohesion. These studies also led to a modification of the contention of Evans-Pritchard's Azande study that witchcraft accusations tend to occur in relationships not governed by structural norms and rules since in many other societies kin, and often close kin, accuse one another.

In the patrilineal societies of Southern Africa (for example Zulu, Swazi, Mpondo, Xhosa and so on) a group of men related through the male line and tracing common descent from a single ancestor four or five generations back occupy a group of homesteads each of which jointly owns land and cattle. On marriage these men bring wives into their own homesteads while their own kinswomen move away on marriage to their husbands' homesteads. Ideally a man will take several wives but in practice only a few senior men are able to do so.

The status of a woman who joins the homestead community as the wife of one of its members varies according to the status of her husband, the status of her father, and in the case of polygynous marriages her position in the order in which he acquired his wives. Because of this multiplicity of criteria it is not surprising that disputes and jealousies arise among the wives.

Also, each wife tries to further the interests of her own children against those of co-wives. Wives are in an ambiguous and contradictory position in this type of social structure. A wife has the duty of producing sons which strengthen the group of kin and ensure its continuity. On the other hand, a particular woman's sons compete for positions with the sons of other wives. In the very act of fulfilling her duty by producing sons a woman simultaneously weakens the group by undermining its solidarity. Furthermore, a man is closely identified with his brothers and half-brothers and with his patrilineal cousins but, on the other hand, he fulfils himself as an individual by marrying and having sons of his own. A wife thus stands at the centre of a conflicting set of values. She provides her husband with the means of creating his own autonomous household yet it is necessary for the group to produce new male members for any individual to achieve full adult status.

Polygyny thus inherently tends to produce tensions and conflicts which are not the consequence of clashes of personality or purely personal factors but of social structural arrangements which place people inevitably in conflict with one another. It is wives who are accused of witchcraft in these societies and usually by their mother-in-law, sister-in-law or brother-in-law. A daughter-in-law quickly comes into conflict with her husband's mother under whose supervision and authority she is. The mother-in-law represents the unity of all her sons, while the wife represents the independence of one particular son her husband.

This pattern of tensions and conflicts, Gluckman argues, is common in patrilineal joint families and produces a variety of notions concerning the inherent evil of women and femininity whether they take the form of witchcraft beliefs or not. In China women were said to compromise male vigour. Hindus believe that a man gives up part of his life and virtue in intercourse. Many Bantu peoples believe in the mystically polluting and harmful powers of menstrual blood and the blood of birth.

Hence the characterisation among Southern Bantu peoples of women as witches. Zulus believe that a woman's desires attract familiars who demand from her the lives of her husband's kin in return for their favours. Wives are believed to be inherently evil and cause misfortunes. Yet they possess ritual powers for good as well.

When a misfortune occurs among the Zulu, a diviner is called. He calls out questions before the assembled community to try to discover what is troubling them. They will clap and shout as he does so and the closer he gets to the cause of the trouble the louder becomes the clapping. Ultimately he will specify the name of an individual who is causing the misfortunes, sickness or whatever through witchcraft. The named individual is likely to be a younger wife of one of the men of the community. The diviner knows very well the kind of tensions that will exist in the community and he is guided by the community in his divination of the causes of the trouble. The community, however, perceives the diviner's activities as entirely objective and the outcome is, in their eyes, due to the diviner's particular skills and special powers.

Divination procedures such as this take on a special significance in some societies. Witchcraft accusations often play a role in the course of fundamental rifts in a community that has grown large and is on the point of division. Fission of the group is a necessity in the economic and ecological conditions which prevail but is nevertheless a contentious and conflictual process which is experienced as destructive of a solidarity which ideally should always be preserved. It is, consequently, traumatic. Rival factions within such a group will attempt to control the divination procedure and produce an outcome which leaves the opposing faction responsible for the heinous act of witchcraft. This justifies a separation of the two factions, either the accused or the accusing faction leaving to establish an independent community, an action normally unthinkable in communities in which the maintenance of solidarity is of overriding importance but which becomes acceptable once one party can be labelled as beyond the pale through use of the evil powers of witcheraft.[3]

Again there is a fundamental conflict of principles of social organisation involved in such situations. Group solidarity should be maintained yet division is a necessary and normal part of the dynamics of such communities. The group is able to split only if some legitimating reason can be found for destroying its solidarity. In such societies radical changes in social arrangements are not contemplated lightly. Any break in continuity is seen as a threatening disturbance full of potential danger likely in itself to bring about misfortunes. This is an expression of the essentially moral nature of the issue. It is a disturbance in the proper relations between people who are highly interdependent upon one another and responsible for one another's fate. If someone falls sick or dies in such a society it is because, in the minds of it members, the social order is not in a healthy condition. But when a group is on the point of inevitable division because of its size a misfortune will be interpreted as a sign of irreparable moral breakdown which warrants and even requires a breakup of the group.

The participants in this process are, of course, not fully aware that the disputes are actually unavoidable or that division is inevitable. Moral breakdown may have occurred but that it is due to deeply rooted contradictions in the very structure of the society is not readily evident to the members of the society. As Gluckman puts it:

> In short a belief of this kind has to be referred to a deep seated conflict of social rules, or principles of organisation, or processes of development, and not to superficial quarrels arising out of divergent interests . . . The essence of these situations is that the people concerned are not aware of these conflicts (1972, p. 18).

It is perhaps to some extent because of this lack of awareness of the deeply rooted nature of the conflicts that the forces at work are conceptualised as insidious, mysterious and intangible. In a sense they are exactly that. They are also difficult to control and to combat, working away in invisible but lethal ways.

Studies carried out in a wide range of societies seem to confirm Gluckman's claims. Among the Nupe of West Africa, for example, it is husbands who accuse wives of witchcraft (Nadel. 1954). Ideally, in this society a wife should be subservient to her husband, bear him children, raise them and look after the home. In reality wives often achieve a good deal of independence. Women frequently engage in trade and market activities which provides them with an independent source of income, often of a significant amount. Instead of the husband supporting his wife she often has to help him out financially. It is often the wife who provides the money for a son's marriage payment to the bride's kin. This is considerably humiliating for men. It is not surprising that given a belief in witchcraft it is women who are said by Nupe men to have harmful witchcraft powers.

In another study Monica Wilson (1951) attempts to show why among the Mpondo of South Africa witches are believed to be motivated by sensual lust, while among the Nyakyusa of Tanzania witches are greedy for milk and meat. The significant factor in the Mpondo case is that because of kinship regulations men are surrounded by many women who are sexually taboo, and at the same time the rules of apartheid banned any sexual contact with white women. This leads to the idea that witches are motivated by sexual desire. In the Nyakyusa case there is a conflict between the obligations a man has to his lineage fellows with whom he holds and sacrifices cattle, on the one hand, and those he has to his age-mates with whom he lives in their own village but with whom he does not own cattle in common. This leads to the idea that witches are greedy for milk and meat.

Studies of witchcraft accusations in Europe have shown similar patterns. Macfarlane's study of witchcraft trials in Essex (1970) in the fifteenth and sixteenth centuries revealed that accusations were largely made against older women, often widows who were neighbours of and had a fairly close relationship, but not one of kinship, with the accuser. Accusations occurred as a result of quarrels between neighhours usually in circumstances where the accuser had failed to give help such as a gift, a loan of food or other things thus causing resentment on the part of the accused who was said to have turned to the use of witchcraft powers in revenge. The accusers were generally moderately well-off villagers and the accused their rather less well-off neighbours, Often the accusation was the final stage in the severing of a relationship. The contradictions involved here were those of the obligation on the part of the better off in small village communities to help the more needy against, on the other hand, the desire to devote resources to personal ends and plans, or in short, as Thomas puts it (1973, p. 662) a 'conflict between neighbourliness and individualism'. This is shown more clearly between 1560 and 1650 when there was a marked increase in the number of witch trials. Economic changes and growth of population had impoverished some villagers and this had placed a heavy burden of aid and assistance on their neighbours. The normal institutions of help to the old and poor church relief, the manorial system, kin and neighbourly ties became very strained. At the same time, the yeoman farmers were under increasing pressure to invest in and improve their land in order to maintain their prosperity. The tensions and conflicts, resentments and breakdown of relationships that resulted led to increasing accusations of witchcraft.

In situations like those outlined above a person has to steer a difficult course between conflicting obligations or between conflicting motivations. To go too far in one or other direction is to invite accusations of witchcraft.

Witchcraft is often associated with a person's actions to the degree that they fail to meet some ideal of moral behaviour or with the powers and capacities of a person as an individual as opposed to commitment to the collectivity. Someone who seems too successful, whose crops grow particularly well, for example, may be said to have witchcraft powers which could he used against others. Such people go too far in the direction of serving their own interests and in a sense may show a disregard of their moral obligations to others in using their talents too much for their own ends. On the other hand, someone whose crops grow very badly compared to others is equally failing in his or her duty to the community which depends to some extent on all contributing adequately to collective production. Individuals must attempt to achieve what Gluckman calls a 'golden mean of morality' (1972, p.33).

This association of witchcraft power with individualism relates closely to the frequently ambivalent character that witchcraft powers are said to have in many societies. Very often men are believed to have powers of witchcraft which can he used for good ends, and especially to combat other evil witches at work in the community. But there is often a fine dividing line between a good and an evil witch. There is also a constant risk that the good witch will be seen to have used his or her powers for selfish ends and thus slide over into the evil category. Monica Wilson (1951) has described such processes among the Nyakyusa. Middleton (1960) has shown how among the Lugbara an elder can utilise the powers of the ancestors to punish recalcitrant subordinates as a legitimate part of his role in controlling group and community affairs but may, if he goes too far, attract an accusation of witchcraft. When a group is on the point of dividing, senior men of different factions who are competing for authority and control will vie with one another in claiming to have caused misfortunes in an attempt to demonstrate and validate their claim to have particularly privileged access to the powers of ancestors and, thereby, strengthen their leadership position. To claim too often to have brought a misfortune on someone, however, carries the danger that the elder will be accused of actually using witchcraft powers for his own selfish ends and not legitimate ancestral power.

This example illustrates the ambivalent character of witchcraft beliefs but it is noticeable that the pattern of accusations here is not like that among the southern Bantu peoples. Wives are not accused and neither are they in other patrilineally organised systems such as the Azande. What accou-nts for such differences in the pattern of accusations? Middleton and Winter (1963) have suggested, on the basis of a comparative examination of a wide range of cases, that witchcraft accusations are made against women where property interests are focused upon them. In the southern Bantu societies each wife in a polygynous household is allocated cattle and land which her own sons will inherit. It is because wives are at the focal point of a separate estate that inherent evil is thought to be mediated through women. In societies where a man's entire estate passes to a single heir who is responsible for administering it on behalf of the whole kinship group (among the Lugbara and Azande estates pass on death from brother to brother before going to the next generation) conflicts seem to be more directly between males and accusations of witchcraft are made directly by one man against another.

Where a society is organised matrilineally again we see a quite different pattern of accusation. Mitchell (1956) and Marwick (1965b) show that among the Yao and Cewa of Malawi it is often brothers who accuse one another. Since in such societies authority and property pass from mother's brother to sister's son, brothers tend to compete with one another for control of their sistérs and their sisters' children in order to establish a basis of independence. Older brothers will try to deny this to their younger brothers who in turn struggle against the authority of the elder brothers. Again there is a conflict between legitimate aspirations and the demands of social solidarity here. Brothers, however, thought to maintain solidarity and these conflicts cannot be openly admitted or pursued. The reality of the situation cannot be seen, or in any case admitted, but is expressed iii a disguised form in terms of accusations of sorcery.

A second frequent pattern of accusations in such societies is that where a man accuses his mother's brother. Maternal uncles wish to control this matrilineal kinswomen but so do these mens's sisters' sons, their nephews, since this will give them a position of authority and independence. Hence the accusations against uncles. The complexity of the ensuing arguments and quarrels may be such that sisters also end up by accusing one another or a brother or their mother's brother.

It is significant that in these instances it is not witchcraft that is the charge but *sorcery*. Attempts to explain why in some societies it is an accusation of witchcraft that is levelled against enemies while in others it is sorcery while in yet others both types of charge might be made have not been very successful. Middleton and Winter (1963) have claimed that where both occur witchcraft is associated with generalised misfortune a long run of bad luck while sorcery is associated with particular misfortunes. By their own admission, however, this association is only some*times* found. Where malevolent evil takes only the form of witchcraft, Middleton and Winter suggest we find that the unilineal kinship principle is used in the constitution of local residential groups which are larger than the domestic household. Where it takes only the form of sorcery some other principle governs the formation of such groups. But as Turner (1964) points out, Middleton and Winter offer only two examples of the former situation and in one it seems that sorcery is in fact sometimes the charge. The root of the problem, according to Turner, is that there is no clear and consistent usage of the terms witchcraft and sorcery by anthropologists, nor is the distinction one which is clearly made in many systems of belief themselves. Traits assigned to witchcraft by one writer are assigned to sorcery by another. In such a situation it is impossible to uncover patterns and associations.

Insightful as many of the anthropological analyses mentioned so far are with regard to the role of witchcraft and sorcery beliefs in the management of tension and conflict, they do tend to suggest that such beliefs are generally positive in their effects and consequently retain a functionalist flavour. The beliefs and mechanisms of accusation facilitate the necessary division of groups which have expanded beyond a viable size but where this is nevertheless a painful and difficult process. While the result of conflicts and tensions the accusations play their part in the resolution of these tensions by breaking bonds which have become shackles and inhibitors of harmonious relations and good order. While acknowledging the important contribution such analyses have made to our understanding of witchcraft we should not be misled into thinking that witchcraft beliefs are always functional. As Mary Douglas (1963) and Vic Turner (1964) have pointed out, an accusation of witchcraft may intensify and magnify hostility and tension in situations which would otherwise remain relatively harmonious and which are not ones which are destined inevitably to result in division and separation. These beliefs generate tensions as often as reflecting them. The incidence of sickness and misfortune in any society is such that accusations are quite likely to occur even in the most harmonious of communities, potentially destroying that harmony. We should not forget that witchcraft is a socially available means of explaining and dealing emotionally with otherwise inexplicable misfortune and particularly death. It is not inevitable that as such it will have positive social consequences. Witchcraft accusations, as Douglas (1970) has pointed out, are attempts to exercise power over others; they are weapons used against enemies.

If witchcraft beliefs are to a large extent explanatory of misfortune, the question is raised as to why in certain societies this particular form of explanation occurs rather than some other Why, for example, do they not occur in modern Western societies, in which people are just as prone to misfortune and where social tensions are just as endemic. One answer to this question might be that in our own type of society good fortune or misfortune can be explained by science and that there is therefore no temptation to link them to the moral state of social relations which prevail. The problem with this is, of course, that science cannot give an explanation for the kind of question the Azande, for example ask in the face of misfortune and which we also are inclined to ask, namely why did it have to happen at all.

In any case, as Douglas (1970) points out, the approach which sees witchcraft as simply providing an explanation of misfortune in the absence of better ways of doing so ignores the fact that in many primitive societies belief in witchcraft does not exist nor is there any resort to supernatural explanations of misfortune. The pygmies of the Congo, for example, are content to do without such explanations. The reason for this, she suggests, is that they are able very easily to move away from one another as soon as undue strain in relations appears. Witchcraft beliefs do not occur where social contacts are sparse and diffuse or where roles are fully ascribed. Where people press close in upon one another, where social interaction is intense but ill-defined, then we should expect to find witchcraft beliefs.

Turning to the absence of beliefs like witchcraft in modern societies Max Gluckman (1972) believes that we cannot explain this non-occurrence in terms of the advance of science and knowledge. He believes it is due to the fact that in modern societies we are not so inextricably bound up in complex cross-cutting networks of relationships and interdependencies as people are in primitive societies. We do not ascribe moral responsibility for misfortune to one another because our relationships are not intense and interdependent. They are, to use Gluekman's terms, simplex whereas in primitive societies they are multiplex.

In modern societies we deal, to a very large extent, with different individuals in different aspects of our lives. Our spouse, grocer, teacher, colleague, vicar, brother, friend, neighbour, local policeman, tax official, chemist, builder, solicitor, chess opponent, are likely to he all different persons. In a primitive society the roles of kinsman, leader, spiritual guide, friend, neighbour, fellow hunter, are likely to be combined in the same person or persons. Where relationships are close, complex and multi-layered in this way an exaggerated emphasis tends to be placed upon the importance of others and their responsibility for one another.

Gluckman agues that this difference between modern and primitive societies has led to a situation where in the former, far from blaming one another for sickness and misfortunes which we have not brought on one another, we are increasingly reluctant to blame one another for the harm we do actually cause. A view has grown to prominence which seeks to treat the criminal as an unfortunate victim of social and personal circumstance. The problem lies in psychology, upbringing, social, physical and mental deprivation, and so on—all factors beyond the control and responsibility of the individual who is less to he punished but rather to receive treatment.

This tendency, Gluckman suggests, may be one which has ultimately resulted from a process of change in which people are separated from dependence on kin and progressively from dependence on any social group a dependence which in pre-modern social systems places a high moral evaluation upon all actions and all feelings.

Spirit Possession

Religion is more than a set of beliefs and practices. It also involves *experience*. Religious experience may take many different forms - faith, inner peace, ecstasy, and so on. One of the most dramatic forms of religious experience is that associated with and attributed to invasion or possession of a human body by a spirit, demon or deity. Signs of possession are such things as trance-like states, odd behaviour, fits, speaking in tongues, wild ecstatic dancing, change of personality, and so on.

When interpreted in religious terms this kind of behaviour may be seen in two ways either as an infliction brought about through possession by a molesting spirit or demon, or as a sign of divine recognition and selection a special visitation on those who are to fulfil the purposes of or act as intermediaries with the spirit world. In actual practice, however, this distinction may he blurred. Anthropological research has shown that the possessed person may make a transition from the category of the strangely afflicted to that of the specially blessed or endowed. The ethnographic data on this has been very usefully reviewed by Lewis (1971), who also discerns certain significant patterns in the data pertaining to spirit possession.

In fact, Lewis is primarily concerned with something which is both narrower and wider than 'spirit possession'. Trance-like states are not always attributed to the invasion of some spirit into a human body. Some cultures attribute trance-like behaviour to the loss of the person's soul. On the other hand, many peoples consider a person to be possessed by a spirit without any trance-like behaviour being manifested. Lewis is primarily concerned with trance states which are attributed to possession by some external spirit or agent.

He distinguishes between two types of possession and two types of cult or set of practices and rituals centring on these types. The first he calls *peripheral cults* since they play no part in upholding the central moral code of the society. They generally involve women or men who are in a largely subordinate and inferior social position. The spirits concerned are seen as largely malicious, capricious and amoral. They are commonly believed to originate from outside the society the deities of other tribes or peoples.

The second type of possession and associated cult is called by Lewis the *central possession religion*. The spirits involved in this type are concerned with morals they intervene in human affairs when misdemeanours have occurred and they uphold and sustain public morality.

Lewis examines a wide range of instances of both of these types and is able to derive some significant generalisations and interpretations.

The first type of cult is extremely common among women and he argues that it is to a large extent a disguised protest on the part of women directed against the dominant sex. It takes the form it does because in the societies in which it occurs women do not have more direct means of furthering their aims.

One of the best examples of this type of cult and situation is that which occurs among the Somali of East Africa, data on which was collected by Lewis while engaged in fieldwork among them. In this largely Muslim society men are very dominant and women highly subordinate to them. Marriage is often precarious and divorce is easy for men. Women cannot enter mosques and are regarded as weak arid submissive creatures. In this society women are often afflicted with possession by spirits which make certain demands through the woman in an authoritative manner and speaking in a special language which has to he interpreted by another woman who is a shaman skilled in such matters.

Typically, Lewis tells us, the afflicted woman is a hard pressed, somewhat neglected wife struggling to bring up a family. Her husband is typically away for long periods. She may have rivals if the husband is polygynous which creates tensions, conflicts and jealousies. The precariousness of the marriage tie makes her life insecure.

The spirits which possess such women are believed to he consumed by greed arid envy. They hunger after dainty food, fine clothing, jewelry, perfume and all sorts of luxuries in short all those sorts of things that women typically crave. They voice their demands for such things through the woman and will leave her alone only when these very costly demands have been met by the woman's husband who also has to pay for a special ritual dance attended by many other women.

In Lewis' opinion this is a strategy employed by women to obtain benefits that they cannot obtain more directly. Somali men are not entirely unaware of this deviousness. Their attitude is somewhat ambivalent. They believe in spirits and in the possibility of possession but when their own wives are possessed they are more inclined to see it as malingering. As Lewis puts it:

> they interpret this affliction as yet another device in the repertoire of deceitful tricks which they consider women regularly employ against men... they regard the opposite sex as possessing a unique endowment of guile and treachery. (1971, p.76)

But possession of this kind is not entirely confined to women. Down-trodden categories of men are also liable to possession. In this case the cult associated with it can he seen as a kind of protest on the part of these groups against the dominant group in society.

How are women who resort to such devices able to get away with it? It is, in fact, very difficult for a husband, whatever he may believe, to do anything other than comply with the demands. He accepts the existence of spirits and of spirit possession in the case of other women and, of course others, men and women, will believe that in the case of his own wife it is real and genuine and that he has an obligation to do whatever is necessary to free her from the affliction. He cannot really ignore these pressures. If the wife insists that the possession is genuine he cannot completely reject it as malingering because the symptoms are real enough. It is certainly not just an act or performance. The woman clearly suffers as a result of it and has, apparently, little control over it. She can successfully claim, to be blameless in the matter.

In any case, Lewis points out, although the demands are expensive, they do not pose any real challenge to the system and to the principle of male authority and superiority. Possession is a way of making demands and expressing dissatisfaction without actually challenging the authority structure and without being personally responsible for one's behaviour. Men, on the other hand, in meeting the demands of the *sprit* can claim that they are not giving way to their wives and are, therefore, not jeopardising their dominant position. The principle of male superiority is preserved.

On the whole, then, a husband will tolerate one or two instances of this spirit possession if they are not too frequent. Otherwise he may beat his wife and if this does not work he may threaten divorce. It is often a matter of a fine balance between the demands made by women and the patience of men.

The fact that men tolerate it all, Lewis suggests, perhaps testifies to a sense of guilt—a feeling that perhaps there is some injustice in the way women are treated and that they do have some cause for complaint.

Getting possessed by a spirit has a marked tendency to become habit forming with some women. Recurrent bouts may occur. Ideally the spirit is exorcised by a female shaman once and for all through ritual procedures, but in some cases the 'cure' turns out to he only temporary and the spirit returns. In time the woman learns to live with the spirit and to 'tame' it. This usually involves more ceremonies, dancing, and so on. Often the woman ends up by becoming a member of a regular circle of women liable to possession under the general direction of a female shaman. Such possession societies hold regular meetings, dances, feasts and ritual performances. Ostensibly for therapeutic purposes these activities really constitute a regular cult which may exclude men from its proceedings. What begins and presents itself as a healing activity becomes a religion. Men accept it as a healing activity while in reality it is a form of religious drama and the basis of a female subculture. What begins as suffering ends up as religious ecstasy.

Women who join such groups may themselves become shamans able to diagnose possession in other women and to understand the dictates of the possessing spirits. Whereas in the early stages of their possession history their symptoms are uncontrolled and involuntary, by this stage they develop into a controlled and regulated pattern. The afflicting spirits have been mastered and can he used for general good, for diagnosis and for healing.

This pattern of development is very typical in spirit possession according to Lewis It is usually in this way that a shaman, male or female, acquires his or her skills and position in the society. A shaman, once in control of powerful spirits can exercise considerable influence. Just as in the case of the Lugbara elder discussed above in the section on witchcraft, a successful shaman can cross the dividing line between legitimate use of ritual sanctions and illegitimate use. A shaman risks being accused of using his or her power over spirits to cause sickness rather than curing it if he or she goes too far in the use of this power. Such an accusation may he a strategy used by opponents to curb the power of shamans if it is thought to be a challenge to other sources of authority. This is especially likely in cases such as the Somali when subordinate men become shamans and if it seems that they may use this alternative basis of power to acquire a position of influence and authority in the community. In a sense they are condemned by their own standards and in their own terms. The powers that enabled them to protest and struggle against the authority structure are turned against them and used to engineer their downfall.

Turning now to the central possession religions, in these, typically, shamans, while in a state of trance and possession by a spirit that they have mastered, are able to diagnose the causes of sickness and misfortune and suggest appropriate cures and remedies, communicate with the spirit world, exercise a degree of control over it by ritual performances thereby ensuring prosperity, punish misdemeanours through their control of spirits, and so on.

The possessing spirits may vary considerably from one instance to another. Where ancestor worship is important the possessing spirit will generally be an ancestor. In such cultures there is frequently a belief in a variety of different spirits which can possess a human being but tribe shamans are only possessed by genuine ancestor spirits. Only well established shamans will he able to tell whether someone newly possessed is so by an ancestor spirit or by a malicious demon. In this way the established shamans can control recruitment to the position of shaman for which there may he considerable competition. Possession of the socially relevant and significant kind is thus confined to a particular circle, faction or elite. Only persons belonging to the appropriate social group or category will be accepted as novice shamans.

The novice shaman will tend to suffer from spirit possession which is as much an affliction in the early stages as it is for members of peripheral cults. Initially there will be attempts to exorcise the spirit. Failure to do so will lead to gradual acceptance that the possession is a permanent thing and that the possessed person, if considered suitable, is a shaman in the making. In time he will learn to live with and master the spirits.

Central possession religions and peripheral cults may coexist alongside one another. Frequently, the central religion involves largely men and the peripheral cult largely women.

Lewis concludes his study with a discussion of the relationship between spirit possession and psychological disorders. Many writers on the subject have sought to explain spirit possession in terms of psychological disorder or abnormality. Lewis disagrees with this interpretation. While many individual shamans may be mildly neurotic or mentally disturbed most are not or at least not seriously so. We 'cannot'. Lewis says, 'meaningfully reduce shamanism and spirit possession as total cultural phenomena to expressions of private fantasies of psychotic individuals' (1971, p. 186).

Lewis prefers to see spirit possession as a culturally defined initiation ritual for those who feel called to the vocation or profession of shaman - an initiation ritual which testifies to the candidate's ability to contact and deal successfully with dangerous and powerful forces. The crucial thing is that a successful shaman must control his spirits and his behaviour. He is not usually a person whose behaviour is beyond his own control in the way that a mentally disturbed person's is.

It has been argued that individuals in traditional societies subject to mental disturbance can, through adopting the role of shaman, control and channel their eccentricities in culturally acceptable and indeed socially useful directions. Rather than becoming a problem for others, as is the case in Western industrial societies, they find a creative and constructive role in which they can be of service to others. Lewis, however, emphasises again that spirit possession and shamanism conform to a culturally defined pattern and are not the idiosyncratic actions of individuals.

Finally, comparison of spirit possession and psychiatric disorder might; suggest the further possibility that the shaman is in some sense a psychiatrist or psychoanalyst. He cures sicknesses which have their roots in the mind. Lewis points out in this regard that shamanism does not confine itself to disorders which are or could be mental in origin but is generally equally concerned with illnesses that clearly have a physiological basis. He considers that it would be more accurate to say that psychiatry and especially psychoanalysis are, in fact, rather limited and imperfect forms of shamanism. It could be argued that the 'truths' of psychoanalysis are as dubious as the interpretations that tribal peoples give of abnormal behaviour and that the latter are consequently, as good as the interpretations of the psychoanalysts. At least both are equally hypothetical. We have to recognise that the idea of spirits of the kind that possess people has much in common with concepts in psychiatry and psychoanalysis such as that of the unconscious. Perhaps they do serve to some extent as concepts which explain abnormal behaviour in a way which allows it to be understood in terms of and related to social tensions and power relationships.

Many studies of spirit possession subsequent to Lewis's book have borne out his main points. A survey of a sample of 114 societies carried out by Greenbaum (1973) found that possession trance was more likely to occur in societies with fixed internal status distinctions and differences of role as occurs, for example, in highly stratified societies and those in which slavery exists. It is the rigidity of social structure, a common feature of such societies, which seems to account for the frequency of spirit possession. Where individuals are denied by the social structure freedom to achieve their aims and where close control over daily activities is imposed, possession trance is likely to be common. In such societies, Greenbaum reasons, social controls make decision making for the individual a risky and dangerous affair. Possession relieves the individual of responsibility for actions by changing the identity of the agent concerned from the human individual to that of the possessing spirit.

A number of studies may be cited in support of this interpretation and which show that possession may be an aid in coping with stressful situations (see Bourguignon, 1976 (Haiti); Macklin, 1077 (New England); Obeyesekere, 1977 (Sri Lanka); Pressel, 1973 (Brazil); Saunders, 1977 (Egypt); Spiro, 1978 (Burma)). Bourguignon, for example, argues that the role playing in spirit possession acts as a form of compensation for those who experience neglect in daily life and whose self respect needs bolstering. Reviewing the range of other studies she claims that possession acts as a safety valve in situations of stress. Possession also allows a degree of power over others to be exercised by those who would never otherwise be in a position to do so. Walker (1972), in another extensive review of the literature, takes a similar view.

Not all recent work, however, supports Lewis. Some have taken issue with other aspects of his analysis. Gomm (1975) questions the extent to which possession can be seen as a challenge to the authority of dominant individuals and groups. The concessions won by the afflicted women, for example, serve only to reinforce their subordination because they are won at the price of accepting it. Morton (1977) shows that those who become regular cult devotees in Ethiopia are often cut off, as a result, from their kin, their friends and their spouses who may divorce them. They become wholly dependent upon the cult leader and often to a greater extent than they were upon husband and kin prior to their career of possession. Wilson (1967) questions whether spirit possession should be seen at all in terms of male-female conflict. Possession, Wilson argues, whether it is of the peripheral cult form or of the central religious form, is rather the result of conflict and tension between ,members of the same *sex*. In the case of peripheral possession which predominantly affects women it is competition between women that is involved. Possession frequently occurs when a man takes an additional wife. This is a threat to the position and status of the first or earlier wives. Possession may be a means of affirming status and of receiving reassurance from the husband of the wife's continuing importance to him. It is a strategy in the face of a threat from another woman. Also, a woman's status varies according to her competence and adequácy as a wife and mother in relation to culturally expected standards and it fluctuates through the life cycle according to whether, for example, she is still capable of bearing children, and so on. These are matters of comparisons and competition between women and not matters of conflict and tension between men and women. Possession of the peripheral type, Wilson argues, just as in the case of central possession religion, may he seen as a form of *rite de passage* whereby a new status or social identity is defined and affirmed.

As for central possession religion and the process by which shamans are recruited Wilson argues, rather less convincingly than in the case of peripheral possession, that the epidemiology is, in fact, much the same. However, his empirical evidence on this is sparse. Also, he goes too far, perhaps, in characterising peripheral possession as a rite de passage. In fact one might criticise Lewis's interpretation from the opposite position to that of Wilson and question whether central possession constitutes a rite de passage. The history of affliction and ultimate control and mastery of spirits is hardly a type of ritual as rites de passage undoubtedly are. It is more a process of personal crisis and development involving stress and psychological difficulty, not unlike peripheral possession, but where the individual concerned, for personal and social reasons, is able to turn the experience into a means of finding a central social role and a position of status in the society, in contrast to those who become involved in peripheral cults. While it might be somewhat extreme to say that shamans are those who would otherwise be classified as clinically mad but are saved from this fate by the socially approved role of shaman, it may well be the case that shamans are people who have suffered mental stress and disturbance which they have come to terms with and overcome in such a way as to give themselves an acknowledged social role one which utilises the insights and capacities that are often gained through traumatic experience. In the same way, these involved in peripheral cults may have found ways of living with their difficulties through the cult, although perhaps, as Wilson suggests, at a cost. It certainly seems odd to liken the acquisition of the centrally significant social role of shaman to the ritual or ceremonial induction of the individual into such a role. It would seem rather more accurate to understand it as the discovery or even creation by the individual of such a role through a process of inner struggle, tension and ultimate catharsis.

Clearly, spirit possession is a varied and complex phenomenon and no single approach, as Walker points out (1972, p. 1) is adequate to explain it. Even Lewis's distinction between central and peripheral types seems to break down in the context of more complex social structures such as that of Brazil and Haiti.[4] Bourguignon (1976) questions Lewis's characterisation of voudou in Haiti as an amoral peripheral protest cult. It may once have embodied an element of protest, she argues, but no longer does so. It is now more like a central morality religion embodying elements of Catholicism and upholding central moral values. However, it differs markedly from the central cults described by Lewis. It does not involve a long period of illness and affliction prior to mediumship. There is no mastering of an originally afflicting spirit and transformation of it into a helpful agent. Much the same is true of the Brazilian cults such as Candomble and Umbanda. In the latter case, Pressel (1973) argues that it has elements of both the central and peripheral types and that this is generally true of possession in more complex social systems.

In some respects Lewis' distinction between central and peripheral possession seems too simple to encompass the complexity that the phenomenon manifests. Jones (1976) has suggested a more elaborate classification based on the work of various fieldworkers in Nepal where alone a considerable diversity of forms is found. Jones distinguishes four types according to whether the possession occurs at designated or undesignated times or in designated or undesignated places. *Reincarnate possession* is for life and therefore undesignated from the point of view of time. In this form an individual reincarnates the spirit of a deceased individual and takes up residence in a monastery or religious centre where he becomes a full-time religious practitioner of divination, curing and apotropaic and other rituals. *Tutelary possession* is the opposite of reincarnate possession. It occurs at designated times but in no particular place. The person possessed calls up a spirit during a seance held wherever circumstances demand and becomes possessed by it for the duration of the ceremony. *Oracular possession* occurs in some sacred place such as a temple, church or monastery (designated in space) and on a designated occasion such as a village festival. Finally, *peripheral possession*, like Lewis' type of this name, is spontaneous and undesignated as to time or place.

These four types, all of which can be found in Nepal, can be related, Jones argues, to features and variations in Nepalese social structure. Initial possession is generally 'peripheral' in type; that is to say it is spontaneous and occurs at no special time and in no special space. Nepalese society, divided as it is by caste and ethnically plural, is such as to deny many people opportunities for self-respect and prestige. Low castes often provide the religious specialists who combat disease and misfortune through control of spirits though their possession is at first involuntary. Women too are more likely to experience possession than men and unmarried women, widows and servants are more likely to than married women with children.

Possession is likely, in many cases, to develop into one of the other three forms. The type of social situation seems crucial in determining which. Reincarnate possession seems particularly appropriate to Tibetan Buddhist communities where the landless typically either turn to trade or enter the monastery. Spirit possession here takes the reincarnate form and is incorporated into the monastic setting.

In the isolated villages of tribal areas of Nepal which lack the complex institutions of temple and monastery and where the influence of Hinduism and Buddhism is superficial, tutelary possession dominates. In these circumstances it is the shaman who plays the primary role.

Oracular possession is found in the Brahmanical communities of western Nepal. In this caste-divided society it provides a means by which socially and economically deprived individuals can achieve some status as an oracular medium in a hierarchical and rigidly divided system in which positions of status are determined hereditarily. It thus resembles, Jones argues, the oracles of the classical slave societies of Greece and Rome.

Whether Jones' typology can fruitfully be applied to other societies remains to be seen. A further complication of the pattern of spirit possession is that possession takes different forms in different societies. The main variation is that it may or may not involve trance (Bourguignon, 1966; 1976). Possession is the invasion of the person by some external spirit. Trance is a change in normal behaviour, personality, perception and so on. These may occur independently in different cultures or even in the same culture. Possession trance occurs when trance states are attributed in the culture to possession. As yet we have little understanding of the reasons for the pattern of variation between societies in this respect. Bourguignon (1976), surveying a wide range of societies, claims that those which have only possession without possession trance tend to be smaller and less complex than those which have possession trance but the relationship is statistical and by no means one to one.

If much, however, remains puzzling and unclear on the question of spirit possession one thing perhaps does emerge from work on the question. Most researchers seem agreed that it is not random in its occurrence but affects individuals who stand in definite structural relationships to others. While it may be related, in many ways, to personality, and quite clearly involves personal difficulties and psychological problems, it is also both socially patterned in its epidemiology, and socially determined in its character.

Chapter-14
Religion in Modern Britain

R. BOCOCK

Chapter-14

Basic concepts

A religion is a complex mixture of beliefs, values, symbols and rituals. Most major religions, such as Christianity, Islam, Hinduism and Buddhism, contain beliefs and values about *this world,* whatever they may say about another, super-empirical one. It is the influence of the empirical and super-empirical beliefs and values of a religion upon the social, economic, political and cultural activities of various groups of people, especially classes and ethnic groups, which is of concern to sociologists and social theorists. In this context Marx's famous proposition that 'religion is the opium of the people' is not, therefore, to be understood as being about the truth value of a particular religion, but rather about what religion does in a society. The issue of central concern to sociologists is not whether a particular religious claim is true or false, but what consequences believing it has for particular groups in specific circumstances.

Religion can be seen as a part of the ideological sphere of a society when it operates in a way which helps to maintain the political, cultural and economic arrangements of that society over time. The ways in which a religion does this may be either by directly teaching that the social, political and economic order is right and God-given, and that it is sinful to try to change it, or they may be more indirect. For example, religions often offer hope about a better future in this life, or in another life, for those oppressed groups who suffer in the present. The ritual and symbolic practices of a religious group may provide comfort to people who experience suffering, pain, poverty and bereavement, By doing this a religion may indirectly help to maintain the social structure (see C. Geertz, 1964; 1966, in this volume).

To focus upon religion as ideology, as this article will do, is not to make derogatory statements about religion, but rather, to take a central concept within social theory and to try to use it to throw some light upon major aspects of religion in modem Britain. To reiterate the point made earlier, such a sociological analysis of religion is not dependent upon making any claims about the truth value of particular religious beliefs and values.

In this article the role of religion in modern Britain will be examined using a number of key concepts derived from sociological theory rooted originally in the works of Marx, Weber and Durkheim. Unless some theoretical framework is used one would become lost in a plethora of material, there being so many sects, churches and religious groups in modern Britain that it would be impossible to cover them all here. The main theoretical concepts to be employed will be derived from the sociology of religion as this area has developed over the last hundred years or so.

Many people, including some sociologists, define modem western societies such as Britain as being 'secular'. In the sense that such modern societies are no longer dominated by religious institutions in the way the Catholic Church dominated life in the Middle Ages in Europe, then it is possible to say that they are more secular. However, such a description can overestimate both the role of the Church in the past and the decline of the influence of religious groups on many people in present day societies. So some definition of religion and the secular is needed which allows for these complications in a way which the notion of secularisation fails to do. It is also important to avoid an over-cognitive definition of religion, such as those definitions which concentrate upon beliefs in supernatural entities as the defining characteristic of religion (see, for example, R. Robertson, 1970). Many people, for instance, participate in ritual occasions, which take place in churches, who do not think of themselves as believers in any clear set of propositions about the supernatural. This is true of rituals such as funerals, some weddings, and some church services such as those at Christmas time, or on Remembrance Sunday.

An important concept in Durkheim's sociology derived from his distinction between the sacred and the profane. 'The sacred' denoted the 'set apart' from the everyday, secular, utilitarian, profane area of social life. Beliefs, values, symbols, places, objects, people, time periods and ritual actions can all be sacred in this sense. The sacred is special, not part of the everyday world. All societies contain a sacred part of social and cultural life, according to Durkheim and Durkheimians, including communist systems (see C. Lane, 1981). This notion of the sacred forms the basis for a useful definition of religion. Religion can be defined analytically as consisting of those beliefs, values, symbols, rituals, social roles, organisations and groups which are concerned with the sacred, the set-apart from everyday life, according to Durkheim.

Another major concept to be used here is that of legitimation, and its converse – de-legitimation, or protest. This concept is part of both later forms of Marxism, and can be found in Weber's sociology (see A. Giddens, 1971). Religions can be seen as legitimating the ruling groups in a social formation, such as Christianity came to do in the Roman Empire after it became an officially recognised religion under the Emperor Constantine. Christianity can be seen as having begun as a protest movement among the Jews whilst they were subjugated to the imperialism of Rome. After its official recognition by the Emperor Constantine, Chrlstianity became an ideology which could be used for the legitimation of rulers. This continued under feudalism and in early capitalism, although protest movements continually emerged, especially after the Bible became available in the vernacular languages of Europe and elsewhere. The tension between a church type of religion which is willing to compromise with ruling groups in a society, and to legitimate their rule, or at least not actively to oppose them, and sects which do not compromise on some values, such as pacifism, but often condemn some aspects of secular life and form a protest movement is, therefore, built-in within Christianity according to most sociologists of religion (see E. Troelstch, 1931).

As an unintended consequence of social and economic change, churches in modern societies such as Britain and the USA have in effect lost, on the whole, the critical, protest element within Christianity. The concept of privatisation introduced by P. Berger (1968) highlighted one of the ways in which Christianity became neutralised. The notion of privatisation refers to the process whereby religion is located in the private sphere of the family and sexual morality. Religious values are seen as irrelevant to economic, political, military or wider social issues, and any claims to apply morality to these areas are seen as ill-founded by most key groups in these activities — unless the religious leaders are willing to legitimate that which the ruling groups do. In this way, privatisation may be said to operate in ways which help to legitimate the power structures in a society and to remove the critical edge of Christianity from general circulation.

There is, however, a contrary process at work within both sects and churches. Some people do recover the protest element in Christianity that is, the inherent protest against social injustice, political oppression, military evils and economic inequality to be found in both the Old and New Testaments. The development of Christian socialism earlier in the twentieth century is one important example; the development of 'liberation theology' in Latin America in the last three decades is another. The critique of communism by Catholics, in countries such as Poland, for instance, is a further development, usually based upon an acceptance of socialism but not in an autocratic form. These are forms of protest within churches and mark a separate phenomenon from sects, in which protest is typically embodied in some supernaturalist form. Sectarian protest usually offers salvation for a chosen elite, but not for everyone, and in this sects are less universalistic than mainstream Christianity is, at least in theological terms.

Finally, it is important to make it explicit that the definition of religion which is used in this article is wider than one based upon religious organisations such as churches and sects. Religion is defined here as those social actions and cultural beliefs which are concerned with the sacred. This provides a wider definition of religion than those which concentrate upon organised groups which hold supernatural beliefs, and enables the sociologist to include other ritual activities such as those of the nation and the state. On the other hand, such a definition avoids including just about all aspects of culture as being religious, a position T. Luckmann approaches in his book, *The Invisible Religion* (1967). This means that a phenomenon such as the Royal Family in Britain is analysed as being a part of the sacred area in the society—although this is not too far removed from organised religion in many situations, in any case. Royalty, in the eyes of many, is assumed to be above party politics. Royalty is 'sacred' and is, therefore, treated as being immune to criticism of the kind which may be made of politicians. This has not always been the case, however, as a number of writers have pointed out – it is a relatively new, post-Victorian phenomenon (see D. Cannadine, 1983).

Religion is also involved in the process of the social regulation of sexuality, the family and marriage through its moral teachings. In some states, under certain historical circumstances, these moral rules form the basis of the laws which regulate these matters. In modern Britain the Royal Family is expected to live by the moral rules of the Church of England, even though some members may lapse from time to time. Such lapses are defined as exactly that - a falling away from maintaining the moral rules they should aim to live by.

In this article there are two areas to be examined — namely the rituals associated with the state and the nation, and the private sphere of the family and the social regulation of sexuality. These are not as unrelated as they may seem to be at first sight. One important link between these two aspects of the social role of religion in modem Britain is the Royal Family. The Royal Family is held up as an example of family life to children and young people, as well as to adults, in numerous ways. For example, the Archbishop of Canterbury wrote in a booklet widely available during the Queen's Silver Jubilee in 1977:

> But at this time we specially celebrate, with thanksgiving to Almighty God, the presence, at the heart of our nation and Commonwealth, of a family which has set standards for us all to follow. This has been — and is — a steadying influence in a day when forces are at work which would break up the family as a strong and loving unit in society; and when that happens, the nation's strength is sapped.

Silver Jubilee, 1977.

One aspect of acquiring an identity and a value system involves the process of being socialised into the ideology of the British nation state and in this the Royal Family and the national ritual events in which it is involved play an important role, especially for children. This is, of course, true in varying degrees for children from a wide variety of cultural and socio-economic class backgrounds, although some may not be socialised in such a manner. In this way it can be seen that there are important links between the two levels and areas of concern here, namely the nation state's ideology and the ideologies to which young people are exposed from the earliest age in their families, and in schools and religious organisations which form a part, therefore, of their sense of individual identity and their views about gender roles, the family and sexual morals. However, it is useful for analytical purposes to try to distinguish the two levels of analysis and to treat them separately. This will be done here.

Civic ritual in Britain

At the level of the nation-state it is important to distinguish two major types of ritual activity which are analytically distinct, though they are often mixed together in empirical cases. The two types are civic ritual on the one hand and religious ritual on the other. In Durkheim's sociology these two were not distinguished analytically and because of this he was unable to distinguish modern nationalism as an ideology, which may have religious overtones or may not, from religious ideologies which cross-cut nation-state borders (see R. Bocock, 1974).

For Durkheim, the sacred was separated off from the profane by 'negative' rituals, and the 'positive' rituals which were then performed in relation to the sacred symbolised the superiority of society over the individual. He wrote in *The Elementaty Forms of the Religious Life* about Australian aborigine totemism. Totemism refers to the practice of giving the name of a material thing, often, but not always, an animal, bird or plant, to the different clans which together constitute a tribal group; for example, the eagle-hawk is the totem of a daft in the Mukwara tribe of Australian aborigines. A clan is a group which operates as a network of kin, even though all its members may not be blood relatives. Durkheim argued that the representation of the totem was regarded as sacred because it symbolised the identity of the clan group. 'So if it is at once the symbol of the god and of the society, is that not because god and the society are one?' Durkheim wrote (See A. Giddens, 1971, p. 109).

In more highly differentiated societies, such as modern Britain, the rituals of national identity in which social group identity is created and maintained over time may or may not involve religious organisations. Similarly, religious ritual may be quite distinct from national, civic rituals, and may generate feelings of loyalty to other collectivities than that of the nation-state. This was thought to be the case in the past in Britain with regard to the religious ritual actions of Roman Catholics, for example. There was a suspicion by some that Catholics owed their allegiance to the Roman pontiff rather than to the British monarch and state officials.

The rituals surrounding and involving the members of the British Royal Family are primarily an example of civic ritual in that they symbolically represent the group, the nation state. However, the British monarch is not only the Head of State, but also Head of the Church of England and the Church of Scotland. This complicates the situation somewhat compared with the situation in the United States or France, for example, where the President is purely the Head of State and where, therefore, the civic ritual is closer to a purer type than is the case with the British situation (see R. Bellah, 1970).

In civic ritual the symbolism used refers to, or represents, the collectivity. In this sense, civic ritual is concerned with particular groups, in this case whole nations or even links between several nations such as England, Scotland and Wales. The fact that Northern Ireland does not easily fit in with this list is significant in that it shows that there has not been the same historical linkage between the civic rituals of the nations which make up Britain and those of the two main communities in Northern Ireland, the Catholics and the Protestants. In Northern Ireland the link between what are called here civic and religious rituals is stronger in the two communities than is the case in Britain, where religious ritual is more differentiated from civic, national identity maintaining ritual.

Religious ritual, as a separate analytical type, refers to the ritual which members of churches or sects use to worship their conception of a deity. The membership of these religious organisations may or may not overlap with a particular nation-state. The Church of England, for instance, had been established by the Tudors to contain everyone in the nation-state in one religious organisation, and it still retains a role as an 'ecclesia', or established Church in this respect in England (M. Yinger, 1970, pp.262-4).

Most modern states in the world contain members of many religious organisations and each of these has its own kind of religious rituals. This can cause trouble if those in power in the major institutions of the state decide that one or more of these religious groups produces some kind of perceived threat to the society. For example, the 'Moonies' and Scientology became suspect groups by some in Britain during the early 1980s (see Media Project 1, on the Unification Church, i.e. the Moonies, in D207 *An Introduction to Sociology,* an Open University second level course).

It is important to retain this distinction between civic and more specifically religious rituals because unless this is done it is not possible to understand or explain conflicts between church leaders and politicians in key offices of state, for instance. The usual pattern in Britain is for the major civic ritual events, such as Remembrance Day or a Jubilee, to have a significant church figure present, usually the Archbishop of Canterbury, and there is little tension about this from either side. There was some tension and conflict over one event, however, which was meant to be a piece of uncontroversial civic ritual as far as the Prime Minister and other ministers of state were concerned. This was over a service of thanksgiving for victory. The service was meant to express thanks to God for Britain's victory over Argentina at the end of the Falklands/Malvinas fighting in 1982. The church authorities at St Paul's cathedral did not want, and did not allow, a nationalistic victory celebration because they thought that the loss of life on both sides was not something to give thanks for. Rather, church leaders wanted to stress comfort for the bereaved on both sides of the conflict and to attempt to begin to make reconciliation between two supposedly Christian states. This led to a sense of tension and conflict of view between the Church and the government. It illustrated that the state authorities could not always assume that they had a 'tame' church in the Church of England or the other denominations involved. Conflict between the Church and state is possible, and in the case of the Falklands service the conflict was concerned with the type of ritual event to have in a specific situation. The disagreement can be seen in terms of whether the ritual should have been primarily civic, in which the feelings and Values of a particular government and of some groups in Britain would be articulated, or whether it should be more in keeping with the feelings and values of the bereaved on both sides in the conflict. This latter focus illustrated that for some church leaders there were wider issues involved concerning the feelings of Christians among the 'enemy', not only those of a triumphant government and of one nation involved in the fighting. Religious ritual quite unexpectedly became significantly different from the civic ritual requirements in this instance (A. Barnett, 1982, p. 90). This example serves to illustrate that the distinction between the two types of ritual is by no means insignificant at the level of practice as well as the theoretical level.

Further back in time there was an interesting controversy about another civic ritual event — the Coronation of Queen Elizabeth II in 1953 — but this time the controversy was among sociologists, not between politicians and church leaders! It is worthwhile re-examining this controversy in sociology for the light it may throw upon some issues which are still important in sociology and social theory more generally. In order to perceive this it is necessary to understand that in the 1950s, in British sociology and in most sociology elsewhere for that matter, there was a general tendency to see rituals as maintaining the society in which they occurred, and to identify the forces and groups for social change as being economic in some unproblematic way. In other words, there was an assumption that rituals were only of interest to conservative sociologists because they served to maintain the status quo, and that radical sociologists should not give much weight to rituals of any kind because they were not the motor of major change, for this was assumed by some to be in the economic sphere. The import of these remarks should become clearer in the next section of this article.

The sociological analysis of the Coronation

One major example of a sociological debate about a major ritual event, namely the Coronation of Queen Elizabeth II in 1953, will be used here to illustrate how the debate between sociologists who used a consensus model and those who used a conflict model affected their respective approaches to the analysis of the Coronation. (The Coronation received some attention from sociologists in the journal, *Sociological Review,* in 1953 in an article by E. Shils and M. Young, and in a critical reply to this by N. Birnbaum which was published in 1955 in the same journal.)

The Coronation took place eight years after the end of World War II, and two years after the end of the 1945-51 Labour government. This historical setting is important to bear in mind because there had been less class conflict during the war years within Britain than before the war. The Labour government had brought in some nationalisation, for example in the coal mining industry and transport, and the welfare state had been developed and established, crucially including the National Health Service. The post-war boom and the coming of affluence still lay in the immediate future for most people, but the effects of the war years and the material problems of the late 1940s were beginning to fade in most people's memories by 1953.

In 1953 television was developing rapidly both geographically and technically, nevertheless many families did not have their own television set and so watched the Coronation with friends or neighbours who did have one. This may or may not have contributed to the way in which the event was perceived by the television audience, in that watching in groups may heighten the impact of what is shared experience. The Coronation did, no doubt, make some extra impact upon people than might otherwise have been the case by being seen in a group (sec D. Chaney, 1983, in this volume). (Also, see the discussion about broadcasting rituals and the state in D209 *The State and Society.)*

One further point worth bearing in mind in this context is that although the Coronation focused specifically upon the monarch as an individual, the Royal Family as a group were involved, too. It is also interesting that the Archbishop of Canterbury mentioned the Royal Family, and not just the Queen, in his article written for the Silver Jubilee in 1977, which I mentioned above. (The celebrations in 1977 were, incidentally, to mark Queen Elizabeth's accession to the throne in 1952 on the death of her father, George VI, the actual coronation being a year later.)

The life-cycle rituals of the central members of the Royal Family also play a major part in the rituals of Britain. Royal weddings are one example of this, for instance the marriage of Prince Charles and Lady Diana in 1981 and of Princess Anne and Captain Mark Phillips in 1973. Royal funerals also evoke the more serious side of Britain's Royal Family life-cycle ritual events, creating important shared collective sentiments.

The Coronation can thus be seen as a major example of a civic ritual event in Britain. The debate which took place about the Coronation in the 1950s still has some important points for a sociological analysis of the place of royal rituals in Britain in the 1980s. I shall return to it following a discussion of the analysis made by Shils and Young mentioned earlier.

Edward Shils and Michael Young (1953) saw the Coronation as a ritual of communion, bringing the whole British nation into a ritualistic dedication to the basic values of its society. The basic values they instanced were: charity, loyalty, justice in the distribution of opportunities and rewards, reasonable respect for authority, and respect for the individual and his freedom. Shils and Young's analysis claimed that many of the population were deeply involved in the ritual, and they saw this involvement as an expression of the people's commitment to the sacred values. The ritual also handled the emotional ambivalence that people have towards moral authority and moral rules. There is no hint, however, of any group whose ambivalence is based on the fact that they disagree with some of the values, or the ways in which these were being interpreted. For example, the value they instance of 'justice in the distribution of opportunities and rewards' is ambiguously worded, but it would seem that even in the euphoria of the Coronation not all were agreed that the actual distribution of rewards was just, although no doubt adhering to the generalised value that justice in the distribution of rewards was desirable. Looking at this analysis later, it seems that Shils and Young were themselves carried away by the seemingly overwhelming consensus about basic British values, and the worth of the society in the early 1950s. The period of high consensus in Britain was short lived. In part it had built up during the Second World War, but was probably not as high as Shils and Young thought even in the Coronation period (see Bocock, 1974).

Shils and Young drew on Emile Durkheim in their analysis of the Coronation, and ignored Max Weber and Karl Marx. They did not see that the Coronation, and other rituals surrounding the Royal Family — such as the giving of honours and decorations and the State Opening of Parliament — serve to legitimate the existing set of families who rule economically, politically (including the new Labour families) and militarily. Yet the nineteenth-century writer William Bagehot, who is quoted by Shils and Young, had argued that this was the case. They failed to draw the conclusion that little has altered since then. According to Bagehot, the monarchy enabled the educated 10,000 to go on governing as before. By commanding their unbounded loyalty, it 'tamed the uncouth labourers of Somersetshire who, in their simplicity, needed a person to symbolize the State'. In this way, 'the English Monarchy strengthens our government with the strength of religion ... It gives now a vast strength to the entire constitution, by enlisting on its behalf the credulous obedience of enormous masses.'

The upsurge in the popularity of the monarchy in England reached its clearest peak in the 1950s, especially at the time of the Coronation. Since then it has been less marked as a phenomenon, but no doubt if there were a national crisis, the monarchy would re-emerge as one of the major symbols of English nationalism. The Church of England can also find that it is itself part of this basic, latent nationalism, and this makes it very difficult for the Church to take clear stands which are critical of the economic and political status quo. The Church of England tends to seek to express a set of core values which overarch the disputes and conflicts in the society, and so to act as a 'reconciler' between disputing parties. The church leaders are most likely to speak out in favour of seeking consensus than in pursuing economic justice through, for example, industrial conflict.

Birnbaum (1955) was critical of Shils and Young's analysis

of the Coronation because it accepted a *unitary* view of the values of British society and assumed there was a consensus about them, rather than acknowledging that *conflict* about values and distribution of wealth and income were and are present in Britain:

> The authors (i.e. Shils and Young) note immediately after remarking on the decline in prestige of the ruling elite, that 'consensus on fundamental values remained'. It is unclear what these fundamental values could have been, since consensus by the authors' own admission did not quite extend to the legitimacy and efficacy of the society's ruling elite or of its economic institutions. Agreements on 'justice' and 'charity' do not seem to have precluded the social conflicts of the past decades. It is a question whether they alone set the limits, undoubtedly present, which kept Britain from civil war. (op. cit., p. 14)

Later in his critical analysis Birnbaum wrote:

> What seems to emerge in the authors' analysis of the Coronation is their own strong feeling of adherence to the official morality of Great Britain — and their preference for conformity to such moralities wherever they appear. In discussing popular response to the Coronation, they tell us that 'antagonism emerged only against the people who did not seem to be joining in the great event or treating with proper respect the important social values — by failing, for instance, to decorate their buildings with proper splendour.' They give no evidence for this assertion, nor any indication of how widespread this aversion might have been. We should also expect them, as social scientists, to show some awareness that such aggression might have been displaced from other spheres, Instead we get what from the language employed seems to be enthusiastic concurrence in it. (op. cit., p. 22)

Norman Birnbaum's critique of the Shils and Young analysis of the Coronation was based upon a sociological theory which did not give any explicit weight to ritual events, and which made no use of the concept of the 'unconscious'. It was based upon a view of human social action as being motivated by a relatively rational pursuit of economic goals by both capitalists and by wage and salary earners. This viewpoint has been a powerful one among many conflict theorists in sociology, but there is no necessary connection, nor historical connection, between the use of a conflict model of capitalist society and rationalistic, economic views of action. There have been social theorists, working in critical theory, and others using more structuralist methods, who have worked with a model of society derived from both Marx and/or Weber, and from Freud. Freud's model makes the *emotional* meanings of religion, ideologies and rituals of importance, just as Marx's model is concerned with the economic and the political (see Bocock, 1983). The two models can be brought together in the analysis of ideology and cultural activities such as rituals without, therefore, assuming that a focus upon rituals and emotions is somehow incompatible with a conflict model of capitalist societies.

In the specific case of the Coronation, and other Royal Family rituals such as weddings, funerals and jubilees, there is no need to deny that many people in the working classes, and in the middle classes, do have positive feelings towards members of the Royal Family and will watch the ritual events on television and in the streets, while still allowing for the point that this does not affect economic and political conflicts in the society.

The precise consequences in terms of the legitimation of the political and economic structure of British society of these royal rituals is then a matter for more empirical investigation. Such rituals help to *construct* a sense of consensus, rather than being seen as simply reflecting a preexisting agreement as Shils and Young (1953) argued.

There seems to be a plausible case for arguing that there is no major, popularly-based social movement for republicanism in Britain, that the monarchy is accepted as either fairly harmless by some or much more positively by others, and that this has some consequences for the legitimacy of the British political system. The American and French Presidents are both elected political figures and the Heads of State for ceremonial occasions. These two roles are distinct in the British system of a hereditary monarch, who is the ceremonial Head of State, and an elected

Prime Minister, who is a politician. Unpopular British Prime Ministers do not produce the problems of conflicting emotions which unpopular Presidents may do. Presidents who are disliked for their policies, or their corruption, are nevertheless treated with the respect due to the Head of State however corrupt they may be. Whether the monarchical system is more stable is difficult to say, but superficially there does seem to be a gain in legitimacy under a monarchy for the constitution as a whole in Britain. Unpopular and corrupt American Presidents helped to enhance the already existing pattern of cynicism, low voting in presidential elections, and a politically apathetic population in the United States during the 1970s.

The comparative stability of the legitimacy of the British constitution is a problem for those who seek radical or revolutionary changes because it makes a radical break very difficult without a major breakdown of economic life, which could lead to a new constitutional settlement based on a republic. Such a legitimation crisis may occur but it seems unlikely, given that Britain has survived worse economic conditions than those of the early 1980s in previous decades of the twentieth century.

New directions

The major issue underlying this ealier debate between sociologists concerned whether Britain was still basically a capitalist society after the Labour government of 1945 or not. Since that time a new issue has developed, raised by feminist writers during the late 1960s and 1970s. This is the issue of patriarchy.

The issues raised about patriarchy by feminists and others have ranged from the fact that men, not women, typically hold the most powerful positions in the major social institutions, including the churches, the armed forces, trade unions, political parties, and industrial companies, to the role of women in the family as mothers and wives. The concept of 'patriarchy' has both a structural aspect – that men hold most of the powerful positions in society, and a cultural or ideological aspect. Juliet Mitchell (1974) defined patriarchy as a culture dominated by the 'Law of the Father' – a term she derived from the French psychoanalyst, Jacques Lacan. In a patriarchal culture dominated by the Law of the Father, gender roles are defined in particular ways such that mothering is seen as work for women, as is most if not all domestic labour (see N. Chodorow, 1978), and fighting in the armed forces is seen as basically a male activity. In a patriarchal culture, women mother; men fight.

A series of institutions can be seen as linked together to make up a major component of British society's patriarchal culture. These are: the nation, the armed forces, the family, the church and the monarchy. Together they could be said to constitute the main part of the archaic heritage of this society, or the central elements of its patriarchal culture. This culture is constituted by certain moral values, beliefs, rituals and symbols which operate within the institutions mentioned. It produces and reproduces the gender roles and definitions of sexuality which most people think of as natural and normal — the heterosexual, monogamous family.

An important component of this ideological structure and set of social practices is the Royal Family. The rituals surrounding not only the monarch but other members of the Royal Family are central events in the 'civil religion' (R. Bellah, 1970) which persists in modern Britain. The recent examples of such royal ritual occasions include the Silver Jubilee in 1977, to celebrate twenty-five years since the Queen came to the throne; the eightieth birthday of the Queen Mother in 1980; and the marriage of Prince Charles and Lady Diana in 1981. There are, in addition to these special events, the regular cycle of royal civic rituals throughout each year, such as the Christmas Day television broadcast by the monarch, the State Opening of Parliament, and the Remembrance Day events.

These rituals are a complicated mix of a number of analytical types of ritual action. The central ones are civic rituals by the Head of State, such as the State Opening of Parliament; life-cycle rituals such as Royal weddings and birthdays; military ritual such as the Trooping of the Colour on the monarch's official birthday; and nationalist communal rituals such as the Remembrance Day ceremonies. These could be said to constitute the civil religion of Britain, to use Bellah's term, rather than being, strictly speaking, religion in the sense of beliefs and rituals which purport to be in contact with the 'holy' or the 'numinous' – as R. Otto (1924) called the special sense of awe which he saw as typifying religious experience and ritual.

'Civil religion' in the United States and Britain is not itself Christianity, according to Bellah, even though it draws upon themes and symbols from Christianity. The 'God' of American civil religion is unitarian, for example, not the complex trinitarian God of Christianity, Bellah argued (Bellah, 1970). A civil religion focuses on a particular nation-state, whereas a major world religion is universalist and does not teach or claim that loyalty to any particular nation-state is a necessary prerequisite for 'salvation'. Civil religions do focus upon generating loyalty to a particular nation state. The Church of England, for example, combines aspects of both types, being a civic religious organisation focused on England, and part of the universal religion of Christianity. Tensions have actually resulted from this dual aspect from time to time, whenever church leaders have stressed universal values and used them to criticise politicians' activities and policies. Politicians have typically expected legitimation from the Church of England, and certainly not criticism. The tension can erupt whenever the church leaders stress universal Christian values of reconciliation, love and the equality of all people in the eyes of God and find fault with particular political actions, for instance, the bombing of civilian targets in the Second World War, which was criticised by Bishop Bell; the criticism of the nuclear deterrent in 'The Church and the Bomb' report in 1982; or the Tory government's handling of unemployment and the 1984 miners' strike criticised by a number of bishops, including the Archbishop of Canterbury. (In this context, it is worth noting that the Church of England still commands attention and retains a latent loyalty among many English people; three out of every five people claimed to be members of the Church of England in a National Opinion Poll carried out for The Times in 1978.)

Within sociology there remain different ways of assessing the significance of 'civil religion'. To those who broadly accept the proposition that consensus over fundamental values is central to any identifiable social system, as Bellah tends to do, then a society's civil religion is of great importance in understanding and explaining how societies such as the United States persist and maintain their basic component values over long time periods. If most people are socialised into these values in the rituals of the civil religion in schools and local communities, and in learning about the major events in the history of their society, then it is not so surprising that the state and the economic mode of production in the society become accepted as legitimate, or unchangeable. It is interesting to note in this context that the Soviet Union has developed its own equivalent civil religion and a socialist 'liturgical' year in the ritual occasions it has developed since the revolution in 1917 (see C. Lane, 1981). It is possible to see these rituals as helping to legitimate the Soviet state and mode of production, to make them appear as unchangeable as those in Britain and the United States appear to be.

Some sociologists (R. Bellah, 1970; P. Berger, 1969; E. Shils and M. Young, 1953) have found that it is useful to adopt a view which also sees the role of civil religion in societies, like those of the United States and Britain, as having some importance in trying to explain why there is a lack of a desire for change of the state, and of the main mode of production, among the working classes in these societies. If it is thought that the civil religion of these societies is popularly-based and accepted in a relatively unconscious way by many people in all classes, then the lack of large-scale, popular-based movements for radical social, economic and political change is seen as more easily explained. The people are caught up in the ideology of the civil religion and they do not, therefore, conceive of change as being either desirable or possible. In this double sense, it can be said the existing system is regarded as legitimate. This proposition may be seen as holding more for the United States than in Britain, or the two societies may be regarded as similar in this regard in spite of the existence of a stronger socialist party in Britain than in the United States.

There are other sociologists and some Marxists who have taken a different view, as Birnbaum did. Some have described their position as being 'materialist' (see, for example, B. Turner, 1983). Such writers do not attach much significance to civic or religious rituals and beliefs in societies such as those of modern, industrial, capitalist societies. For example, it has been argued:

> Societies are held together not simply or even primarily

> by common beliefs and ritual practices, but by a multitude of material factors — force, economic coercion, economic dependency, legal compulsion, economic scarcity, habituation and the exigencies of everyday life. Societies can continue to operate with relatively high levels of conflict, disaffection and indifference to norms in combination with pragmatic acceptance of values. The social cement is constantly eroded and swept away by these circumstances without any ultimate descent into anomy and social chaos. (Turner, 1983, Ch.2, p.61; p.243 in this volume.)

Is it necessary to accept one or other of these positions? Here I wish to argue that there is another position which can be plausibly sustained, and which preserves some of the strengths of both of the analyses which have just been considered above. These were, firstly, that there is a 'civil religion' in modern Britain which plays some part in the ideological sphere in masking the possibility of fundamental change as being either possible or desirable. Secondly, that material factors and class interests are more important than the beliefs, values and rituals associated with civil, or any other kind of religion, in British society. To develop the possibility of a third position, in which ideological factors are *combined with* material ones, rather than *opposed to* one another, with one being treated as more important that the other, it is first of all necessary to clarify the fundamental starting points of the various protagonists involved in the debates.

The most critical point is whether the theory being used in the sociological analysis is one which purports to be materialist or not. If it is not explicitly materialist the chances are that it is implicitly idealist, as in the case of Bellah. This means that ideas, beliefs and values are treated as being more important in analysing social action than material factors such as economic interests and physical force. On a materialist view economic interests are seen as more important than ideas in understanding and explaining social action in a capitalist-based type of society such as that of modem Britain. Physical force is only of marginal significance in such a society in modern conditions. This does not mean that force was not a significant factor in the past in Britain, nor in other societies at present, nor that it may not become important again in the future as a means of maintaining social control in a decaying capitalist Britain on this view.

This difference in starting points has to some extent been overtaken by a new emphasis in philosophy and social theory upon the importance of language. By emphasising language as a central characteristic of the human species, as that which distinguishes humans from all other species which use elementary forms of signal communication rather than the elaborate forms of symbolic communication found in human cultures, recent developments in this area have shifted the ground upon which the debate about materialism and idealism should be conducted. Michel Foucault (1976), for example, emphasised the power relations which are built into various forms of knowledge in what he termed 'discourses'. Words and symbols do not just reflect, or represent, an already established social world. Words, language, or 'discourses' produce and create the social world. Knowledge is a form of power. The creation of organized 'discourses' is part of an expanded notion of the 'political' for Foucault (see also J. Weeks, 1981, chapter 1).

This emphasis upon language entails that both the positions of idealism and materialism need to be changed. Neither can be held in an unmodified form. On the one hand idealism has to be modified to take account of the way in which language is produced in particular discourses within concrete economic and political circumstances, and does not appear outside of the dominant mode of production in any given society. Language, in the form of discourses, is produced, created and maintained in social institutions such as publishing houses; schools, colleges and universities; churches and sects; broadcasting stations, film and television studios and distribution networks. The production of language, or a particular discourse, must be included in the sociology of beliefs and values in ways which has not been done in the past by sociologists inclined towards idealism as their starting point (see R. Williams, 1981).

On the other hand, materialism has to be modified to take account of the new developments about the fundamental role of language in human society. It is not simply one more additional factor to be taken into account in doing sociology. Language use is the key distinguishing feature of the human species. It transforms the relationship between human beings and the natural environment, and this implies that earlier, crudely materialistic views about man as tool-maker, for example, are no longer adequate. This has implications for historical materialism (see A. Giddens, 1981).

The model of the economic, material mode of production, consisting of the social relations of production and the technical means of production, has to be modified to include the means of mental production as being of fundamental importance. That is to say that it is not possible to privilege the position of the production of industrial goods and food beyond the basic means of subsistence, over and above the production of words, symbols and rituals in the means of ideological, or mental, production. For example, the advertising industry in advanced forms of capitalist societies deeply influences the consumption of most material goods from cars and tractors to clothes and food. The world of symbols and language in the broadest sense, including the language of style, fashion and taste, is profoundly intermingled with the world of the production and consumption of material goods. There is no clear dividing line between ideology in the broadest sense and material interests and material desires, for conceptions of what counts as a material interest, or desire, are affected and formed by ideological discourses (see R. Coward and J. Ellis, 1977).

Even physical force and its use, or threatened use, is affected by ideologies. The most potent of the ideologies which affects who kills and maims others, or who gets killed or maimed, in wars are those of nationalism and patriarchal religion. The sense of an ethnic identity is both a political and a religious product. It is perceived competition for material resources between various ethnic communities in the world which lies behind many groups resorting to violence. These perceptions are not given outside any linguistic or symbolic discourse; they are formed and maintained within ideologies about ethnic identity and in the collective rituals of 'civil religions'.

The desirability of fighting, killing, and even of being killed, for a particular ethnic group, or nation, is perpetuated and maintained in civil religion. Patriarchal ideologies socialise males to accept organised violence as a part of the natural order of things. This same discourse maintains that women will 'naturally' stay at home to mother babies and children. These values and beliefs are communicated to people in the civil religion of Britain, with its military ritual occasions, and its rituals of the Royal Family, especially potent in communicating the patriarchal gender divisions — men fight and die for their Queen and country; women mother. The churches are involved in this civil religion too, but they also contain a critical few who argue that warfare, especially nuclear warfare, is evil. Some also think that women should be ordained as priests in the Roman Catholic, Orthodox and Anglican Churches and that the symbolism of 'God' as a father, a male, should be replaced with symbolism which portrays 'God' as female, or as both male and female (P. Nichols,1981).

Material factors do not exist outside human discourses. Both economic, material, interests of classes and the use of physical force and violence by organised groups, are located within concrete discourses produced in social institutions in a particular historical situation. Religious organisations are involved in the production and reproduction of these discourses in the beliefs, values, symbols and rituals of the particular religious tradition in which they are placed. Civil religion is an important component of these processes in Britain as it is elsewhere in the world. It produces a sense of ethnic identity among each generation and reproduces commitment to the nation for older members of the nations which make up modem Britain. Civil religion is not completely successful in these tasks, but nor is it empty and without efficacy.

The social location of religion

The social location of religion in a society like that of modern Britain has quite specific elements to it. The most important of these elements is that it is clearly differentiated from the economic sphere and that it is located in the private sphere of the family. Religious institutions have become differentiated from the economic sphere. No one could understand how to implement the kind of moral theology that was once developed by the church about a just price or a just wage, nor the sinfulness of taking interest for money loaned to someone else, in a modern capitalist economic system. The economic sphere has become quite separate from the moral control of religious institutions under capitalism (see R.H. Tawney, 1926). This contrasts, incidentally, with some forms of Islam, which do seek to control economic activity by religious precepts.

The arts, technology and sciences have also become differentiated from religious institutions and from control by the hierarchy of the church. There are attempts made to control by law both spheres, however, as can be seen in the attempts by some social organisations to control television, theatre and cinema on the basis of a puritanical interpretation of Christian morality. This surfaces periodically in different guises in Britain, from the finding of the editor of *Gay News* guilty of blasphemy for publishing a poem in 1977, a decision upheld in the House of Lords in 1979 (not 1579, nor 1679, but 1979); to an unsuccessful attempt in 1982 to have a play at the National Theatre banned (*The Romans in Britain*) because it contained a homosexual rape scene; to attempts to control videos of films at home because children may see them and be exposed to sex and violence (see J. Weeks, 1981, in this volume).

In the spheres of science and technology there have been attempts to bring some of the developments here under moral control. For example, there have been groups telling doctors not to perform abortions, and Christian protests over the development of birth control. In the United States there have been a number of skirmishes over the activities of groups which try to prevent Darwin's theory of evolution being taught in schools and colleges, or which try to teach a Biblical version of creation alongside Darwin's version of evolution, as though the two were of equal intellectual and scientific merit. There is also a strong Christian involvement in the Campaign for Nuclear Disarmament — a more significant attempt to control the use of modern technology.

These examples are, however, exceptions. They are newsworthy and strange in the eyes of many people in the societies in which they have occurred because they appear to be left-overs from an earlier historical epoch. Today, many assume religion belongs in the private sphere, not in the public arena.

Church leaders should not be political, it is asserted, especially by Conservatives.

Religion is a matter of personal choice, not something which should be imposed upon others in modern consumer orientated societies, such as Britain or the United States. However, in the family, moral values and religious beliefs and practices may be taught to children. On the whole, religion is seen as a matter of adult freedom of choice in modem societies.

As was seen in relation to the role of the Royal Family in Britain, there is still a place for official religion on state ritual occasions. Religious symbolism is used in Britain and the United States as a means of legitimation of the state. In everyday political affairs it is seen as unnecessary for politicians to appeal to religious beliefs and values. Indeed it is an implicit rule that British politicians should not try to claim that they are more 'Christian' than anyone else in the general run of political affairs. Religion is mentioned on certain special occasions only, such as a new Prime Minister taking office. One major difficulty which has faced Christian socialists, for example, is that they appear to be claiming to be more moral, more properly religious, than others, and this appears to reflect badly upon the proponents of that perspective because they appear to have 'a holier than thou' aura about them.

One sociologist of religion, Peter Berger, has argued that there is a tendency towards the institutional separation of state and religion in most societies. He wrote, for example, in The Social Reality of Religion (1969):

> The global tendency seems to be in all cases the emergence of a state emancipated from the sway of either religious institutions or religious rationales of political action. This is also true in those 'antiquarian' cases in which the same political secularization continues to be decorated with the traditional symbols of religio-political unity, as in England or Sweden. Indeed, the anachronism of the traditional symbols in these cases only serves to underline the actuality of the secularization that has taken place despite them. (Berger, op. cit., p. 128)

Berger wrote his book before the Iranian revolution of 1979 in which a religious movement did act in politics and provided a religious rationale for their revolution. The point which he made seems mistaken and Berger over-emphasised the split between religion and politics in the modern world. Some powerful ideologies in the modern world do mix religious values and symbols with a more political-economic ideology, as in the various forms of religious socialism, Iranian Islam and in American Republicanism in the 1980s.

As was illustrated by the Coronation and events involving the Royal Family generally, there does seem to be some popular basis to these ritual events in that many people from all socio-economic classes do become involved in these activities even if it is only by watching them on television and reading about them in newspapers and magazines. Berger may perceive these rituals as 'anachronisms' but this is a statement more about his own response than about those of many of the citizens of Britain. For a sociologist who used a phenomenological approach this was a curious lapse in that he failed to pay attention to the meanings of the rituals to the people themselves, but rather imposed his own upon them. Sociologists have not done detailed research on this area in Britain or in the United States.

If these rituals are seen as a means by which a sense of identity is produced among British children and revitalised among adults, then their importance and appeal can be more properly assessed. This sense of national identity is separate from the state as such, although political figures are interested in trying to use any existing means of identity production and reproduction to legitimate their structures and activities. The Royal Family ritual events can be seen as a component of national identity maintenance, and as part of the process of the legitimation of state offices. This is rarely made explicit in the post-war period as it was in the writings of earlier generations, as was illustrated with the quotation from Bagehot earlier in this article.

Religion in a modern capitalist society is pushed increasingly, however, into the private sphere of the family and marriage as its major site of operation, where it can be seen as having a residual role in the morality of sexuality and marital relationships. Even if people reject the sexual and marital morality of the major churches, as there is evidence they do, especially in the case of lay Roman Catholics who reject the Church's teaching on birth control, and many members of the Church of England reject the idea of not remarrying divorced people in churches, for example, there is at the very least some residual acceptance that religious institutions are legitimately involved in this area among some people (see B. Wilson, 1982, chapter 6, especially pp. 161-5).

Religion, therefore, may be said to have a residual role left over from the past at the level of maintaining a sense of national identity and partially legitimating the state. It is at the level of the private sphere of the family, the key social institution concerned with the reproduction of patriarchal ideology, however, that religious institutions have their major social base in a society such as Britain. In other societies, however, such as Poland in the late 1970s and early 1980s, religion's role in carrying a sense of national identity in distinction to the state and communist government of Poland was strong.

Berger analyses the situation of religion in modem capitalist societies as follows:

> One of the essential traits is that of 'individualization'. This means that privatized religion is a matter of the 'choice' or 'preference' of the individual or the nuclear family, *ipso facto* lacking in common, binding quality. Such private religiosity, however 'real' it may be to the individuals who adopt it, cannot any longer fulfill the classical task of religion, that of constructing a common world within which all of social life receives ultimate meaning binding on everybody. Instead, this religiosity is limited to specific enclaves of social life that may be effectively segregated from the secularised sections of modern society. The values pertaining to private religiosity are, typically, irrelevant to institutional contexts other than the private sphere. (Berger, 1969, pp. 132-3)

The plausibility of traditional belief in religions is lost in the minds of millions of people in urban industrial societies, both capitalist and communist, according to Berger. He argued that the rational, bureaucratic forms of work required in any modern and complex society affect people's general consciousness in ways which make it very difficult for moral and ideological directives from the Church to have any impact. In large part this is because appeals pitched at a level of generality common in moral statements of this kind are impossible to apply in most work situations not because the people are immoral, but because no one could apply them in a concrete situation. The everyday routines of bureaucratic organisations and industrial plants do not leave room for either individual initiatives nor deviations from the planned routines. This type of consciousness, Berger seemed to imply, is carried outside the work situation so that religious beliefs, values and symbols lose plausibility in a widespread form in such societies. This is not because people have been converted to some other ideology, Berger would argue, but that no ideology can take root in such a situation. People live in a world deprived of any overall meaning system of any kind. They do, however, continue to search for identity and meaning at a personal level and use the wide variety of religious organisations available in modern pluralist cultures to do so. They may shift from Catholicism to a Buddhist group to an oriental sect and back again in a very short time-span.

In Berger's analysis there is a market place of competing religious roads to salvation from which an individual in a modern city may choose. Or the individual may use secular therapy to try to find some purpose and meaning, some sense of identity, for themselves. The only difference seems to be that religious solutions are usually free of any fees, while those of therapy cost the individual a cash sum for the professional service rendered (see P. Berger, 1969).

The analysis which Peter Berger provided of the process of increasing privatisation of religion in modem societies, that is, the link between religion and the family, highlighted one aspect of the sociological situation of religious institutions, but at the same time it obscured another. At the comparative historical level at which Berger pitched his analysis, it appeared that religious institutions had less and less direct moral influence upon political, military and economic affairs in conditions of advanced capitalism, and that the family, the private sphere, had become the only site where religious-based moral values appeared appropriate and legitimate. However, another aspect of the process was missed in this type of analysis. This additional feature of the social situation of religious morality had been discussed before Berger as 'the social control function of religion'.

Berger was attempting to move away from the teleological aspects of functionalism towards a sociology based upon a phenomenological sensitivity to subjective meaning. This led him to make religions of central importance as providers of meaning in the past, and to provide a sociological account of the loss of plausibility of traditional religious meanings under conditions of advanced consumer capitalism. This type of approach does show why there is a search for meaning outside the traditional denominations and churches of Christianity in the west and a growth of new sects and cults, especially among the generations who have grown up since the end of the Second World War. If someone is searching for a satisfactory meaning system and identity, the old organisations of Christianity appear too certain of themselves to welcome searchers. They are catering for those who have a sense of collective identity which they seek to revitalise in church rituals. They claim to know too much and so thrust it upon people rather than to encourage a personal search. Berger's approach does highlight some of the reasons for the growth of new religious groups in modern capitalist societies such as Britain and the United States in the 1960s and 1970s.

During this same period, however, events moved on. Changes took place in western capitalism which intertwined with changes in social theory and in sociology. For example, at the time Berger was writing, the United States was involved in a war in South-East Asia which it lost. However, a whole generation of young Americans and West Europeans had learned some lessons about the role of the military in the United States and its influence in political circles as a result of their experiences in protesting about that war. In Europe similar lessons were drawn in both West Germany, Britain and Prance. The main conclusion of all the various events of the late 1960s was that, for the time being, a major change of the system was not possible, and that change had to begin elsewhere — not in the large organisational structures of modern capitalism but in everyday experience.

The main consequence of these perceptions of the political situation in western capitalism was to produce new kinds of social movements outside the orthodox political parties. The prime example of the new type of movement has been the women's movement. This led to an interest in issues concerned with gender and sexuality primarily as these affect women (see, for example, J. Mitchell, 1974). The main impact upon men so far has been through the groups concerned with male homosexuality, although there have been attempts to create a men's movement for all men, heterosexuals included (see A. Tolson, 1978). There have also been groups interested in studying the influence of the media in both conventional political terms, and in less conventional terms, by exploring how common sense is constructed and perpetuated as an ideology. These substantive issues have led to the development of new social theories. These theories are new in the sense that they have involved novel ways of reading, or understanding, earlier theorists, especially Marx and Freud, Berger's phenomenological style of doing sociology of religion was overtaken by these new developments.

The use made of the work of Michel Foucault, on the other hand, has increased – at least in Britain in the late 1970s and early 1980s. Foucault concentrated upon the concept of 'power' as a generalised capacity in a society, not as a concept whose central focus is upon the state and its repressive apparatuses of control and violence, as in Weberian sociology, for instance. As mentioned earlier, Foucault's approach emphasises 'discourses' and the social construction of categories which create the worlds in which people live. In the private sphere which was of concern to Berger, various discourses penetrate to regulate sexuality. This is something omitted by Berger, but is the central focus for Foucault. The discourse created by the Catholic Church, and other religious organisations, especially since the reformation and the counter-reformation, spoke endlessly about sexuality in order to regulate it. This detailed control of sexuality applied mainly to elites, educated people, rather than to the great majority of the faithful who went to confessions very infrequently. Poucault, however, went on to argue that, nevertheless, an ideal was created of the ideal the good Christian should aim to achieve. He said:

> An imperative was established: not only will you confess to acts contravening the law, but you will seek to transform your desire, your every desire, into discourse. Insofar as possible, nothing was meant to elude this dictum, even if the words it employed had to be carefully neutralised. The Christian pastoral prescribed as a fundamental duty the task of passing everything having to do with sex through the endless mill of speech. (Foucault, 1979, p. 21)

Foucault quotes one of the confessors: 'Tell everything, not only consummated acts, but sensual touchings, all impure gazes, all obscene remarks ... all consenting thoughts' (ibid.).

This Christian tradition of speaking about sexuality frequently as a major area of sin, while forbidding certain words to be used and cloaking everything in decent expressions, has been continued in the 1970s both by the Catholic Church and by lay Protestants and Catholics alike, especially in both Britain and the United States (see J. Weeks, 1981).

The Christian churches have become split over the issues raised by the women's movement, by gays and by sexual liberationists. Some, both among the ordained elites in the churches and among the laity, are on the side of maintaining the traditional archaic heritage of Christianity, as is especially true of those who produce the Vatican documents about sexuality, and of the National Viewers' and Listeners' Association whose secretary is Mrs Mary Whitehouse as the standard bearer of decency (J. Weeks, 1981, in this volume). Others, again both among ordained and lay people, take a more liberationist view on matters concerning birth control, divorce and re-marriage, abortion, pre-marital sexual intercourse, homosexuality, lesbianism and the ordination of women. These people are also, but not necessarily, involved in the peace movement against nuclear weapons. The peace movement in Britain has had Christians involved in it since the late 1950s, from Canon Collins to Mgr Bruce Kent (see F. Parkin, 1968, on the earlier phase).

The focus upon 'discourses' has produced a new way of conceptualising the importance of religious organisations' texts, whether these are sermons, articles in magazines and church newspapers, prayers, or explicit moral rules and guidelines. Such texts can be seen not as a left-over from some earlier, supposedly more religious period of history, but as one way in which social regulation takes place in modern societies. Religious organisations still have power in the sense that they can generate discourse which is real in its social effects upon members, and maybe others less directly, especially in the sphere of sexuality, gender roles and, to some extent, in the area of the organised preparation for war. The consequence of churches' discourse about sexuality has been to make what had, to a large extent, been a private matter into a public one. The churches were involved in turning private troubles into public issues long before the more recent social movements among women and gay people tried to do so.

Conclusion

Religion in modern Britain has been analysed here at the level of the nation-state as a complex mixture of a civil religion and as part of a universal world religion. The Royal Family is a central component of British civil religion and forms a focus for ritual activity and the revitalisation of loyalty to the nation-state. In this sense it is a major component of the ideological practices which help to legitimate the state, the constitution, governments, law and the armed forces by bringing them into contact with the 'sacred'.

The social location of religion was discussed using the concept of privatisation. Religion is seen by most people as being especially relevant to the family, sexual behaviour and gender issues. The Royal Family is involved in this aspect, too, by supposedly epitomising how family life ought to be conducted. The concept of patriarchy, which has been developed by feminists and others, was used as one way of providing a theoretical link between the ideology of the nation-state and that of the private sphere. Britain's civil religion can be seen as expressing in its teachings, in its values, in its social practices and in its organisations such as the Churches of England and Scotland, a form of patriarchal ideology. This ideology fundamentally centres upon two main themes: men should be willing and able to fight, kill and die; women should desire to be wives and mothers.

Britain's civil religion, therefore, legitimates the state and patriarchal ideology by symbolically representing and expressing in its social practices these themes which perpetuate traditional definitions of gender. The universal religion of Christianity has historically been involved in doing this work of legitimation in other societies, too, but Christians are increasingly challenging this role. Tensions between church leaders and politicians result from this dual aspect of the churches in Britain — namely that they are both part of the civil religion of the nation-state, and part of a wider, more universalistic, world religion which contains the values of love, reconciliation, justice, equality, peace and joy for all.

References

Althusser, L. (1971) *Lenin and Philosophy and Other Essays,* London, New Left Books.

Archbishop of Canterbury (1977) *Silver Jubilee,* London, The Queen's Silver Jubilee Trust.

Badcock, C. (1980) *The Psychoanalysis of Culture,* Oxford, Basil Blackwell.

Barnett, A. (1982) *Iron Britannia,* London, Allison and Busby.

Bellah, R. (1970) 'Civil religion in America', in *Beyond Belief,* New York and London, Harper and Row.

Berger, P. L. (1969) *The Social Reality of Religion,* London, Faber and Faber.

Birnbaum, N. (1955) 'Monarchs and sociologists', in *Sociological Review,* Vol.3.

Bocock, R. (1974) *Ritual in Industrial Society,* London, George Allen and Unwin.

Bocock, R. (1983) *Sigmund Freud,,* London and New York, Tavistock and Ellis Horwood.

Cannadine, D. (1983) 'The context, performance and meaning of ritual: the British monarchy and the invention of tradition, c. 1820-1977', in E. Hobsbawm et al., *The Invention of Tradition,* Cambridge University Press.

Chaney, D. (1983) 'A symbolic mirror of ourselves: civic ritual in mass society', *Media, Culture and Society,* Vol.5, pp. 119-35.

Chodorow, N. (1978) *The Reproduction of Mothering:*

Psychoanalysis and the Sociology of Gender, Berkeley, California, Berkeley University Press.

Coward, R. and Ellis, I. (1977) *Language and Materialism,* London, Routledge and Kegan Paul.

Durkheim, E. (1912) *The Elementary Forms of the Religious Life,* translated by J. Ward Swain, New York, Collier Books, first published in paperback by Collier in 1961.

Erikson, E. (1974) *Identity: Youth and Crisis,* London, Faber and Faber, first published in England in 1968.

Foucault, M. (1978) *The History of Sexuality.* Volume 1: *An Introduction,* London, Allen Lane; translation copyright Random House Inc., New York, 1978.

Freud, S. (1908) 'Civilized sexual morality and modern nervous illness', in *Collected Papers,* and reprinted in *An Introduction to Sociology,* edited by Bocock, R. et al., 1980, London, Fontana.

Freud, S. (1912) *Totem and Taboo,* Standard Edition, Vol. 13, London, Hogarth Press. Freud, S. (1923) *The Ego and the Id,* Standard Edition, Vol. 19, London, Hogarth Press.

Giddens, A. (1971) *Capitalism and Modern Social Theory,* Cambridge University Press.

Giddens, A. (1981)A *Contemporary Critique of Historical Materialism,* London, Macmillan.

Goffman, E. (1963) *Stigma: the Management of Spoiled Identity,* Englewood Cliffs, N. J., Prentice Hall.

Klapp, O. (19691 *Collective Search for Identity,* New York and London, Holt, Rinehart and Winston Inc.

Lacan, J. (1977) *Ecrits: a Selection,* London, Tavistock Publications. Lane, C. (1981) *The Rites of Rulers: Ritual In Industrial Society: the Soviet Case,* Cambridge University Press.

Lane, C. (1983) 'Women in socialist society with special reference to the German Democratic Republic', in *Sociology,* Vol. 17, No. 4, pp. 489-505.

Luckmann, T. (1967) *The Invisible Religion: the Problem of Religion in Modern Society,* London and New York, Macmillan.

Maclntyre, A. (1967) *Secularization and Moral Change,* Oxford University Press. Martin, D. (1978) *The Dilemmas of*

Contemporary Religion, Oxford, Basil Blackwell.

Marx, K. (1845) 'Theses on Feuerbach', in On *Religion,* London, Lawrence and Wishart.

Mitchell, J. (1974) *Psychoanalysis and Feminism,* Harmondsworth, Penguin Books.

Nichols, P. (1981) *The Pope's Divisions,* Harmondsworth, Penguin Books.

Otto, R. (1924) *The Idea of the Holy,* Harmondsworth, Penguin Books edition, 1959:

Parkin F. (1968) *Middle Class Radicalism,* Manchester University Press.

Robertson, R. (1970) *The Sociological Interpretation of Religion,* Oxford, Basil Blackwell.

Shils, E. and Young, M. (1953) 'The meaning of the coronation', *Sociological Review,* Vol. 1, pp. 63-82.

Tawney, R.H. (1926) *Religion and the Rise of Capitalism,* Harmondsworth, Penguin Books.

Troelstch, E. (1931) *The Social Teachings of the Christian Churches,* translated by O. Wyon, London, George Allen and Unwin.

Tolson, A. (1978) *The Limits of Masculinity,* London, Tavistock.

Turner, B.S. (1983) *Religion and Social Theory,* London, Heinemann Educational Books.

Weeks, J. (1981) *Sex, Politics and Society,* London, Longmans.

Williams, R. (1981) *Culture,* London, Fontana.

Wilson, B. (1982) *Religion in Sociological Perspective,* Oxford University Press.

Yinger, M. (1970) *The Scientific Study of Religion,* London and New York, Collier-Macmillan Limited.